YOUR OWN WAY IN MUSIC

Also by Nancy Uscher

The Schirmer Guide to Schools of Music and Conservatories Throughout the World

YOUR OWN WAY IN *M*USIC

A CAREER AND RESOURCE GUIDE

Nancy Uscher

St. Martin's Press • *New York*

Design by Judith Dannecker

Library of Congress Cataloging-in-Publication Data

Uscher, Nancy.
      Your own way in music / by Nancy Uscher.
            p.   cm.
      ISBN 0-312-05186-7
            1. Music—Vocational guidance.   2. Music trade—United States.
      I. Title.
      ML3790.U8   1990
      780'.23—dc20   90-37305
                                                                          CIP

First Edition: November 1990

10 9 8 7 6 5 4 3 2 1

To my wonderful parents, Ida and Milton Uscher
and my precious daughter Alessandra
who came into the world as this book went to press

CONTENTS

ACKNOWLEDGMENTS

I am deeply grateful to friends and colleagues who were extremely generous with information and ideas for the book. Heartfelt thanks go to Janice L. Gorn, Laurence Dreyfus, Jerrold Ross, Samuel Adler, Gunther Schuller, Howard Klein, Richard Adams, John Duffy, Tom Knab, William Lincer, Paul Schuback, Lukas Foss, William Thomas McKinley, Beverly Wright, Fran Richard, Richard Clark, Jesse Rosen, Isabelle Ganz, Elizabeth Ostrow, Andrew Manshel, Dean Stein, Richard Kaplan, Mary Hammann, Robert Lindsay, Michael Levine, Jeff Gertler, William L. Monical, William Adler, Esther Rosenberg, Paul Goldberg, Frank Donaruma, and my sister, Janet U. Gorkin. Further thanks are in order to my editor, George Witte, and my agent, Susan Zeckendorf, for believing in this project from the time it was proposed. I wish to thank all of those I interviewed for the book, many of whose profiles appear in the text. I learned a great deal from them and often received the inspiration needed to keep going during the hard times. Finally, my husband, Bill Barrett, provided all kinds of help with the book, but none more important than his constant loving encouragement and support.

FOREWORD

As this book neared completion, tumultuous changes were overtaking Eastern Europe. Among them, playwright Vaclav Havel was elected president of Czechoslovakia. In February 1990 the new Czech president visited U.S. President George Bush and addressed the United States Congress. On February 22, an American tribute to Havel took place at the Cathedral of St. John the Divine in New York. I was privileged to participate in this moving event and will never forget it. The evening was not only a celebration of democracy, but also a time for artists to rejoice. One of their own had been chosen as a world leader.

Among the words spoken in tribute to Havel by a host of distinguished artists were these, part of a speech by the actor Ron Silver. I quote them here because they have a profound relevance for all artists. As musicians, in whatever career we choose, may we always live with the dignity they inspire.

He [Havel] has dedicated his life to reminding us of something timeless and universal. Vaclav Havel has shown the world that art matters. He has reminded us that art is not an end in itself, but it is a means of addressing humanity. He has reminded us that artists speak to people in ways that politicians cannot, and he has reminded us that art has the power to define us, to challenge us, and to make us explore the frontiers of human existence.

INTRODUCTION

Being a musician is a wonderful and brutal life, with incredible rewards and big disappointments. Dull, it isn't. We have a lot of control over our destinies, but musicians can't always see that fact. Lew Waldeck, a wise man in charge of symphony orchestras, opera, and ballet at the American Federation of Musicians, says that to better our lot we all have to give up the "garret" mentality. "We have to get down off that stage and say good-bye to the image of *La Bohème*'s consumptive Mimi," he says. It isn't easy to shed an identity so firmly ingrained in our beings.

Perhaps we can't do and be everything we want. But I am convinced the things we *really* badly want we can get. While writing this book, listening to one person's life story after another, I very often felt overwhelmed by the indomitable journey of the spirit. What circuitous routes people have taken to become who they are! Tough journeys sometimes, with lots of rejection along the way. But how things happened was entrancing, and these musicians' rites of passage are examples of the great contributions we are all capable of making.

This is not a book which focuses on superstars. I had little interest in writing about that segment of the music community. They usually have career patterns tightly controlled by their managements and determined by a great deal of complex political maneuvering on their behalf. In America one is likely to hear the same soloists over and over again, with little opportunity for fresh blood except when replacements are called in for emergencies.

I'm not much interested in the Wall Street brokerage house mentality of the biggest, most powerful agents at establishments like Columbia Artists Management and International Creative Management. Granted, they do work hard to get their clients plenty of money from concerts, recording contracts, and video projects. On the level of music as big business they have a kind of monopoly. But I'm skeptical of the role these managers have played in helping their clients gain recognition. That task is usually the domain of expensive public relations firms. How much talent is there in the music management field? I think, more times than not, it is the illustrious clients who help the careers of the agents. David Rubin, professor of journalism and mass communications at New York University, talks about the classical music industry's elitist "cylinder" and the finite number of people within it. Their lives all seem to fit the same basic blueprint.

What fascinates me are the original, varied careers many gifted musicians in our profession have carved out for themselves. I'm more interested in thinking, intelligent people outside this "cylinder" who have found ingenious ways to run their own lives. I'm interested in people who grow during their careers. Some make career changes in mid-life. These are the people who have made writing this book such an inspiring challenge. They have charted new territory, made special contributions, and have earned recognition from developing their gifts to the fullest.

In a calling where self-expression and creativity are so connected to the life of the professional, the approach to finding a satisfying niche for oneself may be more personal and individual than in other professions. Yes, there are positions in symphony orchestras for those trained as instrumentalists, and jobs advertised for music administrators, music therapists, ethnomusicologists, musicologists, music ministers, and all sorts of traditional employment categories. All of these are described in the book, with concrete information about how to train for these jobs, hear about available openings, and be successful in them. Considerations of salary and contract arrangements are far too complicated to cover in a book intended as a source of creative ideas and resources. However, there are plenty of texts focusing on the more "businessy" side of music, and these are listed here in the Resource Guide.

It takes quite a lot of original thinking to stay content and financially solvent—alas, probably never rich—in a profession that generally has less social status than the occupations of law, medicine, or business. All my life I have been inspired by musicians who delight in their work and refuse to give up, even when beset by career disappointments or financial struggles. For these dedicated colleagues, there is always a project on the horizon.

"At Juilliard I was so frustrated . . . I felt like I had to fit into a mold in order to have a career in music," a colleague recently confided, recalling her days as a student. My hope is that those who don't easily fit into a "mold" or traditional career slot will get as much help from this book as those who do. In the end, what really matters is that each of us gets to experience at least a part of the dream which brought us to this most beautiful of professions in the first place.

YOUR OWN WAY IN MUSIC

PART

I

GETTING YOUR
SKILLS TOGETHER

A Music-Inspired Career: Charting the Course

I STEPPED off the plane in Suva, Fiji, ready to present a lecture and recital at the University of the South Pacific. Ueta Solomona, dressed in the typical native skirt men wear in Fiji, greeted me with a most enthusiastic welcome. He had invited me, but this was our first meeting. During the ride to the university in his jeep I was surprised to learn he had gone to college in the United States. Traveling from Western Samoa on a Fulbright scholarship in 1959, he earned a Bachelor of Music degree in music education at the State University College of New York at Fredonia. Upon return to his native Western Samoa, he created a music curriculum in the schools, introducing Western instruments and fashioning a program in Western and Samoan music. He also formed an orchestra on the island. Solomona joined the faculty of the University of the South Pacific in 1976, teaching music at the main campus in Fiji and creating programs at university centres in the Solomon Islands, Tuvalu, Tonga, and Western Samoa. Solomona struggles to build his department. At this point he *is* the music department. In Suva he has the same headaches with budget and campus politics afflicting most university department heads the world over.

As Solomona told his story, what struck me so deeply was the sense of purpose and accomplishment in his life. He originated a school curriculum from scratch on his native Pacific island and then created a university music department. How fortunate he was to have turned his university education into a viable contribution to his own culture. Solomona has more than once made something from nothing.

Many musicians I interviewed, like Ueta Solomona, have made important contributions to their profession. They may not be rich and famous, but the precious quality these vital artists have in common is the gift of creativity. Their original ideas have made a strong impact. "I've always had the habit of dreaming about something and letting my heart lead," says ethnomusicologist Marcia Herndon in Berkeley, California, who started a valuable music research institute; filmmaker Allan Miller creates films that humanize musicians, taking them "out of the remote community of strangers" for audiences; Anthony Seeger, current director of the Smithsonian Institution's Folkways Records, helped to establish one of the first ethnomusicology degree programs in South America; and David Greenberg, a French horn player turned acoustician, travels the world as a consultant to the major concert halls. All of these musicians derive enormous pleasure from their work.

Creativity, excitement from learning something new, determination to make a difference, and the feeling of fulfillment that comes from making an impact on other people's lives are building blocks to a healthy career. Confidence and pride in past accomplishments encourage new steps forward. These elements are deplorably absent in the lives of too many artists struggling in a society that has not yet learned to appreciate them enough.

No book can teach creativity. But there are resources which can help musicians help themselves. This book describes the wealth of what is available. Its most important task, though, is to trigger the reader's imagination. To show musicians how they can take control of their own lives without waiting for the telephone to ring. To profile those who have been creative and resourceful in carving out careers and who are an inspiration to us all. To show that there is a lot of work to be done in the arts and that, contrary to popular opinion, there are plenty of jobs out there for musicians. But there is a catch to all of this. We musicians must be clever, original, and aggressive enough to seize opportunities even when they are not handed to us on silver platters—and we can be pretty sure they won't be. Some job slots are invisible. As the composer Samuel Adler says, we must "create our own vacancies." Viola professor William Lincer believes that "musicians should aggressively seek help from corporations to enable every small town in America to have its own orchestra. Germans raise money to have an orchestra in almost every city in the country—paying musicians good salaries and generous benefits. Why can't it happen here in the U.S.?" He warns that "a lot has to be done, or music is just going to die."

Conditions have never been worse in the conventional job market for professional musicians. Gunther Schuller, the eminent American composer-conductor, has given lots of thought to problems plaguing the music profession. He concludes: "The numbers are all wrong." There are too many graduates with music degrees and not enough positions. He points to an amazing thirty to forty thousand composers in this country, not even including jazz and popular composers. Only a small fraction of these can ever expect to find positions teaching at American universities, let alone live on their composing. So what do we do? Withdraw the opportunity for students to develop their gifts? Or accept the dismal reality and figure out how to make things better? The former, in my opinion, would mark the beginning of the end of civilization.

In the early 1970s Peter Mennin, then president of the Juilliard School, told BMI head Ed Cramer, "I don't tell my students anything about after college. My only job is to make them the best musicians they can be." A fair point of view at the time, perhaps. But times have changed. That comment rings of irresponsibility to my late-twentieth-century ears.

Students need help, and not just with learning the fingerings for their instruments. What responsibility do institutions have to the thousands of conservatory and music school graduates in America each year? Shouldn't career issues be discussed *before* a student enters the job market? A few institutions incorporate career courses into the academic structure. More should. Such curricula can have a practical component—i.e., writing resumes and tackling grant applications—but at their best can begin to teach a new kind of creative thinking. Embracing a fresh philosophy about careers can spawn valuable ideas about alternatives outside the traditional choices. Self-discovery—uncovering gifts and career inclinations beyond the obvious talents displayed early in life—can open up a whole new range of professional options.

Some schools have begun to address career concerns. Oberlin College offers a course called "Professional Development of Musicians." Manhattan School of Music has two courses: "Business of Music," and, for jazz musicians, "Business of Commercial Music." New England Conservatory has a course entitled "Career Skills." These courses help students take control of their professional lives.

What Color Is Your Parachute? by Richard Nelson Bolles is not about music. But it is a very original book, updated annually, discussing the process of knowing oneself—and how to use that knowledge to explore the job market. This book is assigned reading for Oberlin's career course. Developed by Jean James, the semester starts off by teaching how to undertake a job search. James, a musician who has also worked with career development in medicine and law, says job searching is basically the same for all professions. Skills such as networking are invaluable to all careers.

In James's course, outside speakers lecture on different aspects of career development. Students are taught to create resumes, press packets, and grant applications. During one class students are asked what they like and don't like about various publicity photographs. Critical faculties are awakened. Class requirements include making career contacts and writing a report explaining career intentions for two to three years after college. These exercises are designed to get students thinking about their own destinies.

The Manhattan School of Music is a rare school; it has long recognized the need to teach students career skills. The placement office helps students prepare materials and be aware of an array of professional opportunities. Says Dean Richard E. Adams, who originated the school's career curriculum: "As a rule, musicians don't have enough industry awareness. I encourage the students to pick up a music periodical they know nothing about: *Entertainment Business, Show Business,* or *Backstage.* The most exciting artists are the most aware artists. I tell my students that when they go to an interview to sell themselves, they've got to have something to talk about. Know about current events. Don't be an unenlightened critter."

The "Career Skills" course at the New England Conservatory, which was originated in 1986 by Robin Wheeler, is required. The first semester consists of lectures by guests on such topics as music therapy, conducting, public relations, and financial concerns. The second semester is devoted to group projects in which the students do research on their own interests and make contacts with useful people. A series of self-help pamphlets covering topics such as resumes, a bibliography of music resources, and financial management for musicians has been developed by the Conservatory's placement office.

These courses help students become aware of what awaits them in the real world. But there are numerous ways to structure curricula designed to make musicians more astute. Why not focus on topics such as audience-building, the history of philanthropy in America, the government and the arts, history of censorship of the arts, or a global perspective on the arts?

Back to Gunther Schuller. He speaks of educating the "total" or "complete" musician using role models from the sixteenth, seventeenth, and eighteenth centuries, when it was common for a musician to be versatile. Rarely did the best specialize. The creative and recreative sides of music were integrated. Paul Hindemith, the composer/Yale professor/violist/conductor, revived this ideal during the twentieth century. He is not alone. Among them: Schuller, who without so much as a college diploma performed, composed, conducted, and headed the New England Conservatory while becoming a respected scholar on the history of jazz; oboist/composer/

conductor Heinz Holliger; composition professor/composer/conductor/educator Samuel Adler; composer/conductor/cultural leader Morton Gould; and conductor/composer/pianists Leonard Bernstein and Lukas Foss. Why list all these categories? The label *musician* should be sufficient. Curiosity, the insatiable thirst for knowledge that knocks down artificial barriers, should be welcomed. Performers should be encouraged to do research and write their own program notes. Musicologists should perform or at least have extensive contact with those who do. (Incidentally, they would also make qualified music critics.) A fourth-grade music teacher in the public schools, charged with the awesome task of introducing music to future generations, should have a grasp on music surpassing the usual "education" orientation. As Schuller puts it: "The higher the tree grows, the deeper its roots must be anchored, lest it fall over."

Some musicians succeed without formal music training at the university level, especially performers who have had fine private teachers. But at their best, undergraduate and graduate studies create a protected environment where there is plenty of time to spend in practice rooms and libraries. With the proper inspiration and guidance, these years can be a glorious time of discovery. What criteria should determine a student's choice of school? For an instrumentalist or composer, of prime importance is the major teacher/mentor who will help to create and guide good work habits and the value system by which a student makes choices about a life in music. Likewise, in the more academic professions, mentors, particularly at the graduate level, can help shape a student's life and career. In recent years, musicology, ethnomusicology, and music theory have become more intertwined, and offerings in university music departments reflect this. Boundaries are less defined than in the past. As Phi Beta Kappa Professor of the Year in 1988–89, Samuel Adler toured many American universities. While traveling, he thought about what qualities really matter in choosing a school. He came up with the following list:

- the teacher
- peer competition to provide a challenge
- an environment conducive to an individual's liking
- reputation of the school
- location

Never let it be said that to become a fine musician one need go to a conservatory, rather than a liberal arts college or university. Why not go to both? This is a list of distinguished musicians who included liberal arts in their educations: pianists Ursula Oppens, Philip Moll, and Emanuel Ax; cellist Yo-Yo Ma; violinist Eugene Drucker; and Eastman School of Music director Robert Freeman. And who says you can't go back to school later in life? Years after graduating from the Royal Academy of Music in London, English conductor Simon Rattle took time from his global career to read English at Oxford University. Here is a musician who understands the importance of self-renewal and growth.

Does it really matter where you go to school? Well, it is nice to have the prestige of an Ivy League school on your resume when seeking an academic career. It probably will help. We all know that good and inspired training is essential for a performer. But getting a good education and knowing about resources, opportunities, and all the rest of it is only the beginning.

Ultimately it is the knowledge of how to educate one's self, think creatively, and continue to grow, independent of any institution, that endures. This kind of drive permeates the lives of Ueta Solomona from Fiji and many others who have fashioned interesting and satisfying careers in music.

Carving out an original career or sticking with a great idea is not without its struggles. But those who have managed to hang in there, often under great financial hardships, have learned the best lesson of all: using every ounce of your potential and making an impact on other people's lives has its own amazing rewards.

Knowing About Career Resources

MAGNIFICENT resources abound for musicians. Knowing about them is important. Making use of them is even more important. The various resources discussed here—grants, research basics, resume formats, computers, publishing outlets, professional associations, instrument archives, and literature about the music profession—are great career boosters. With the material in this chapter I attempt to serve a wide range of musicians. What is new and informative to a young performer may appear excruciatingly under-detailed and even banal to a graduate student in musicology. The tradeoff in addressing many musicians is that not every part of the book will be relevant for each discipline. But there is a certain common ground among the music-related professions. Scholars and performers alike can take pleasure in the great libraries, reference works, and instrument collections that benefit us all. And virtually every music career has some kind of society or association providing an entrée to a network of professionals. The Resource Guide contains addresses and telephone numbers of all the organizations discussed here.

GETTING MONEY FOR A GREAT IDEA

Putting ambitions and aspirations into motion takes a lot of imagination and courage. It usually also takes money and help from people. There are

9

ways to find money, whether it be for a New York recital, a research project
in Japan, or for a book about opera. The first step is knowing how to do
research about what is available.

HOW CAN INDIVIDUALS FIND MONEY?

Foundations are reluctant to fund individuals. This problem will be spelled
out in considerable detail in chapter 5. Service organizations, which get
money from foundations to fund individuals by the "trickle down" theory,
will be dealt with in chapter 6. Still, there *are* foundations that do give
money directly to individuals. We may not be talking about huge sums.
Extensive research, letter-writing, and telephoning may yield as little as a
hundred dollars here and a hundred dollars there. But that may be sufficient
for your project. Consider my own experience.

In 1986 I was seeking funding for a research trip to Budapest, Hungary,
in connection with my book *The Schirmer Guide to Schools of Music and
Conservatories Throughout the World.* My research revealed that the International Research & Exchanges Board (IREX) of Princeton, New Jersey,
underwrote projects in Eastern European countries. Although it was far
from clear whether my plans qualified under the published guidelines, I
called IREX's offices and spoke with the program specialist for Hungary.
Almost as an afterthought, I asked her to keep me in mind if she came
across any other possible funding sources. Well! Less than twenty-four
hours later she left a message on my answering machine with the name
and telephone number of the Soros Foundation, a foundation whose
objective is to promote—guess what?—Hungarian culture. Eventually,
the Soros Foundation provided me with room and board for my week's
stay in Budapest, as well as a guide. It was worth maybe $800, not a large
figure but sufficient for me to live comfortably and accomplish my research
goals.

There are several lessons here. Published guidelines aren't chiseled in
granite. People in the business of grant-giving often know of other sources
but sometimes have to have their memories jogged. No matter how obscure
your project, there probably is a funding source out there somewhere that
specializes in it.

Here is how you find out about the world of philanthropy. There may
be more information here than you really *want* to know. Not everything
will be directly relevant to individuals. But it is *always* better to know more
than less.

THE FOUNDATION CENTER

The Foundation Center collects and distributes information about the $7.4 billion given away each year by thirty thousand grantmaking foundations in the United States. The center operates its own reference collections in New York, Washington, D.C., Cleveland, and San Francisco and has over 180 cooperating libraries across the United States. Careful scrutiny of the center's materials can identify appropriate funding sources for a particular project, whether it be in performance, musicology, or another music discipline. In a catalogue listing publications for sale, a few titles in particular are worth noting. *Foundation Fundamentals* is a thorough overview of the philanthropic world, with a particularly valuable section (Appendix E) entitled "National Organizations Serving Grantseekers and Grantmakers." Appendix G lists cooperating collections in libraries. *Foundation Grants to Individuals* and *The Foundation Directory* are the center's primary sources for individuals and non-profit organizations. *Grants for Arts and Cultural Programs* is geared to the needs of non-profit cultural organizations. These books are available at most libraries or can be ordered by phone, prepaid on a credit card.

The Foundation Directory, Foundation Grants Index and *The National Data Book of Foundations* are also online databases available through DIALOG Information Services, Inc. A personal computer user with a modem can connect directly to DIALOG, although it can be very expensive. (Many public libraries also offer searches on DIALOG.) All database services, including information about Telecommunications Cooperative Network (TCN) and ALANET, are listed in a brochure printed by the center.

Literature about grants is usually written with a non-profit audience in mind. There is little around with direct bearing on those without that magical tax-exempt designation (more about this in chapter 5). But don't despair. There *is* a source after all: *Foundation Grants to Individuals*. Chock full of help, it offers a valuable introduction and a terrific bibliography of materials on sources for scholarships, fellowships, loans, and grants. A marketing officer at the Foundation Center suggested using *Foundation Grants to Individuals* in conjunction with the *National Guide to Funding in Arts and Culture*. This approach thoroughly covers the territory of arts funding by foundations.

There is more. Want detail? To find out the particulars about a foundation, you can look at its tax return. Information returns filed by foundations with the IRS, called 990's, are stored at the center on microfiche, organized by state, then alphabetically by foundation name. The employer identification number listed in any of the reference materials is also the IRS identifying number. If not at the Foundation Center, returns can be requested directly from the IRS or from the specific foundation.

The center will not give out the addresses or telephone numbers of any foundations over the phone. After being refused the telephone number of a small foundation in Massachusetts, I phoned the Worcester, Massachusetts public library, which has a Grants Resource Center, one of the many such cooperating collections. I got the number. For an annual membership fee of hundreds of dollars, clearly beyond the means of most musicians, one can become a member of the Foundation Center's Associates Program. This program is intended for officers of organizations and consultants, and not for individual grantseekers. Associates are provided answers over the telephone, and access to a "Grantmaker Updates" service which tracks changes taking place in the foundation world on a weekly basis.

THE GRANTSMANSHIP CENTER

The Grantsmanship Center in Los Angeles is a resource offering seminars and workshops, primarily for executives of nonprofit organizations. The center, which has a reference library, publishes a helpful proposal-writing guide, which shows an accepted format and style of proposals for grants. This is an excellent research tool for individual artists, as are other of the Center's publications, listed in the *Whole Nonprofit Catalog*.

COUNCIL ON FOUNDATIONS

This is a Washington, D.C.–based organization that can answer questions about U.S. foundations. The Council is a national membership foundation representing independent, community, and company-sponsored corporate contributions programs and foundations. Even though this is not an association geared to individuals, it will take telephone inquiries about obscure or hard-to-locate foundations.

GRANTS LITERATURE

The book *Money for Artists: A Guide to Grants and Awards for Individual Artists* is one of that rare breed of books focusing on money for *people* instead of organizations. General material about the subject can be gleaned from *Directory of Research Grants 1990*, published annually by Oryx Press. Another such book is *The Grants Register* by St. Martin's Press. In books like these, you might find a grant "in the cracks" that is much less competitive, albeit less prestigious, than, for example, the coveted Guggenheim Award. Remember: The research category of arts and humanities includes music. Likewise, a guideline announcing "nonfiction writing" grants may well be open to projects with music topics. *Grants for the Arts* (1980) by Virginia L. White, although out of date, is still a worthwhile reference. There are a number of interesting topics discussed, among them the history of government involvement with the arts.

STATE AND LOCAL/REGIONAL ARTS COUNCILS

Another source of funding for artists comes from state and regional arts councils. Information about a number of these organizations, such as New York Foundation of the Arts, Arts Midwest, and United Arts, is contained in this book, and a list of all state arts councils is found in the Resource Guide. The National Assembly of State Arts Councils and the National Assembly of Local Arts Councils, both based in Washington, D.C., are advocacy and information clearinghouses. Both publish useful resources explaining the programs and policies of the country's arts councils. The National Association of Artists' Organizations, another Washington, D.C., arts advocacy association, publishes a valuable directory. Keep informed about funding policies of regional and state agencies. Although, like foundations, they are more likely to fund nonprofit entities, some do help individual artists through sponsorship of residencies and artists' colonies.

FINANCING MUSICAL INSTRUMENTS

Instruments are much more than "tools" of the performers' trade: they become the souls of their players. When it comes to stringed instruments, some of the finest instruments today cost more than $1 million and at least tens of thousands of dollars. How do performers afford them? Needless to say, most musicians don't earn enough money to pay off six-figure loans.

Nigel Brown, a creative music-loving investment manager at the Cambridge, England, firm of N.W. Brown, has come up with an imaginative solution which he calls "multiple ownership." Put simply, it is selling shares of a highly priced instrument to investors. As Brown outlines the scheme, a trust would be created with, for example, $10,000 contributed by fifty investors, for a total of $500,000. The money would be used to buy a fine instrument by a maker such as a Stradivarius or Amati for a promising musician. The musician would be responsible for paying insurance and maintaining the instrument but otherwise would use the instrument for free.

Investors would be free to sell their shares to anyone at whatever price could be obtained. The musician would have the right of first refusal. At some point in the distant future, if the musician should stop playing or trade up to another instrument, the original instrument would be sold and the proceeds distributed to the investors. "So long as there is a capital gain in the end, investors should be happy to take this in lieu of income," Brown says. In effect, instruments are being treated like racehorses or oil wells to be syndicated.

"My basic idea is that musicians should eventually own the instruments they play. The musician, if given enough time, should be able to buy out the investors subject to a successful career," he explains. Brown, who collects a fee for his service, has arranged trusts for several musicians and is considering implementing his ideas on a larger scale.

THE CHECK IS IN THE MAIL

One day I got a check for $1,000 in the mail, from someone I had never met, for a research project on music schools. Does it sound a little like that TV show "The Millionaire?" Honestly, it happened. It can happen to you. There are no formulas. Just be aware that there are some wealthy people in this world who can and will fund worthy projects. Usually such a gift is the result of some networking that has gone on in your behalf, with or without your knowledge. The situation is reminiscent of the magnificent MacArthur Award program, given exclusively through nomination, where creative people receive thousands of dollars based on past accomplishments. A private patron is found this way: An admirer of your work—it could be your uncle, cousin, old family friend, or former professor—has spoken glowingly about you to someone or to someone who knows someone who knows someone. The wealthy person at the end of the line has been convinced that contributing to you will be an investment worth making. Of course, the patron we are talking about is a special human being with a quality value system. And one day the money is given. As simple as that.

SAYING WHO YOU ARE

RESUMES: CHOOSING THE STYLE

Whether you are a musicologist or a performer you will need a resume or curriculum vitae to introduce yourself professionally, whether for a college teaching position, orchestral position, or international festival. There are a variety of accepted styles. If you have two disciplines, musicology and performance, two resumes may be in order. Constantly updating a resume to keep it current is of primary importance. The Manhattan School of Music has printed resume-construction books for its students. The guide, called *Resume Basics*, by Dean Richard E. Adams and revised by James Gandre and Mark LaPorte, offers several options. For an instrumentalist:

Name   Address and Telephone
Instrument

Orchestral Experience
Concerto Engagements
Recordings
Honors
Principal Teachers
Education

Name
Instrument
Address and Telephone
Orchestral Experience
Solo/Chamber Music
Major Teachers
Education
Festivals

For a singer:

Name   Address and Telephone
Voice Type Height, Weight, Eyes, and Hair Profile

Opera Performances
Orchestral Engagements

Voice Teachers
Education

Name
Voice Type

Address and   Height, Weight, Hair, and Eyes Profile
Telephone

Opera Performances
Roles Studied
Training
Festivals
Special Skills

Here are some others.
An editor of a music magazine in England sent me this resume format:

Name
Address
Date of Birth

Education
Career Details
Current Positions
Other Professional Interests

An ethnomusicologist sent a resume with the following format:

Name   Date updated
Address
Place of Birth
Citizenship
Social Security Number
Passport Number
Current Employer
Position
Subdisciplines
Degrees
Languages
Professional Employment Experience
Field Work Experience
Other Professional Experience

Fellowships, Prizes, and Awards
Publications
Short Articles and Reviews
Papers Presented at Meetings and Congresses

A freelance writer on music subjects and musician suggests:

Name, Address, and Telephone
Publications
Selected Articles
Teaching Background
Solo Recordings
Orchestral Positions
Selected Solo Recitals
Selected Festivals

Basil N. Tschaikov, the Director of the National Centre for Orchestral Studies in London, England, suggests this format for an orchestral applicant's curriculum vitae:

Name	Instrument
Home Address	Current Address
	Telephone
Marital Status	Nationality
Date of Birth	Age

General Education
Musical Education
Orchestral Experience
Referees (Name, address, and telephone of references)

*B*EING LITERATE ABOUT MUSIC

Writing about music? Whether an idea has come through a performance project, or a newly defended doctoral dissertation is ripe for several spinoff articles, a comprehensive list of publishing outlets will be useful. Three reference works combined cover most music and general publishing outlets: *Literary Market Place* lists all university presses and commercial book publishers; *Musical America: International Directory of the Performing Arts* lists most music journals and magazines in the United States and around the world; and *Writer's Market* lists all general subject magazines. Each of these references publishes a new edition annually. Another way to keep current with new music periodicals is to peruse the periodical shelf in the arts division of a major library. At the General Library and Museum of the Performing Arts at New York's Lincoln Center, the third-floor music research division is a haven for music researchers. The shelf of journals in this library is stocked with important periodicals.

Don't limit yourself to American publications. There are wonderful periodicals in English-speaking countries that welcome contributions. Here are some examples, all published in London: *Tempo* Magazine, published by Boosey & Hawkes, is a superb journal focusing on modern music; *The Strad* has articles about string players, instruments, and repertoire; *Opera's* subject matter is self-explanatory; *The Musical Times* and *Classical Music Magazine* cover a variety of musical subjects; and *The Gramophone* is a periodical featuring classical record reviews. *Early Music* deals with performance practice on period instruments.

The Chicago Manual of Style and *The Writer's Handbook* by Janice L. Gorn are two invaluable tools for good writing form. *Introduction to Music Research* by Ruth T. Watanabe has style rules directed specifically to music topics.

COMPUTERS: FILES FOR EVERY OCCASION

There are some veteran writers who do very well on typewriters that have served them so loyally over the years. But a computer certainly makes life easier. There are two basic classifications of computer hardware: the graphic kind and the digital models. They have numerous uses for musicians, from turning out scores to word processing to data management. Two popular word processing software programs are Word Perfect from SSI Software (used to write this book) and Nota Bene from Dragonfly Software—often favored by scholars because of its facility with foreign languages. Word processing is helpful for storing and updating resumes, and producing repertoire lists, sample programs, program notes, articles and reviews, and research notes. Everything can be changed and updated easily without constant retyping. Andrew Tobias's Managing Your Money data management software offers the mechanics of controlling and managing data with programs to do accounting and give reminders about daily events. Is the cost of a computer a problem? The price of no-name IBM compatible clones keeps dropping. Many libraries arrange free time to work at computers. All you have to do is bring your own disks. Laptop computers, which keep getting lighter in weight and less expensive, are useful for jet-setting scholars. Keep in mind that in entering some countries, including the United States, computers must be officially registered with customs.

A BIBLIOGRAPHIC ODYSSEY

THE BARE BONES OF MUSIC RESEARCH

Doing research resembles the work of a private detective or an investigative journalist: a satisfying quest resulting in answers to important questions. Music scholars spend their lives doing research. But practitioners in other genres of music also need to undertake research projects from time to time. A good music library has everything a musician needs to research program notes, or find out about music literature, composers, instruments, etc., ad infinitum. For less experienced music researchers, knowing about some basic resources will make the job easier. *Music Reference and Research Materials*, fourth edition, by the late Vincent H. Duckles and Michael A. Keller; *Introduction to Music Research* by Ruth T. Watanabe; and *Library Research Guide to Music* by John E. Druesedow, Jr., give an overview of bibliographic tools of the music library. *Grove's Dictionary of Music and Musicians* (1980, sixth edition) has been available for a decade, but this twenty-volume reference work is still considered the definitive music research tool in any language. The spinoffs of the dictionary are the *New Grove Dictionary of Musical Instruments*, *New Grove Dictionary of American Music*, and *New Grove Dictionary of Jazz*. *Modern Music Librarianship*, a series of essays dedicated to Ruth T. Watanabe, has interesting bibliographic information.

If you are doing research for program notes, two books will answer questions about composers' important dates: *Baker's Biographical Dictionary*, published by Schirmer Books, and *Performing Arts Biography Master Index*. Is chamber music your passion? Don't forget to look at the marvelous *Cobbett's Cyclopedic Survey of Chamber Music*, second edition, three volumes, and the *Guide to Chamber Music* by Melvin Berger. When searching for material, remember that music librarians are trained to be helpful. They know how to tackle research inquiries and can often save a researcher valuable time.

DOCTORAL DISSERTATIONS

Doctoral dissertations are a great source of esoteric information. Two dissertations I consulted while writing this book were Quentin Gerard Marty's "Influences of Selected Family Background, Training, and Career Preparation Factors on the Career Development of Symphony Orchestra Musicians: A Pilot Study," (The University of Rochester, Eastman School of Music, 1982), and Ellen Parker's "An Investigation of the Practices of Selected Manhattan-Based Corporations and Private Foundations in Assessing the Eligibility of Performing Arts Groups for Funding" (New York University, 1988). The detailed material found in these was unavailable elsewhere. Want to know what has been written? University Microfilms International publishes an indexed catalog of doctoral dissertations about music, *Recent Studies in Music*. Most libraries have University Microfilm Dissertation Abstracts. Dissertations can be ordered through university library networks, or purchased by order form or telephone request, with hard cover or paper binding.

NATIONAL RESEARCH MONUMENTS

THE LIBRARY OF CONGRESS

Everyone knows about the Library of Congress, founded in 1800. Researchers from other countries come to Washington, D.C., specifically to use its resources. The Music Division had its beginning in 1815 when Congress bought items from Thomas Jefferson's personal music collection for the library. Under the tenure of George Theodore Sonneck, appointed chief of the division in 1902, an impressive research collection was assembled. Since then, a continuing expansion of resources has made this collection one of the most important in the world. The holdings include more than four million pieces of music, three hundred thousand books and pamphlets, and three hundred and fifty thousand recordings. Materials in the division are international in scope and diverse in genre. Special collections include the Dayton C. Miller Flute Collection of sixteen hundred flutes and books, treatises, and photographs; the Rachmaninoff Archives, detailing the life and accomplishments of Sergei Rachmaninoff; the George Gershwin Collection, containing a number of Gershwin's original manuscripts, including *Porgy and Bess*, *An American In Paris*, and the first and second versions of *Rhapsody in Blue*; and the Jascha Heifetz Collection, including autograph manuscripts of violin concertos commissioned by Heifetz. *The Music Division: A Guide to Its Collections and Services* handbook contains details about the collections.

Serious music researchers who have been unsuccessful finding information elsewhere can be helped by telephone inquiry to the library's music division. But telephone assistance is limited, since the music librarians in this grand institution are also busy helping people present at the library.

THE SMITHSONIAN INSTITUTION

The Smithsonian Institution is a magnificent resource. Comprised of fourteen museums, all located in Washington, D.C., music is omnipresent around the institution. The National Museum of American History has a division of Musical History. This division, which documents the history of American music, houses the Collection of Musical Instruments. The collection, of approximately twenty-five hundred instruments, has European and American instruments from the sixteenth century to the present. The strengths of the collection are keyboard instruments from the seventeenth century to the present, and archival material documenting the history of American music. The archives of Duke Ellington, acquired through his son Mercer Ellington, contain scrapbooks and a large manuscript collection. The Robert and Margaret Hazen Band Ephemera Collection illustrates the role of the band in American history. The DeVincent Sheet Music Collection features band arrangements of small-theater dance music from the late nineteenth and early twentieth centuries. A collection of business ephemera holds American music trade catalogs including Steinway and Chickering factory number books on microfilm. The division sponsors twenty period instruments concerts a year called "Music in Original Instruments at the Smithsonian." The Department of Anthropology in the Museum of Natural History also has a large collection of instruments from Asia, Africa, and Oceania, and of the American Indian, stored by geographical area. There are some instruments in the Natural Museum of African Art as well. The Festival of American Folk Life is sponsored by the Office of Folk Life Programs. In the festival, presenters, usually with ethnomusicological backgrounds, interpret the performances, introducing the musicians and giving background material about the events. Folkways Records has been part of the Smithsonian since 1987. Its catalog includes folk, blues, children's music, jazz, and world music titles. The Smithsonian Press produces recordings of performances on period instruments. Public programs at the institution include such events as the Duke Ellington Festival.

PROFESSIONAL AFFILIATIONS

PROFESSIONAL SOCIETIES

Numerous associations exist for professional musicians. They assume an important role particularly in the scholarly disciplines, providing a vehicle for the dissemination of important research. Most professional groups have conferences and symposia where scholarly work is discussed and debated. The role of each organization in its particular specialty area varies greatly. The American Musicological Society is an integral part of the musicology discipline and major organ of communication, but Early Music America is more a trade organization, promoting scholarly and commercial aspects of the period instrument movement. With an entirely different perspective, the American Federation of Violin Makers defines "professional" more strictly than other associations and is without student membership. Like every career resource, the value a professional society can have for a musician is dictated by the extent of that person's imagination and re-sourcefulness. A survey of the major organizations follows.

AMERICAN CHORAL DIRECTORS ASSOCIATION

Founded in 1959, the American Choral Directors Association (ACDA) currently has a membership of fourteen thousand choral conductors who represent about one million singers. It is divided into seven regional groups. Once a member of the national organization, regional membership is automatic. Conventions, major events for ACDA, alternate every year between national and regional sponsorship. Projects being considered include a job placement service, a commissioning program, institutes of choral research, and international outreach to directors in Central and South America. The official publication, *Choral Journal*, appears ten times annually. ACDA is one of the few professional organizations which has student chapters in high schools, colleges, and universities.

AMERICAN FEDERATION OF VIOLIN AND BOW MAKERS

The American Federation of Violin and Bow Makers was founded in 1980. The organization's primary goal is to elevate professional standards of craftsmanship and ethical conduct on a national level.

This organization is different from the other associations listed here: membership, currently about eighty, is open only to professionals who have fulfilled specific requirements. Members must have had three years of luthier (violin maker) training, three years as a journeyman (apprentice to a recognized violin maker), and three years of experience running a violin-making shop. The Federation has designed programs to help develop technical skills and knowledge of its membership through seminars and annual meeting events. In addition, the Federation sponsors competitions and exhibitions as a forum for makers, musicians, and the general public to meet and exchange information. To assist in the recovery of lost or stolen instruments and bows, the Federation maintains a computer-organized registry that is distributed to a national network of makers and law enforcement agencies.

THE AMERICAN MUSICAL INSTRUMENT SOCIETY

The American Musical Instrument Society (AMIS) is an international association founded in 1971 to promote the study of history, design, and use of musical instruments from all cultures and periods. The society's publications are the annual *AMIS Journal*, and the *AMIS Newsletter* which is issued three times a year. There is a committee for career development.

AMERICAN MUSICOLOGICAL SOCIETY

The American Musicological Society (AMS) was founded in 1934 to advance "research in the various fields of music as a branch of learning and scholarship." In 1951 the association became a member of the American Council of Learned Societies. The membership includes 3,600 individuals and 1,250 institutional subscribers from forty countries.

In 1948 the *Journal of the American Musicological Society* was established. Published three times a year, this periodical describes the findings of significant musicological research. Other AMS publications are a newsletter containing items of interest to members, the annual directory, and a 1985 handbook called *The Ph.D. and Your Career: A Guide for Musicologists.*

AMS cooperates with such groups as the International Musicological Society, the Music Library Association, the Society for Music Theory, the Society for Ethnomusicology, the Sonneck Society, and the College Music Society in conferences involving projects of common interest. Increasing interaction among the societies representing varied music disciplines has been described by leading scholars as "the wave of the future."

A fact not widely known is that performers are welcome to participate in AMS events. Those with interesting lecture-recitals, e.g., music of women or aspects of the contemporary idiom, can showcase at AMS national conventions. Noon-time and evening recitals run throughout the three- or four-day conference. Sometimes as many as four or five noon presentations are scheduled simultaneously, and audiences for evening concerts often fill a hall of eight hundred or more seats. Although performers do not get paid, sometimes they share in proceeds from ticket sales. The *real* pay-off, however, is in valuable exposure. Usually about two thousand college professors from all over the country attend. Contacts from such a distinguished group may well come in handy when applying for a university teaching position.

AMERICAN STRING TEACHERS ASSOCIATION

The American String Teachers Association (ASTA), with a membership of seven thousand, is made up of professional and amateur violinists, violists, cellists, bass players, harpists, and guitarists. Annual events are the ASTA National Solo Competition and the national convention. Summer workshops offering study and performance events are cosponsored by ASTA. The main journal, published quarterly, is the *American String Teacher*. The ASTA Media Resource Center, housed at Ohio State University, has educational rental videos available. The international counterparts to ASTA are ESTA, umbrella organization to fourteen European chapters, JASTA in Japan and AUSTA in Australia.

AUDIO ENGINEERING SOCIETY

The Audio Engineering Society (AES) was founded by a group of engineers in 1948. An organization was needed that would help with the exchange of technical audio information, thus furthering the science of "audio craft." In 1953 a journal, *Audio Engineering*, was established. The magazine, which is now called *The Journal of the Audio Engineering Society*, served as a catalyst for the society's international profile. Conventions are held each year in the United States and in Europe. Other AES publications are *Anthologies* of selected Journal papers, and *The Cumulative Index*.

COLLEGE MUSIC SOCIETY

A professional musician either teaching at a university or interested in an academic affiliation will benefit by the services offered by the College Music Society (CMS). The society represents over six thousand music teachers in colleges and universities in the United States, Canada, and Europe. Through annual national and regional conferences, CMS provides a forum to consider special interest topics and interdisciplinary issues germane to music teaching in higher education institutions. *The College Music Society Newsletter* and *Music Faculty Vacancy List* are sent to members. The latter is a comprehensive job bank for openings in music at the university level, constantly updated by the 24 hour telephone Vacancy Hot-Line Service. *College Music Symposium* is an annual publication. The CMS *Directory of Music Faculties in Colleges and Universities, U.S. and Canada*, lists about twenty seven thousand music faculty at more than fifteen hundred institutions.

EARLY MUSIC AMERICA

Early Music America, founded in 1986, promotes the performance and recording of music on period instruments. With a membership of about fourteen hundred, the society holds an annual members' meeting. The publication *Historical Performance* is published twice a year and a news bulletin is sent to members each month.

MUSIC CRITICS ASSOCIATION

The Music Critics Association (MCA) was founded in 1957. Its goals are to establish standards of criticism, collaborate with other organizations, and sponsor educational activities. MCA Educational Activities Inc. is responsible for institutes and workshops that have been organized over the years, such as those in Aspen, Colorado; the Smithsonian Institution and John F. Kennedy Center for the Performing Arts in Washington, D.C.; and Santa Fe, New Mexico. A newsletter is published three times a year and special events, such as the 1987 public symposium "Music Criticism in America's Press" are documented with leaflets.

MUSIC EDUCATORS NATIONAL CONFERENCE

The Music Educators National Conference (MENC), founded in 1907, has a membership of fifty-seven thousand. The organization is dedicated to improving the quality of, and influencing public opinion about, music education in the United States. Involved in developing a national policy for all the arts, MENC has worked with the American Council for the Arts in forming the Ad Hoc National Educational Working Group. The meetings of this umbrella group for twenty-five organizations resulted in The Philadelphia Resolution, which presented a platform on lobbying for arts in the schools. Each MENC member receives the *Journal of Research in Music Education* quarterly, *General Music Today* three times a year, and *Update: The Applications of Research in Music Education* in the fall and spring. MENC has a number of other publications, including a several-page leaflet called *Careers in Music*.

MUSIC LIBRARY ASSOCIATION

The Music Library Association (MLA) was organized in 1931 by a small group of prominent librarians and musicologists. MLA provides a forum

for studying the concerns affecting music libraries and their patrons. Publications of MLA include the journal *Notes*, and the "Directory of Library
School Offerings in Music Librarianship."

NATIONAL ASSOCIATION OF JAZZ EDUCATORS

The National Association of Jazz Educators (NAJE), with a current membership of about seven thousand, was founded in 1968. An associated
organization of the Music Educators National Conference, its main goal
is to promote understanding and appreciation of the jazz idiom. NAJE
Young Talent Winners, young jazz players from around the country, are
selected each year to receive scholarships and to perform at the annual
January conference of the association. The association's publication, *Jazz
Educators Journal*, is published six times a year.

NATIONAL ASSOCIATION FOR MUSIC THERAPY INC.

Founded in 1950, the National Association of Music Therapy (NAMT)
promotes the therapeutic use of music in hospital, educational, and community settings, and the advancement of education, training, and research
in the profession. NAMT establishes criteria for the professional registration
of music therapists. All members who complete an accredited university
course and a six-month clinical internship can apply to be certified as a
Registered Music Therapist. All members receive the *Journal of Music
Therapy*, which discusses developments in the profession.

NORTH AMERICAN SOCIETY OF TEACHERS OF THE
ALEXANDER TECHNIQUE

This society deals with matters in the United States connected to teaching
the Alexander Technique, a method of physical therapy created by F.M.
Alexander (1869–1955). Its goals are to establish and maintain standards
for certification and training courses, provide services to members, and
educate the public about the Alexander Technique.

SOCIETY FOR ETHNOMUSICOLOGY

The Society for Ethnomusicology, like the American Musicological Society a constituent member of the American Council of Learned Societies,
is concerned with the advancement of research, study, and performance
in all historical periods and in all cultural contexts. Founded in 1956, the
society has an international membership of scholars, performers, publishers, and librarians in a number of disciplines within the social sciences

and humanities. The society publishes the journal *Ethnomusicology* three times a year, *SEM Newsletter*, and a Special Series of monographs, bibliographies, and discographies.

SOCIETY OF MUSIC THEORY

The Society of Music Theory (SMT) was founded in 1977. The society currently has a membership of about eight hundred, including one hundred from Canada and other countries, plus two hundred library memberships. One of the precursors of SMT was the Music Theory Society of New York State. This and other regional associations still operate independently of SMT, the sole national organization. The biannual official journal is *Music Theory Spectrum*, not to be confused with the *Journal of Music Theory*, formerly called *Yale Journal for Music Theory*, which was established in 1957. SMT also publishes a newsletter.

INSTRUMENT ASSOCIATIONS

If you play an instrument there is probably a society for you. Here are some examples: International Horn Society, International Double Reed Society, American Harp Society, American Accordionists' Association Inc., American Guild of Organists, American Recorder Society, American Viola Society, International Society of Bassists, International Trombone Association, National Flute Association, Lute Society of America, Violoncello Society Inc., Viola da Gamba Society of America, Violin Society of America, and Young Keyboard Artists Association.

What are some reasons for joining them? The societies are great sources about new repertoire for your instrument and new makers of your instrument. They are also good for making contacts. You might meet a colleague who has a fifty-year-old edition of a piece no longer in print. Annual or biannual conferences provide performance opportunities. At these events it is possible to try out repertoire not appropriate for a New York debut. The occasion of a conference recital may be a good time to commission a work for your instrument. A lesser-known composer might welcome the chance for such exposure, where many other potential performers will be listening. Competitions for scholarships and other awards, as well as career symposia, are sponsored by instrumental associations. The events usually get covered by music magazines in the United States and abroad.

All the professional societies and instrument associations are listed in *Musical America* and *Gale's Directory of Associations*.

ARCHIVES OF MUSICAL INSTRUMENTS

Archives of musical instruments are usually found in museums or affiliated with universities. Museums are more likely to be concerned with appearance of the instrument as an art object while a university might be more science-oriented, analyzing the instrument's mechanical faculties. Collections are not always in large urban centers. While travelling through Ann Arbor, Michigan, or Vermillion, South Dakota, you can find some unexpected treasures. A list of major collections of musical instruments in the United States follows.

THE MUSEUM OF FINE ARTS, BOSTON, MUSICAL INSTRUMENTS COLLECTION

The Boston Fine Arts Museum Collection of Instruments was created with the gift of 560 instruments from William Lindsey of Boston in 1917. Known as the Canon Francis W. Galpin Collection of instruments, it had been purchased and renamed by Lindsey as a memorial to his daughter, Leslie Lindsey Mason, who went down on the Lusitania during her honeymoon. Over the years, the museum collection has doubled in size, with the addition of collections from Edwin M. Ripin; Peggy Stuart Coolidge, a composer; and B. Allen Rowlland. This collection traces the development of keyboard instruments in European art music from the early sixteenth century. Other highlights are seventeenth- and eighteenth-century European art instruments; a collection of eighteenth- and nineteenth-century instruments made in New England; and East Asian instruments from China, Japan, and Korea. A document describing the Leslie Lindsey Mason Collection, *European Musical Instruments*, by Nicholas Bessaraboff, was published in 1941. The museum's *Catalog of Keyboard Instruments* is to be published in 1991.

THE METROPOLITAN MUSEUM OF ART

The Crosby Brown Collection of Musical Instruments at the Metropolitan Museum of Art in New York, featuring about five thousand instruments from antiquity to the present, celebrated its centennial in 1989. One of the principles guiding the formation of this collection was the goal to represent all parts of the world as completely as possible. Families of instruments have been preserved, among them the viola da braccio and viola da gamba, balalaika, transverse flute (with and without keys), recorder of the Renaissance and of the Baroque, galoubet, ocarina, clarinet, saxophone, sarrusophone, cromorne, oboe and its ancestor the shawm, bassoon, cornet a bouquin, Russian horn, trombone, helicon, brass saxhorn (with rotary valves and with piston valves), and saxhorn with bell over shoulder. The Crosby Brown Collection became the basis for introducing concerts of early music to the museum in 1941. Since that time, the museum has become one of New York's major concert presenters.

THE SHRINE TO MUSIC MUSEUM

The Shrine to Music Museum & Center for Study of the History of Musical Instruments in Vermillion, South Dakota, was founded in 1973. The Arne B. Larson Collection of Musical Instruments & Library forms the nucleus of the museum's holdings. This encyclopedic museum of five thousand instruments is an academic support unit of the University of South Dakota and part of the university's College of Fine Arts. In conjunction with the museum, the university's department of music offers the master of music degree in the history of musical instruments.

In 1984 the museum purchased the Witten-Rawlins Collection. Documenting the early history of north Italian string instrument makers from 1540–1793, the collection includes not only a violin made by Antonio Stradivarius, but one of the two existing guitars by the maker as well. A recent acquisition is a rare lira de braccio, made by Francesco Linarol of Venice in 1563. The Wayne Sorenson Collection of fine nineteenth-century woodwind instruments was acquired in 1982–83. The History of American Instrument Making collection has a woodwinds and brass archive of trade manufacturers' catalogs. The museum publishes *The Shrine to Music Museum Newsletter* and *The Shrine to Music Museum: A Pictorial Souvenir.*

STEARNS COLLECTION OF MUSICAL INSTRUMENTS

Frederick Stearns was a nineteenth-century Detroit pharmacist who became a serious collector of musical instruments and natural history artifacts. In 1899 the Stearns Collection, then consisting of one thousand four hundred instruments from all parts of the world, was donated to the University of Michigan. Since that time the collection has grown to over two thousand Western and non-Western instruments dating from the fifteenth century to the present. The instruments are displayed, and also used in performance by the university community. The Collection's original catalog was compiled in 1921 by Albert Stanley. James Borders has compiled the first volume of the new catalog, entitled *European and American*

Wind and Percussion Instruments, published by the University of Michigan Press.

YALE UNIVERSITY COLLECTION OF MUSICAL INSTRUMENTS

The Yale University Collection of Musical Instruments is an independent member of the Yale community of museums. Established in 1900, the collection now features about one thousand instruments. The genesis of the collection was a large portion of the Morris Steinert collection of historical musical instruments. Steinert, the Steinway piano representative for New England and co-founder of the New Haven Symphony, donated his collection to Yale University in gratitude to the institution for providing rehearsal space for the New Haven Symphony. Since then, the collections of Emil Herrmann, Robyna Neilson Ketchum, and Belle Skinner, as well as Iva Herman's flute collection, have been added. The current collection has a comprehensive selection of historical keyboard instruments from the European Art tradition, a collection of bells, a collection of flutes, and assorted ethnic instruments.

MUSIC COLLECTIONS LITERATURE

The *Survey of Musical Instruments Collections in the United States and Canada* (1974, MLA), edited by William Lichtenwanger, Dale Higbee, Cynthia Adams Hoover, and Phillip T. Young; and the *International Directory of Musical Instrument Collections* (1977), edited by Jean Jenkins, are two important resources on the subject. The entry entitled "Collections" in the *Grove's Dictionary of Music and Musicians* (1980, sixth edition) is an excellent overview of the major collections.

MUSIC CAREER LITERATURE

PERIODICALS

All the professional organizations, service organizations (listed in chapter 6), and the state arts councils publish bulletins, newsletters, and magazines. The money going into these "paper trails" represents a huge portion of operating budgets. Sometimes it seems like too much paper-pushing and too many mailings. We may well wonder: Where are the cash grants we all want? The only thing to do is to *use* these printed materials. Be creative with them. Let them find jobs and opportunities for you. Many are free for the asking.

NEWSLETTERS FROM STATE ARTS COUNCILS

Neither North Dakota nor Nebraska ever figured strongly in my quest for a meaningful career in music. In fact, I have never been in either state. But each of them has a useful newsletter published by its council on the arts. Not only do they have local information, but lists of national grants, competitions, and awards are regular features.

A typical "Opportunities" section of North Dakota's newsletter, for instance, listed a new Jazz Referral Service, the first of its kind, which will enable members of the jazz community to share information through Arts Midwest's computer bank; and seminars for presenters, touring artists, and artists' management.

From Nebraska's *Flatwater Arts Companion* I have found out about new arts books through in-depth book reviews on the back page.

FYI: FOR YOUR INFORMATION

This newsletter is published quarterly by the New York Foundation of the Arts. Unfortunately, the Center for Arts, which had co-published *FYI*, has closed. This newsletter has a ton of practical information for artists. Items range from "Short Reports" to descriptions of job placement bureaus to book reviews to news about other newsletters for artists to information about artist residencies, international activities, grants, and competitions.

LIVING MUSIC

This two-sided, one-page quarterly print-out, published by California's Minuscule University Press Inc., gives lots of career help. For example, a recent issue featured an article entitled "How to Get Your Work Played by the University Conductor." Discussion of making contacts, performing rights licenses, delivering quality materials, getting paid for the work, and correct etiquette upon acceptance or rejection of a score or proposal is all valuable information for a young composer.

BOOKS

The following is a list of books to help guide musicians: *Supporting Yourself as an Artist* by Deborah A. Hoover and *Performing Artists Handbook* by Janice Papolos were two invaluable career helps to me as I prepared this book for publication. Others are *Hollywood Studio Musicians: Their Work and Careers in the Recording Industry* by Robert F. Faulkner, *Inside the Music Business: Music in Contemporary Life* by Michael Fink, *Insights on Jazz: A Musician's Guide to Increasing Performance Opportunities* by Willard V. Jenkins, Jr., *Guide to Competitions* by the Concert Artists Guild, *Whole Arts Directory* by Cynthia Navaretta, and *How to Submit Music Manuscripts to Publishers* by Norman Ward.

Business of music books, emphasizing contract and copyright law and other such issues, are another type of career help, more practical than conceptual in scope. They will address important practical concerns. Foremost among them are *Music Business Handbook and Career Guide* by David Baskerville, *This Business of Music* by Sidney Shemel and William M. Krasilovsky, *The Music Business: Career Opportunities and Self-Defense* by Dick Weissman, and the *Encyclopedia of the Music Business* by Harvey Rachlin.

CHAPTER

3

Orchestral Auditions

NO responsible book on music careers should be without a chapter on orchestral auditions. According to the American Symphony Orchestra League, there are forty-seven major orchestras in the United States with annual operating incomes exceeding $3.4 million. Many pay musicians a minimum annual salary of $50,000. Playing in an orchestra is a fine, respectable occupation for an instrumentalist. Many orchestral musicians also teach, give recitals, make recordings, and have busy, fulfilling lives.

Yet this is a frustrating chapter to write. Competition for orchestral positions has become so fierce that excellent preparation may not be enough to get the job. So much is out of the auditioner's hands. When two hundred excellent contenders try out for a position, there is an element of chance operating as well, a little like a roulette game. One experienced auditioner calls it a "crap shoot." Sometimes no one gets the job because the judges can't find a particular candidate who stands out—probably because most players are so qualified! This book's theme is that musicians can take control of their own lives and help themselves enormously. The world of orchestral auditions is one arena where the young ambitious musician may encounter a lot of undeserved rejection. The former principal cellist of a leading American opera company voices a legitimate complaint about orchestral auditions: "The problem is they are not auditioning your ability to play in an orchestra. Once when auditioning for the San Francisco Symphony, in the finals I was asked to play a passage from Mendelssohn's *Italian Symphony*. It was marked pianissimo. I did my best to play softly, as indicated. Edo de Waart, the conductor, remarked: 'Can you play it louder? You'll never hear that in a big hall.' Yet if someone in a section *did* play that passage loudly, the person would stick out like a sore thumb."

On a more positive note, with perseverance and good solid preparation, anything can happen. A violinist in the Chicago Symphony auditioned three times before being chosen. The first bassoonist of a major American orchestra got the job on the fifth audition. Determination is essential if this is your chosen career path.

Auditioning is a skill *separate* from one's actual playing ability. It can be learned and even tolerated through good judgment, logic, and experience. William Lincer, a Juilliard professor who was principal violist of the New York Philharmonic for thirty-five years, has prepared many students for auditions. A major problem he sees is that "kids have inadequate instruments. They don't sound in a big hall." He offers a basic piece of advice: "When auditioning, you must play like a soloist, regardless of the dynamic, even in the orchestral excerpts."

Invest the considerable time, money, and effort involved in an audition only *if you really want the position*. A half-hearted effort will only make you angry and disappointed later that you hadn't given the experience your best shot.

FINDING OUT ABOUT ORCHESTRAL AUDITIONS

The monthly publication of the American Federation of Musicians, the New York-based *International Musician*, is sent free to members of all locals affiliated with the American Federation of Musicians (See chapter 6). The back page contains up-to-date lists of job openings and addresses to which resumes should be sent. The American Symphony Orchestra League, based in Washington, D.C., also offers a comprehensive orchestral job openings list to its members. The following is a typical listing in the *International Musician*. (See page 35.)

Foreign orchestral auditions are listed in *International Musician* and in the German magazine *Das Orchestra*, a Schott publication based in Mainz.

SAN FRANCISCO SYMPHONY

Herbert Blomstedt, Music Director
Announces the following vacancies for the 1990/91 season:

SECTION 1st VIOLIN
SECTION 2nd VIOLIN
SECOND FLUTE

Audition Dates

Section 1st Violin
Section 2nd Violin   April 29&30,1990
Second Flute   May 6&7, 1990.

Application deadline for these auditions is February 9, 1990.
Send one-page resumes to:
Joshua Feldman
Orchestra Personnel Manager
San Francisco Symphony
Davies Symphony Hall
San Francisco, CA 94102-4575

The Audition Committee of the San Francisco Symphony Orchestra reserves the right to dismiss immediately any candidate not meeting the highest professional standards at these auditions.

• • • • • • • • • • • • • • • • • • • •

Only the most highly qualified candidates should apply. The San Francisco Symphony is an Equal Opportunity Employer.

AUDITION FORMATS AND PROCEDURES: SCREENS, AND ALL THE REST OF IT

The year: 1966. The telephone rang in the apartment of the legendary American bassist Frederick Zimmermann, for many years a prominent bass player in the New York Philharmonic. The voice on the other end glumly announced the decision. "Fred, we have no choice. This is the third time she's auditioned and she's *STILL* the best. We have to let her in this time. There is nothing else to be done now." Zimmermann, who had been pacing the floor for hours, breathed a sigh of relief. History was being made. The first woman ever was about to become a member of a string section in the New York Philharmonic. It was Zimmermann's own student, Orin O'Brien. He had watched through two previous auditions as his male colleagues refused to admit the obvious. A person who plays the best deserves the job regardless of sex, race, or religion. O'Brien also credits conductor Leonard Bernstein for his courage in accepting her as a member of the orchestra.

Those were the days before the advent of the screen. Since that era, in an effort to make auditions fairer, i.e., less discriminatory against women and blacks, many orchestras have begun "behind the screen" auditions, at least for the preliminary round. Screens are some type of removable wall that separates the person auditioning from the listeners. Women are encouraged to wear flat shoes to do away with any tell-tale signs of gender. The New York Philharmonic writes candidates:

> You may play from your own music if you wish, otherwise, the music will be provided. Also, you will play behind a screen to provide anonymity; women, please do not wear heels which make an obvious sound.

Although there are certain similarities among audition procedures, each orchestra has its own routines. The Metropolitan Opera Orchestra and the Montreal Symphony use screens for the whole audition process, including finals. On the other hand, the Cleveland Orchestra doesn't use the screen at all, nor does the Los Angeles Philharmonic, which has the highest number of minority personnel of any major U.S. orchestra. Screen or no screen, there are more women than ever before in American symphony orchestras today, many in principal positions. Certainly, we have come a long way since Orin O'Brien was admitted to the New York Philharmonic. There are other variations in the audition procedure. Most orchestra committees hear only the prepared solo and orchestral excerpts. Others, such as the New York Philharmonic and Cleveland Orchestra, ask candidates for sight-reading that is not sent with the audition material.

Sometimes the preliminaries and final auditions are held on one day. In other cases, preliminaries and semifinals are held on one day, and at a later date finalists are flown back at the expense of the orchestra for the last round. Sometimes a trial period playing in the orchestra is part of the final audition. For a recent concertmaster opening in the St. Louis Symphony Orchestra, several candidates served two-week stints in the leader's chair before the position was filled.

Auditions can be tough. A cellist now in a major U.S. orchestra described a grueling day in Washington, D.C. "All the eighty applicants for the cello position of the National Symphony Orchestra were herded together into one room to warm up. . . . Those of us who were successful in the preliminaries had to wait for hours, without anywhere to go for lunch or dinner (because you didn't know when you'd next be called to play) until the final round. I was so tired and hungry by the time I was called to play that I was unable to repeat the strong impression I made hours earlier."

The lesson? Know beforehand as much as you can about an audition. A particular orchestra's auditioning "style" can be described to you by colleagues who have auditioned there previously. If this cellist had known what to expect in Washington, she might have brought food with her and requested a place to nap. These factors might have pulled her "over the top." As it was, she came in second for the job.

THE TAPED RESUME

A section violin position in the San Francisco Symphony Orchestra elicited 357 resumes. The Cleveland Orchestra had nearly one hundred fifty applicants for each of three openings: second violin, principal trumpet, and piccolo. A recent flute position in the New York Philharmonic drew hundreds of applicants. Yes, the audition circuit seems to have gotten a little out of hand. Never before has there been such a great supply of well-qualified instrumentalists to fill the relatively small number of orchestral jobs available. Because of this, many orchestras now require a resume tape before the live audition. The New York Philharmonic actually calls its tape stage the preliminary audition. Candidates are invited from those who submit tapes. In guidelines for a position in the Boston Symphony Orchestra, the following tape specifications were given:

GUIDELINES FOR MAKING AND SUBMITTING
CASSETTE TAPES FOR PRELIMINARY AUDITIONS

For the best possible representation of your playing on this tape, we strongly suggest that you consider taping in a professional studio with a professional sound engineer. (This can be done at a modest cost —no extravagant set-ups or equipment is necessary.) However, if this is impractical or impossible we ask that you observe and conform to the following guidelines so that insofar as it is possible all applicants' tapes can be considered fairly.

Only audio tapes will be accepted.

I. *Equipment*

Because the quality of recorded sound to some extent may affect the audition committee's judgment, we strongly recommend the following:

1. Cassette recorder--a very high-quality recorder in good working order with Dolby B (a retail value probably in excess of approximately $200.)

2. Microphones--such as: pairs of AKG 414, 451, Neumann U87, KM84, KM86, Schoeps SKM 52U, Shure SM81, or Neumann SM69, AKG C24, Schoeps SKS 501U, or an equivalent,

high-quality microphone. These are all available at fine audio equipment stores or can be rented for a modest cost.

3. Tape--please use Maxell UDXL II C60 or an equivalent hi-bias (Type II) tape.

II. *Settings and Acoustics*

1. Record using Dolby B.

2. Set VU (Volume) meters so that your loudest passages peak at 0. Do not overload or under-record your tape. And please do not use automatic level setters.

3. Be sure to record in *quiet* surroundings (i.e., no background noise). Avoid churches, large halls, and bathrooms. A room of at least 20' × 30' with at least a 10' ceiling is suggested, and of comfortable acoustics.

4. Record in *STEREO*. Either a stereo microphone or a closely placed pair on a stereo bar should be used.

Suggested placement:

Two uni-directional microphones placed 90° apart with the sound source approximately 8' away (in the middle of the angle) either in one of the following configurations:

A. (using 2 microphones)   -or-   B: (can be done with 2 microphones or with a stereo microphone)

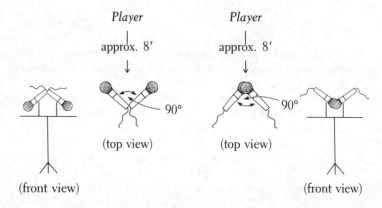

Player
approx. 8'

(top view)

(front view)

Player
approx. 8'

(top view)

(front view)

NOTE: Each instrument makes sound in a different manner. The microphone placement should be in a location and angled to get direct sound. Try several positions and *listen* to a playback to find which best represents your instrument's sound. Avoid close miking.

III. *Taping Procedure* (The performance pitch of the Boston Symphony Orchestra is A = 442. Please record at this pitch if possible.)

1. So that we may play back your tape at the pitch to which our audition committee is accustomed, please play on your instrument and record about five seconds of the A to which your instrument is tuned.

2. Then, record *only* those orchestral excerpts and prescribed solo passages Xeroxed on the enclosed Preliminary Tape Audition Repertoire list. Record in the sequence listed, #1 sequentially through the last excerpt listed.

3. Leave approximately 5 seconds blank between excerpts.

4. Please play all excerpts straight through (rests are to be metered where practical) with *no* editing done on the tape. You may stop playing and re-record any excerpt at will. But please submit a tape that is representative of your normal performance and thereby avoid what otherwise might be a fruitless and costly trip to audition live. Allow yourself 40–45 minutes to make your tape.

5. Do not use piano accompaniment in recording any of this material.

6. LISTEN objectively to your tape to ensure that it conveys a realistic and true representation of your playing and the sound of your instrument. We suggest listening on a machine other than the one used for recording so that any technical flaws in your cassette recorder (such as tape speed) will be apparent to you.

7. Rewind the tape to the beginning before sending.

8. Print your name on the *label* of the cassette itself (not on the box) together with the make and model numbers of the microphone and cassette recorder used.

IV. Please submit your cassette prior to the deadline date to:

LYNN LARSEN
Boston Symphony Orchestra
Symphony Hall
301 Massachusetts Ave.
Boston, Ma. 02115

Tape directives vary with different orchestras, but these guidelines are typical.

WHAT IF YOU ARE NOT INVITED?

Sometimes on the basis of a taped or printed resume, a candidate is *not* invited to the audition. This happened to a young player after applying to the Cleveland Orchestra for an associate principal horn position. He was not pleased. A rebuttal followed. He wrote to the orchestra that he *was* a qualified candidate. "I want to audition," he wrote, "and I don't think you'll be sorry you heard me." The orchestra reconsidered and invited him. Out of the 127 players who came to audition, he got the job.

The New York Philharmonic's form letter telling a player the taped resume wasn't accepted has an "escape" clause:

> . . . on occasion there may be extenuating circumstances be-
> yond an applicant's control that would cause a tape to be not fully
> representative of one's playing. If you feel that is true in your case
> and would like to audition, you must submit a letter stating your
> desire to do so and provide us with two musical references in
> support of this re-application.

The lesson from all this? You can fight to get invited to an audition if you want the job badly enough.

PREPARING FOR THE AUDITION

An audition should be like a performance as much as possible, communicating one's art as musically and convincingly as possible. Unfortunately an audition is *more* difficult than a performance because the time is so limited—anywhere from one minute to half an hour to create a very important first impression. Yes, I mean one minute. According to legend, conductor George Szell listened to a violinist tune up for a Cleveland Orchestra audition years ago and said "thank you"—before the candidate played a note! Szell was not satisfied with the tuning!

Some orchestras specify the repertoire they want to hear. For example, many German orchestras ask violinists for a Mozart concerto, and violists for the Stamitz or Hoffmeister Concertos. If there is a choice of works, select a piece that shows off your particular strengths. It is usually unwise to choose the most difficult work written for your instrument. The audition committee likes to hear contrast, melodic lyricism and fast passages show different sides of one's playing ability.

ORCHESTRAL EXCERPTS

Before the audition you usually will be sent a list of orchestral excerpts and the music for the selected parts. Obtain the entire parts from which the excerpts were chosen. Learn whole parts, not just excerpts. This will shed light on the musical context of the selected bars. Technical perfection is not enough; your renditions must also demonstrate musical understanding. Listen to several recordings of each piece to analyze the varied tempi and musical ideas of different conductors. Why not play your part of each piece along with a recording? In the event that you haven't yet performed a particular work, this exercise will give you a sense of how the part fits into the total orchestral texture. Studying the score of each required work is also an important tool for being fluent with the music. For each instrument, certain excerpts always seem to be requested by audition committees of the different orchestras—so much so that the personnel managers of major American orchestras actually got together and compiled a listing. Called *Facing the Maestro*, it can be ordered through the American Symphony Orchestra League.

Another preparation technique is dressing up for the audition and doing practice runs—straight through—for yourself and later for small groups of colleagues. Hear the music in your head before you begin a selection. Never take a tempo faster than what you can handle cleanly and with good articulation.

WHAT IS THE AUDITION COMMITTEE LISTENING FOR?

A member of the Chicago Symphony explained: "When I'm listening to a candidate's audition, I ask myself: Do I love that sound enough to want it to become part of the Chicago Symphony? If I like what I hear, I listen carefully to what the player does with it." The audition committee naturally enough wants its orchestra to maintain the highest possible standard, and even to keep getting better. What are the listeners focusing on? The obvious components, like intonation, rhythm, and articulation, must be flawless. Categories listed on the "score sheets" at New York Philharmonic auditions, for example, are solo selection, tone, technique, intonation, rhythm, reading, musicianship, and additional remarks. But it is good musicality and phrasing, an expression going beyond the purely technical requirements of the music, which is likely to be the trademark of the winner.

AFTER THE AUDITION

The winning candidate feels a just reward for the great effort that has gone into the long, hard preparation. What about the vast majority who don't win? One member of a leading American orchestra advises, "If you take the trouble to go to an audition, bring as much as you can away from the experience." Before joining one of the world's great orchestras, this player was unsuccessful in a number of auditions. He always tried to get comments from members of the audition committee afterward, either by going to the orchestra's personnel manager to request a list of comments, or by telephoning the members individually. Recently, he was a judge at an audition with ninety candidates. No one got the job. To his astonishment, only two bothered to contact him for feedback afterward.

Joseph Alessi, principal trombone of the New York Philharmonic, welcomes dialogue with candidates after an audition. "When I've been on audition committees, I and most of my colleagues take notes on each player. I file the notes away and keep them for months." After a recent New York Philharmonic audition for assistant first and third trumpet, two people phoned Alessi, and he was able to refer to his audition notes.

TUNING THE FINE POINTS

In May 1982, while living in Israel, I participated in a workshop-masterclass with Leonard Bernstein and a small, then-unestablished orchestra from the desert town of Beersheva. The Jerusalem Music Center was crammed with young conductors and other listeners wanting to hear the class. As he chatted with young colleagues, Bernstein noted that some of the most famous orchestras, although superb, were often less flexible in accepting his musical ideas than younger, lesser-known groups. At one point he suggested an unorthodox way for the violins to make a crescendo (on a down-bow). Instead of balking at the idea, they tried it and were successful. He asked the ensemble to improvise a composition from watching his gestures. Because of the unbelievable attentiveness of the group, the piece was a huge success, full of dynamic contrast and drama.

The point of this story? During the final phase of an audition, a candidate may be asked to play the same passage more than one way. A conductor likes to see quick response in working with the orchestra. The qualities displayed by the small group in Israel—concentration, open-mindedness, flexibility—will impress the committee listeners and conductor in the final cut.

FINAL THOUGHTS

Flutist Samuel Baron, one of the most inspiring musicians around, once said something I think about often: "Each concert is a dress rehearsal for the next." The same can be said for the audition process. Our musical lives are a continuum. We will always be performing and auditioning for something! No matter what happens, the odds are that sometimes we'll be successful and sometimes not. The process of growth and renewal should never stop.

STARTING OUT IN ORCHESTRAS: CAREER RESOURCES

What better preparation for an audition than becoming familiar with the orchestral repertoire? There are some orchestras that were founded for the purpose of training young musicians. As the end of the twentieth century nears, the connection between performance groups and composers seems to grow stronger. As a result, composers also benefit from programs offered by these training orchestras.

NEW WORLD SYMPHONY
The New World Symphony (NWS) is a Miami-based orchestra that had its genesis through the National Foundation for the Advancement of Artists. Conceived as a bridge between a musician's studies and entry into the profession, the 86-member orchestra began functioning in 1987. Twenty-one alumni from the NWS are now gainfully employed in professional orchestras. Selection for NWS is by national audition. Competition is considerable: In its first year, one thousand applicants auditioned. Members, who must re-audition annually, receive free housing and a stipend of $300 a week, renewable for up to three years. The chamber music program enables NWS members to perform in small groups as well as in the orchestra. New World Symphony concert appearances in the last few

years have included a four-week residency in Orange County, California, a five-city Florida tour, performances in Big Sky, Montana, and an international tour in Paris and cities in South America. The current music director of the New World Symphony is Michael Tilson Thomas.

NATIONAL ORCHESTRAL ASSOCIATION

From the year of its founding in 1939 to the late 1970s, the New York-based National Orchestral Association (NOA) was an orchestra composed of conservatory students. Founded by music patron Mary Flagler Cary and conductor Leon Barzin, the National Orchestral Association rehearsed several afternoons a week and performed public concerts. In exchange for participation, each player earned scholarship funds toward tuition and a living stipend. During this era NOA was fully funded by Cary and conducted exclusively by Barzin. The goal of the organization was to prepare college-age music students for orchestral lives. As conservatory orchestras started becoming a stronger force within music schools, NOA lost purpose. In the last several years its focus has shifted to the performance of contemporary music.

The New Music Orchestral Project is sponsored by the NOA in cooperation with the Manhattan School of Music. The national search for orchestral scores that have never been performed culminates in an annual Carnegie Hall concert of premieres. This is one competition where composers' scores are judged anonymously. Distinguished jurors narrow a group of three hundred scores to fifteen. The copying and editing costs of the fifteen chosen works are covered by NOA. The pieces are taped in a private reading by the orchestra. An invaluable service to the composer is the agent role played by NOA. Tapes and scores of the chosen works are sent to different conductors in an effort to secure other performances for the works. At the same time, NOA players get exposure to performing contemporary orchestral literature under the baton of music director Jorge Mester.

NEW YORK YOUTH ORCHESTRA

Not only young performers benefit from the New York Youth Orchestra. Composers starting out get their works played and novice conductors learn the professional ropes of planning rehearsal time and dealing with management. The group in New York, comprised of players age twelve to twenty-two, is representative of youth orchestras throughout the country. There is now a Youth Orchestra division of the American Symphony Orchestra League to which they all belong. Each year at the annual Carnegie Hall concert the new work of a young American is performed.

The piece is chosen by a panel of distinguished composers from among over ninety submissions. According to director Barry Goldberg, "This program is a springboard for a young composer, a bouncing-off point for a career." The winning composer is awarded $1,000, expenses for producing the score up to $2,000, and the Carnegie Hall performance. But perhaps the most educational part is the rehearsal process. The composer attends five rehearsals and therefore becomes part of the process, answering questions, correcting the score, and witnessing the transformation of the notes into music.

NEW YORK PHILHARMONIC MUSIC ASSISTANCE FUND
ORCHESTRA FELLOWSHIP PROGRAM

Fellowships in orchestras throughout the United States are available to African-American players of stringed instruments who have earned a degree in music. Fellows, who are chosen by audition, receive a monthly stipend of $2,500 for undertaking the following activities: rehearsals and performances with the orchestra, coaching with distinguished artists for future auditions, and intensive summer study. Fellowships are for a one-year period with an option to be renewed.

CHAPTER

4

Ready to Perform

PUBLICITY materials, including a good photograph, brochure, and press kit, are essential tools for a performer's career identity. Maybe a New York or London recital debut is the next step in your career. How do you find out about concert spaces? Is it necessary for a performer to have a manager? What is entailed in touring as a soloist or with an orchestra? This chapter will address these fundamental issues.

PHOTOGRAPHS: A PICTURE IS WORTH A THOUSAND WORDS

THE IMAGE

As a performing musician, your face and body language blend with the sound of your instrument or voice to create a total image of *you*, the musician. The photographs you use in publicity can have a beneficial—or detrimental—effect on your career.

FINDING A PHOTOGRAPHER

Several years ago, I needed pictures for a new brochure. Several colleagues made recommendations about photographers. The same name popped up a few times. I saw a sample of her work, and phoned. She seemed dedicated and honest, and was willing to spend all the time necessary for a productive session.

A performer enters into an important relationship with a photographer. Comfort with the person, or lack of it, shows up in the pictures. Going by one's instincts in these situations is important. The feeling must be right.

RECOLLECTIONS FROM A SESSION

My photographer had advised me to come "armed" with five different outfits, each with a different color, style, and "message." Each top provided a new frame for the face. The first question: "Which angle of your face do you dislike vehemently, if any?" I told her in no uncertain terms! "Fine—we won't waste pictures on that," she said. Our session began with makeup. She did it all for me, from a box of wonders any six-year-old girl could only dream about. Thank goodness I had come directly from having my hair cut and blow-dried. It looked neat. Otherwise, she would have spent more time putting that part of me in place. Makeup ready, outfit No. 1, SHOOT! On it went until five exchanges of clothes, many rolls of film, and seven hours had passed. She had ideas. I had ideas. We worked as a team. At the end we were both exhausted.

During the session, I tried to be myself. I tried not to look posed. But therein lies the psychological know-how of a good photographer, literally clicking into the psyche of the subject. As a technique of getting to know you, the photographer will call out instructions—look here, there, up, down—and in doing so will find out what elicits the most natural response. Don't forget that the picture will ultimately be speaking for you to people you've never met.

After a few days, the contact sheets were ready. Family and friends gave me feedback. I had my own impressions. After seeing the 8 × 10 enlargements of the several I had selected, two were chosen for immediate use. The decision was made to have my name printed under each picture on the print, which costs a little more. While the most expensive promotional material isn't a prerequisite for success, scrimping and saving now may result in paying later. More than a half decade has now passed: The pictures have been used in two new brochures, in newspapers from Cuba to Australia, and in recital programs, books, posters, and even a video slide show.

LAST-MINUTE TIPS

Before your session, think how your instrument can be used creatively to enhance your photograph. Consider sites for shooting out of the photog-

rapher's studio. My chamber group in Israel had our photo session over-looking the walls of the old city of Jerusalem. Never close your imagination to what might work best.

BROCHURES: A SELLING TOOL
IN THE MARKETPLACE

STYLES

The dictionary defines brochure as a "pamphlet, booklet, treatise or article published in such form." In the music world, a brochure (or leaflet, as it is called across the Atlantic) can mean anything from a single sheet of paper to a multi-page spread. Sizes vary. It can be general promotional material about an artist, or an advertisement for a specific recital or event. One commonly used type of brochure is a sheet with a photograph on one side and biography, reviews, and anything else which describes what one does on the backside. (See example on pages 50–51) Note that on the brochure's back the reader can find out how and where to reach you, either directly or through management. This is a good general style of brochure because its use is versatile. If an important recital comes along, a graphic designer can include the specifics of the concert in blank space, called the imprint space, on either side of the brochure. (In my sample brochure, the imprint space is used to describe my lectures as a music career consultant.) Think of all the money that will be saved by avoiding the expense of a special recital brochure!

CHOOSING A GRAPHIC DESIGNER

Many of the decisions you will be making about your brochure on paper, typeface, photograph, color, format, and copy will be made with the help of a graphic designer. As with a photographer, to find the best person, ask colleagues for recommendations. Ask those whose brochures you like. Get suggestions from your photographer. Find out costs for the design of the brochure and printing from prospective candidates. It pays to print more copies rather than fewer, as printing costs get lower per copy the more there are printed. You may be asked to supply brochures to presenters and others doing publicity for you. Visit prospective designers to discuss ideas for layout, format, and other technical details. Obviously, go with the most creative artist at the best price.

COPY FOR THE BROCHURE

Who will write the biography? No one knows you better, knows better what your gifts are and what you are trying to accomplish in life, than you. If you are unsure about your writing skills, dictate thoughts to a more literate friend, whose copy you can later edit.

Don't make the brochure too long. People tend not to read material that is too cluttered. It's better not to list your entire repertoire. Write "repertoire list available upon request." Then print an attractively designed list to be sent later.

Your graphic designer can advise you about the layout of review excerpts. Avoid using one-word quotes: ". . . Amazing . . ." looks rather suspicious and may raise questions about what came before and after. Always put the name of the newspaper underneath the review.

Have all the brochure copy in a completed, edited version before you present it to the graphic designer. Changes after typesetting are costly.

violist

NANCY USCHER

"Unforgettable performance . . .
joyously lyrical . . .
fluid technique and tonal warmth."
The Washington Post

COLOR ME . . .

Adding a color to black and white copy can dress up your message. A New York manager once advised me against using a color for a brochure. She liked the stark drama of black and white. I didn't. Lavender was woven into the design of my brochure and the resulting image was what I wanted.

PRACTICAL POINTERS

As far as dimensions are concerned, you will want the brochure to fit into racks at concert halls and music stores. You'll also want it to fold easily in a long envelope for bulk mailing.

Don't be dismayed at the number of times the mechanical (the final, technically-exact copy of everything to appear in the brochure, minus the picture) needs to be corrected. The big problems have been solved, but all the little things need to be sorted out also before the final draft goes to the printer. Reviewing spellings and getting periods and commas in the right place is a tedious but necessary process. Before the printing, the graphic artist will send the proof sheet to you for final approval. Be patient through this final stage! When you're spending thousands of dollars on an important career tool, you want it to be right.

In the end, your brochure should be a nicely organized presentation. An effectively designed product can make a lasting impression of you on the concert presenter, radio producer, or whoever is getting to know about you.

PRESS KIT

A press kit is your introduction to any media outlet, whether it be newspapers, magazines, or radio, as well as a means to get concert engagements. The publicity brochure can be pasted to the folder cover of the kit. The contents should include a good 8 × 10 black and white glossy photograph, a narrative biography—if the kit is without a publicity brochure—and newspaper reviews. Each review should have the name of the publication and date. A resume isn't necessary for the kit; a biography serves the same purpose. An experienced New York manager warns never to send a press kit to newspaper critics who you hope will attend your recital, only a press release answering the questions who, what, where, when, and why. On the other hand, a press kit would be an appropriate introduction for someone writing a feature article or a presenter doing advance publicity for your appearance.

RECITALS

WHERE TO GIVE A RECITAL? THINK CREATIVELY

The life blood of a performer's existence is communicating to an audience. Giving recitals is a beautiful way to grow, become confident, and at the same time, give others lots of pleasure. A recital can be a major affair, such as a New York debut, or it can be a more informal event in someone's living room. There are all kinds of possibilities in between. Most countries in the world have embassies in Washington, D.C., and consulates in New York and other major cities. They frequently sponsor cultural events. Why not propose a concert of French music to the French consulate, or an evening of Finnish music to the Finnish embassy? Arts councils of countries such as Canada and Australia will pay their own composers to write a piece for you. The concert's centerpiece can be the world premiere of a piece by a young up-and-coming composer from the country whose music is being celebrated. Although you will not earn big money, usually there is a small honorarium, and excellent exposure. The event could lead the way to an invitation abroad. Other concert opportunities? Consult the list of associations in chapter 2. Many sponsor concerts. Take a look in the newsletters and music periodicals discussed throughout the book. There are plenty of interesting ideas waiting to be discovered.

THE VALUE OF A NEW YORK OR LONDON RECITAL DEBUT

As recently as 1950, a New York debut could "make or break" a young artist. Debuts were no small events, usually taking place in significant venues such as New York's Town Hall or London's Wigmore Hall. Debuts were attended by at least one and usually several influential newspaper critics. What was written the day after the concert affected the artist for many years to come. Times have changed. Careers are no longer dependent on debuts, and critics cannot be counted on to come to them. A successful debut can be an auspicious beginning to a career, but there are no guarantees.

Organizations such as Young Concert Artists, Concert Artists Guild, and International Artists sponsor New York debuts of musicians who win rigorous competitions organized for this purpose. These management groups also help develop their artists' careers for a year or more after the debut. Some artists set up debuts for themselves. The cost is substantial. Renting one of the major New York halls, i.e., Merkin Hall, Weill Recital Hall, Kaufmann Concert Hall at the 92nd Street Y, Alice Tully Hall, Town Hall, or Kathryn Miller Theater at Columbia University, is just the beginning of the expense. Hall costs vary from about $1,000 to about $5,000. Each location's recital contract includes different terms. Be sure to read the small print about what rehearsals and services are and are not included in the stated fee before making a final decision. London halls tend to be a bit less expensive. The total costs for a New York recital, with or without a manager, will probably not be less than $5,000 and depending on which hall is chosen, can be as much as $20,000. Halls usually need to be booked at least one year in advance.

Although there are no guarantees about the aftermath of a debut, one thing is sure. If you feel ready for the plunge, the recital is a great personal milestone. The event *may* lead to other opportunities because of the exposure it generates. More than anything else, the personal growth and self-confidence gained are invaluable career boosters. However, unlike the past era, it alone can no longer "make or break" an artist.

REPRESENTATION FOR THE RECITAL

Any individual can rent a New York or London recital hall for a concert. But the only person sure to be at the concert is the performer. Getting an audience to come is a long-term, painstaking process that requires months of effort and imagination. Although the work to promote a recital can be done without management, it may be worthwhile to hire someone to help. Competition winners of the debut contests have built-in representation from their sponsors. What does it cost to hire someone to produce your recital, put it all together for you? The ball-park figure in New York is at least $5,000 for labor only, but it varies quite a bit. Besides renting the hall, which is not included in that figure, a representative's duties are putting together the press kit, writing press releases for newspapers, getting radio exposure for the artist on classical showcase programs with interviews and recital previews, sending out invitations for complimentary tickets, being the call-back number for any inquiries about the recital and, perhaps most important, getting a *New York Times* critic there. Having recital representation makes particular sense if you are living out of New York during the months before the event. New York Recital Associates, Inc. has been presenting New York recitals since 1963 and enjoys a very fine reputation. Beverly Wright & Associates is another firm highly regarded for New York recital presentation. The Resource Guide lists others. It is very important that you are comfortable with the person helping you. Be sure to interview prospective candidates before making a commitment.

For a London recital, it is customary to use a concert agent. I recommend it. The *British Music Yearbook* has a huge list from which to choose. A London recital, either in the Wigmore Hall or the South Bank's Purcell Room, is a slightly cheaper affair than the New York debut.

Remember: By taking on the recital project, the manager is *not* taking you on as a regular client. This should all be made very clear before contracts are signed.

ALL THE FREE PUBLICITY YOU CAN GET . . .

Part of the fun and value of planning the recital is getting your name and picture around as much as possible. Whether or not someone is helping out, you'll want to be very creative about getting exposure. Make a list of all the publications that give free listings of upcoming cultural events. A writer from one of these magazines or papers might even be interested in writing a profile or doing an interview. If you are writing your own press release, keep it clear and succinct. Stick to the essential details of the recital; avoid the temptation to tell your life story! Be sure the press release answers the following questions: who, what, when, where, why it is significant, and who can be contacted for further information. Send it about three months before the concert date and include a glossy 8 × 10 photograph with each package. Make sure your name is on it. Don't ask for the photograph back. Send another reminder six weeks before the concert. Remember your hometown paper. The story about your recital will rank in the "Hometown Musician Hits Stardom" category. The alumni magazine of your alma mater will be glad to print an announcement of your next appearance. Distinguished graduates read it. Your notice may get considerable attention and even attract new audience members. The American Federation of Musicians trade paper, *International Musician*, is another source of publicity. Find out publishing timetables for the different periodicals, since often news items must be sent months in advance. Contact all radio stations with classical music programming. Playing and being interviewed is a great showcase for upcoming concerts. A large segment of the population is faithful to these shows.

For visual advertising, enlargements of the recital brochure can be plastered all over New York: in record and music shops, on poles and buildings near Lincoln Center and Carnegie Hall, and on campuses of universities in the metropolitan area. Perhaps you'll sell some tickets to your recital. However, this goal should not be a priority. Energy is better spent getting the right people there, whether or not they are paying customers. Put all of your mailing lists together. Include family, friends, and all the important, influential people you know personally or have heard about. Send each person a cordial invitation which can later be exchanged for two complimentary tickets at the box office. If a manager is handling the mailing, the invited guest can phone to request the tickets. An enthusiastic house full of your family and friends provides a much more vibrant recital audience than a sparse group of ticket buyers.

PROGRAMMING IS AN ART

Be imaginative with programming for your recital. Explore all possible repertoire for your instrument. Consult books that have lists of repertoire, read newsletters of your instrument's society, and write to all the different music publishers to get their latest (free!) catalogues. There is even a research institute in Philadelphia, Musicdata Inc., whose only job is to keep track of music in print, Most major libraries subscribe to this service. Keep informed about small chamber works for your instrument. It adds zest to include one piece with a guest artist on a solo recital. A more diverse program may attract a bigger audience. Select the finest repertoire from different periods and cultures.

Why not get one of your favorite composer-colleagues to write and dedicate a piece to you for your recital? You will be making history as well as news, adding a new work to your instrument's repertory, and giving the composer valuable exposure. The commission will be another important vehicle for publicity. Also try to find unusual works—American premieres. Come up with a balanced, intriguing array of works. As a final check for shaping the best possible program, ask yourself: If *you* were a non-musician sitting in the audience, would there be enough variety to keep you interested?

Program notes are important, extremely important! They educate the listener by setting the historical stage for each piece. As the performer, you know exactly why the works on the program have been selected. Each work has a special meaning in the context of the whole program. Who else has that unique perspective? The recital will be enhanced and made personal with notes you contribute.

Before you give a major New York or London recital, it is a good idea to try out the program several times, enough times to get confident but not so many that the program feels stale.

MENTAL AND PHYSICAL EXERCISES: PREPARATION FOR THE PERFORMER

In the weeks before my New York recital debut I had a few sessions with an Alexander Technique teacher (whose method is described in chapter 14) specializing in work with musicians. The routine of going to someone for help before the big event served me well. The Feldenkreis Method is another approach used by musicians. A *Soprano on Her Head: Discovering the Performer Within* by Eloise Ristad uses unorthodox means to tackle problems of technique, interpretation, and stage fright. The books *The Inner Game of Tennis* by W. Timothy Gallwey and *The Inner Game of Music* by Barry Green with W. Timothy Gallwey talk about focusing and concentrating under pressure. Many of today's health centers offer yoga-relaxation-breathing seminars which can be useful to musicians, especially as a routine to fall back on during times of particular stress.

*A*FTER THE RECITAL

The entire recital experience will surely contribute to your identity as a musician and to your self-confidence. Once it is over, there is usually a letdown, and then you can't wait to get up and do it again! While considering future career steps, there may be thoughts of getting concert management.

TO HAVE MANAGEMENT OR NOT TO HAVE IT

The head of a well-known management agency in New York told me the following tale: "A young man in a piano-duo phoned me at the recommendation of a mutual friend. I thought to myself: 'That's all I need—another duo-piano team!' I was determined not to take them. The guy suggested meeting for lunch, and the fact is that I was utterly charmed by these two people. In spite of my previous resolution I did take them on." The man in that piano team knew he and his partner were ready for management, wanted it badly, and knew how to act relaxed at the moment when an overzealous attitude could have scared management away. These musicians convinced the manager of their worth *before she had heard a note of their playing.*

When I returned to the United States after six years abroad, and with my New York and London debuts behind me, I invested in a new edition of *Musical America*, the definitive listing of all American managers and all artists represented by them. I made a list of all the managers who didn't have a violist on their rosters and started phoning. With most, I didn't get very far. "We're not adding any names . . . especially not a violist—so difficult to sell, you know." My fifth call was to a well-known management with a long list of famous singers, but just a few instrumentalists. By chance, and lucky for me, the person who answered happened to be in charge of building a new instrumentalists division. We had a pleasant talk and I offered to send a press packet and record. At lunch the next week we made a two-year commitment.

If you really want management, can show a number of past accomplishments, and do your homework, you will find management. Whether you will reap anything from it is another issue. No one will guarantee you a list of engagements. You may not even get a single one. You will get your name in *Musical America*, which has been called "the largest book of unemployed musicians in the world."

THE ADVANTAGES AND DISADVANTAGES OF HAVING REPRESENTATION

In the old days managers sought out the artist. It still happens to the few pianists and violinists who win major competitions and when a famous performer or teacher decides to stand behind the career of a young artist. But those situations are rare. Impresario Sol Hurok once ruled the music business with an iron fist. Now there are hundreds of managements and artist representatives. How do they all make a living? Many don't.

To generate income, some of the smaller managers take a hefty retainer from the client without any guarantee of concerts. The recital industry in the United States has almost dried up. Concerts are hard to find. Booking success is dependent on an agent's contacts. Very few agents are as brutally honest as they should be about the probable outcome for the artist. There are no guarantees that even a big, prestigious management will find concerts for an artist. A young musician who has been with a very prominent New York agency for the last two years complains, "The term *management* can be misleading. They don't really manage, guide or advise you. They are not career builders, but if your career happens to grow, the management will be happy to take a commission along the way!" His major disappointment? "My management likes to give the impression of being all-powerful and won't admit limitations. I wish they could say 'this is what we can do and this is what we can't,' but they prefer to carry on a mystique. They don't even realize they're not telling their clients what they need to know." An alternative to concert management is hiring an administrative assistant: someone handling business correspondence, working out concert and traveling arrangements (for concerts you have found for yourself), providing a mailing address and perhaps negotiating concert fees according to your instructions. Then *you* will have control over the situation. You list the tasks to be accomplished and pay accordingly. Results will be tangible.

WARNING ABOUT PAYING FOR INCOMPETENCE

Most managements take from ten to twenty percent commission on engagements they find. Usually, if you get a small appearance for yourself, the agent won't ask for a cut, but this must be agreed upon beforehand. If a special publicity push is done on your behalf, i.e., mass mailings about your availability for solo recitals, you will be asked to pay the expenses. Managers who get paid a retainer instead of a percentage commission per engagement have, in my opinion, little motivation to find concert dates. Sometimes the price tag gets awfully big. The more that is promised, the greater the disappointment when no engagements materialize. One New York office I knew had the audacity to charge an hourly rate for secretarial services on top of a huge retainer. Each client was paying big bucks for the clerk's on-the-job computer training.

Thousands of dollars can be taken by unsavory managements for doing much of what *you* can do for yourself. There are publications in which you can list yourself as available for engagements. *Musical America* is one. Another is the Maine-based *Artscan*, a national catalog of performing artists. With or without management, unless you are well known, presenters won't come to you. The hard work is coming up with creative performance projects, writing letters, sending out materials, placing follow-up calls and more follow-up calls, and facing a good bit of rejection. But with perseverance the yeses are bound to come.

TOURING

LIFE ON TOUR

Morton Gould once told me about an experience he had on the road with the legendary Boston Pops conductor Arthur Fiedler. They both happened to be giving concerts in the same part of the Midwest. One night they found themselves in a particularly small town in Indiana where they knew no one. They arrived already exhausted by a day of travel and hadn't eaten dinner before the concert. Afterward, the town closed up! Not even a coffee shop was open. Starved, they found their small, deserted motel. Fiedler happened to be carrying an open half bottle of Scotch. They took glasses from the bathroom and sat down on a broken bed with the glasses full of the only food they had. Fiedler looked at Gould, and said, "And this is what they call the glamorous life?" The touring life has an exciting, glamorous aura outside the arts world, but like most things, it is a mixed blessing. You do get paid to see the world, but too much time away from home can take its toll emotionally. Nevertheless, globe-trotting is a great way to get exposure, and if periods away from home aren't too long, the touring life can indeed be stimulating and exciting.

FINANCIAL ARRANGEMENTS ON TOUR

Most of the big artists have a set fee per concert and are usually required to pay their own transportation costs. But managements are often in charge of making transportation arrangements and being sure all goes smoothly. Columbia Artists has a community concerts series for which artists are usually paid a weekly salary and per diem, rather than a fee per concert. On these tours, the mileage per day between engagements can be un-realistically high. Too much travel on a concert day can be brutal. Playing under these conditions is unacceptable. Artists should scrutinize all such itineraries carefully with atlas in hand before signing any contracts!

Touring with an orchestra can be stimulating and lucrative. Major orchestras stay in good quality hotels that are paid for by the orchestra.

TOURING TIPS

- Bring along some good books for buses, trains, planes, and airport waiting.
- Eat as normally as possible. Avoid excessive amounts of sugar and caffeine. Try to keep late night (after concerts) eating to a minimum.
- Maintain a regular exercise routine. Jogging, fast walking, bicycle riding, or swimming will help to balance the long periods of sitting and waiting.
- Contact friends in advance who live in cities where you will be visiting with particulars of your stay there. Often you are only in a place for twenty-four hours, and by the time you arrive at your

hotel, it may be too late to phone. This way, the friend can take the initiative and contact you.

- Do research about the places you'll be visiting so if there is free time you can enjoy sightseeing. But don't forget where your priorities are. If the choice is between a good nap or visiting a museum on the afternoon before an important evening concert, it may be wiser to opt for the snooze.
- Most important, enjoy yourself. Enjoy meeting new people, going to music shops in foreign countries to peruse new repertoire, and exploring new parts of the world.

SUPPORT FOR THE MUSICIAN

CHAPTER 5

Indian Chief Syndrome: The Role of Foundations and Corporations in Getting the Arts Paid for in America

WHILE reviewing material about the Mary Flagler Cary Trust, I was surprised to see an orchestral record on which I played listed in the "projects funded" section. I remember the circumstances of the session quite well. In 1988 the Brooklyn Philharmonic recorded Lukas Foss's *Orpheus* in the Great Hall at New York's Cooper Union. The soloists were violinists Yehudi Menuhin and Edna Michel. Some of the trivial details remain rather vivid, such as Lukas's irritation with the record jacket photographer for using valuable recording time to take pictures. But I never wondered who was paying for the record. We musicians are often unaware of the key players in arts funding: what they do, how they got to be where they are. For years I had seen James D. Wolfensohn around Carnegie Hall during concerts. However, it wasn't until he appeared on the cover of *Forbes* magazine that I realized he was one of the world's most successful investment bankers. Musicians are not expected to know these things, of course; we assume fund-raising is the business of an orchestra's development office. We players exist solely to play our instruments beautifully.

Since most of the heavy-hitting foundations and corporations fund only nonprofit organizations, the perceptive reader might well ask what a chapter about institutional giving is doing in a book geared to individuals. Well, for one thing, it's nice to know why payroll checks don't (usually) bounce. Quite simply, being aware of the priorities and changing strategies of the funding world gives musicians more control over their lives. John Mc-

Laughlin, former director of arts education and originating artists' programs at the American Council for the Arts, says he is amazed that artists are not more in touch with the broader world of fund-raising and legislative issues. "They don't even know how to protect themselves," he says. It just makes good sense for those of us out there performing, composing, and teaching to know the way large money-giving entities operate: who runs them, their goals, their methods for screening candidates, and their predictions about future arts support. Understanding the funding process empowers music-makers. We can take a more informed role in applying for money. It leads us to a position of greater strength. Besides, as novices without preconceived ideas, we view goings-on in the philanthropic world with a freshness that may lead us to insights even the experts don't have.

In the United States, where government gives relatively little to the arts, foundations and corporations have become almost by default a major support system for artists. Although individual donors contribute the most to the arts in the United States, arts organizations get a hefty percentage of their operating costs from foundations and corporations.

Large entities like the Rockefeller Foundation, the Ford Foundation, Exxon, and Consolidated Edison prefer to fund 501(C)(3) organizations. This is the all-important section of the Internal Revenue Code that establishes the tax-exempt status of charitable organizations, such as symphonies, and makes contributions to them tax-deductible by the donor.

What are the mysterious forces affecting the world of charitable giving? The best explanation I can offer goes back to a game we played as children at summer camp. It was called Indian Chief and this is how it worked. About ten children sat cross-legged around a circle, one of them chosen as the chief. An eleventh child was "it" and sat in the middle. The designated chief would lead the activities of the circle as imperceptibly as possible, first clapping hands, then clapping thighs, and so forth. "It" 's job was to discover who was calling the shots. At first glance, it wasn't even clear there was a leader at all. Everyone just did the same thing, and yet, lo and behold, the above-the-head clapping would turn into knee clapping. In the world of foundations, major funders rally to the same types of projects, but it is hard to know who influenced whom. One philanthropy champions an idea and another follows suit. Then another decides to give money to the same cause. Before you can say "Indian Chief," a grand foundation policy is established. The only difference is that in the game there actually was a leader. In the foundation world, there is more likely a bunch of decisions based on political undercurrents or a foundation officer's whim.

Nevertheless, we are very fortunate to have foundations willing to contribute to culture. They support great programs initiated by organizations like Meet the Composer and Affiliate Artists. We artists get jobs because of it. But there are no agencies to review policy or monitor funding patterns. This, of course, can be good. Or bad. Just how does influence work in the arts?

Howard Klein, who trained as a concert pianist and now works as a consultant to foundations, headed the arts program at the Rockefeller Foundation for ten of his twenty years there. He contends that policy is determined not by the amount given by a foundation but by what the money is spent on. "When a foundation is doing its job properly, a small amount of money it gives can have enormous impact," he says. "Individual donors may be providing eighty percent of funding to an orchestra. But the foundation that is supplying twenty percent will have the policy impact if an innovative or a trend-setting idea is implemented with that money." He cites a trenchant example: "Mobil has influenced the look of American public television through its support of 'Masterpiece Theater.' It wasn't a Washington policy decision, it wasn't a public television subscriber decision, and it wasn't even a public television management decision. Mobil could specify what it wanted to do."

There are groups around that are vaguely connected to policy-making. But mainly they furnish meeting places for grantmakers to sit around and discuss issues. Artists are usually excluded from this process. So it is a bit like heads of states talking among themselves without being aware of the needs and ideas of the citizens. One such group is Grantmakers on the Arts. Officially called "an affinity organization of the Council on Foundations," it is a body of private grantmakers from major entities like the Rockefeller, Ford, Mellon, and Bush Foundations who come together for educational purposes, sponsoring conferences and seminars. The meetings are not open to grant-seekers. One recent conference of Grantmakers on the Arts held at the Art Institute of Chicago focused on funding individual artists. The official newsletter is sent to five thousand private grantmakers and to state arts councils. Again, there is an exclusivity in the audience privy to this information. Other communications networks are local. A typical example is the New York Regional Association of Grantmakers, which includes grantmakers in the arts as well as other fields. These committees simply provide a way for grantmakers to chat about grants issues. There are also nameless informal get-togethers, such as thirty New York-based corporate and foundation associates who meet for lunch once a month. In this setting, grantmakers pick each other's brains about organizations applying for grants—another example of the Indian Chief theory.

One group that tries to come up with some cogent answers to troubling arts questions is the Independent Committee on Arts Policy. This loosely-structured New York-based organization of about thirty distinguished individuals, among whom half are artists, was created to respond to questions about culture in American life. Among its members are the historian Arthur M. Schlesinger, Jr.; Howard Klein; Schuyler G. Chapin, former artistic head of the Metropolitan Opera; authors Toni Morrison and Susan Sontag; and composers Ellen Taaffe Zwilich and Peter Schickele. The committee, which meets periodically to discuss arts concerns, prepared a nonpartisan policy statement for the two presidential candidates in the 1988 election. The impact, if any, has yet to be seen.

Grants for Arts and Cultural Programs (1988 edition), published by the Foundation Center, lists 6,475 grants of $5,000 or more with a total annual value of $320,515,210 made by 390 charitable foundations. Only a small percentage of these is set aside for music projects. Among the foundations below, the Mary Flagler Cary Trust provides an inspiring tale of how a foundation can enrich the lives of musicians and serve a community's cultural needs. Although the Ford and Rockefeller Foundations have been committed to arts support, support for music has decreased. Pew Charitable Trusts is one organization that is seriously committed to music: it is one of the largest supporters of the discipline in the United States. The Bush Foundation has set an interesting precedent with its Fellowship Program. Unhappily, however, executives of music organizations are disheartened about diminished funds for the arts from large foundations and businesses, particularly as money is dwindling from the government and individual donors as well.

*M*ARY FLAGLER CARY TRUST

Mary Flagler Cary, a wealthy, devoted patron of the arts in New York, died in 1967 and left funds for a fifty-year charitable trust. Ending in the year 2018, the trust supports two of her special interests: music and the conservation of natural resources. Her music collection of autograph manuscripts, autograph letters, and other musical memorabilia was donated in its entirety to New York City's Pierpont Morgan Library.

The life of Mary Flagler, born in 1901, was greatly influenced by her parents' love of music. Her father, Harry Harkness Flagler, was for many years president of the New York Symphony and in 1928 became the first president of the New York Philharmonic. With conductor Leon Barzin, Cary founded the National Orchestral Association (NOA) in 1931, a music project to which she was devoted until her death. After Cary's death, the trust continued to underwrite the major portion of NOA's annual budget. But in the late 1970s the trust began to modify its music program to reflect changes in the careers of young musicians. Many conservatory graduates were settling in New York to pursue free-lance careers rather than joining full-time orchestras. The trustees observed that the eclectic mix of New York ensembles together offered the city a more varied range of programs than more mainstream institutions could provide. At the same time, the free-lance life presented a practicable career alternative for musicians. During 1979–80, the Cary Trust began to spread support among a number of New York undertakings: performances, commissions of composers, and recordings.

During the last decade, the trust, with more than $100 million in assets, has focused on contemporary music performance by New York ensembles. In 1987 it initiated a program for commissioning new music, awarding $200,000 to seventeen ensembles for the composing of thirty-one works. Seventeen organizations were awarded a total of $250,000 for the recording of twenty-seven composers' works. Included in this package were nine new piano works commissioned for Peter Serkin by New York's 92nd Street Y, an example of how an individual can benefit directly through support for a non-profit institution. In 1989 the trust commissioned opera, music theater, dance, and theater. Specific objectives were to help compensate composers and librettists for creative work, build the music repertoire, and increase the audience for new music. Program Director Gayle Morgan has been widely credited as the impetus behind the Cary Trust's venturesome policies, an example of how one person can have a positive impact on an arts community.

THE FORD FOUNDATION

The Ford Foundation, founded in 1936 by car czar Henry Ford, has a reputation for being responsive to the arts and humanities. In 1955, the then-president of the Foundation, Rowan Gaither, Jr., stated, "Because cultural affairs are such an important part of American life, they are particularly appropriate for support by a foundation." The nearly $34 million that the foundation spent in 1987 on education and culture are divided among three categories: funding of new performance art, promoting cultural diversity by funding minority artists, and preserving of documents. The last category is being phased out. Funding which goes abroad is routed through twelve field offices in Asia, Africa, and Latin America. The address list of these offices could be a useful reference for ethnomusicologists and others interested in the cultural resources of developing countries. In its U.S. funding, Ford Foundation interests include Hispanic theater and black and Hispanic art museums. Programs of the American Symphony Orchestra League (ASOL) and the Music Assistance Fund of the New York Philharmonic that address the low representation of minorities in U.S. orchestras have been supported.

The broad philosophy of The Ford Foundation is "to seize opportunities as they present themselves. . . . things go in cycles. . . . be open to a variety of opportunities."

What does all this jargon really mean? Whatever the foundation decides it means. And policies can change on a whim, without an easily understood reason. All because there is a dearth of philanthropic leadership and a lack of creative thinking in the world of corporate funding as a whole.

THE ROCKEFELLER FOUNDATION

The Rockefeller Foundation, founded by oil magnate John D. Rockefeller in 1913, had a lot to do with the construction of Lincoln Center and the novel idea of putting a conglomerate of arts organizations in one place. This pioneering outlook in arts support took on a new character under the twenty-year tenure of Howard Klein, who lobbied for support of *individual* artists. The main focus was on the creative person. As Klein stresses, "Work is to be seen and heard. The individual artist must be the central initiating point." The results were indeed trend-setting. Klein consulted with a number of distinguished artists during his years at the foundation. Many worthy projects were started because of this one man. In 1974, after two years of committee meetings to plan an agenda and repertoire with performers, musicologists, and others from various arenas of the music world, the Recorded Anthology of American Music was on its way. This project to produce one hundred records on the New World Records label was the first nonprofit record venture in American history. In 1976, the International American Music Competition was held for the first time at the Kennedy Center in Washington. In 1981 the competition was moved to Carnegie Hall. The foundation collaborated with Meet the

Composer to bring composers in residence to major orchestras in the United States in 1982. The program "had great impact, paid the composers well, and did not cost a lot," Klein says. "It changed a lot about orchestras: educated managements, brought interesting work to orchestral players, educated audiences, changed the scope of programming, and provided a networking mechanism for composers and conductors." These Rockefeller Foundation-initiated enterprises were fresh, real life stories about how far-ranging, even slightly wacky ideas came to fruition. As a practical postscript, they brought musical employment to hundreds of individual artists.

But then, due to internal political machinations at the Rockefeller Foundation, guidelines changed. Significant music projects initiated during Klein's era have gradually disappeared. According to Ellen Buchwalter, a program associate of the foundation, "Guidelines change to reflect changing priorities in the field . . . they mirror the field, gently moving the field itself." According to its documents, in future years the Rockefeller Foundation will emphasize "increasing artistic experimentation of cross culture" and "international themes." Allegedly, jazz composers, a "Music of the Americas" program, and American artists participating in international festivals will be the beneficiaries. However, as we enter the 1990s, the word is that much of the arts commitment will be transferred to a big environment campaign.

The lesson in all this? That anything can change any time. A foundation committed to some cause can next year be committed to another. That one person—in this case, Howard Klein—can make a difference, even in the bureaucratic world of foundations. When he first arrived at the Rockefeller Foundation, Klein asked a foundation executive, "But what about the guidelines, what are the guidelines?" "*You* are the guidelines," he was told.

*T*HE PEW CHARITABLE TRUSTS

The Philadelphia-based Pew Charitable Trusts consist of seven individual charitable trusts established between 1948 and 1979 by the four surviving children of Joseph N. Pew, founder of Sun Oil Company. Although the trusts give to national programs, of particular interest are projects "which heighten awareness and appreciation of Philadelphia's diverse cultural resources." Grants announced during 1987 included $350,000 for the Philadelphia Orchestra Association; $300,000 for Opera America (Opera for the 80's and Beyond); $30,000 to the Jazz Society of Philadelphia; $180,000 to The Philadelphia Singers, Inc.; $250,000 to Concerto Soloists of Philadelphia; $350,000 to the American Music Theater Festival; and $450,000 to Meet the Composer in support of the Composers/Choreographers Collaboration Project.

THE BUSH FOUNDATION

The Bush Foundation was founded by Archibald Granville Bush and his wife, Edyth Bassler Bush, in 1953. Based in St. Paul, Minnesota, this foundation performs an unusual service. It gives fellowships to individual artists working in the visual arts, literature, music composition and choreography. Since 1976, the Fellowships for Artists Program has funded creative artists at a level which enables them to work full-time, for a period of six to eighteen months. Stipends and cost allowances authorized for fifteen artist fellowships in 1988 totalled $480,000. Applicants must be at least twenty-five years old, and residents of Minnesota, North Dakota, or South Dakota.

WHAT NOW?

These foundations are among the leading arts philanthropies. Each has special qualities, and the amounts of money given are considerable. But there is a major flaw. Funding principles tend to lack a forward-looking perspective. "Intercultural" and "new art" are buzz words used by many of the biggest philanthropies. Because of tax considerations, there is a taboo against offering individual artist fellowships. Should financial matters get the upper hand over creative discovery? In describing the stagnant views endemic in many foundation board rooms, one philanthropy-watcher observed, "They are jumping on the bandwagon. No. They should build the bandwagon and take it to the top of the hill."

How can a future agenda keep pace with the flowing of artists' creative juices? One example of how it has been done is the support given to Meet the Composer's original projects. Why not consider ideas that haven't been discussed before? Bring in artists and hold marathon brain-storming sessions. Howard Klein is passionate about the subject: "A foundation should look fifty years ahead, not ten years behind. Foundations should be able to afford to take risks. Whatever happened to the lunatic fringe?" Artists cannot do the job alone. Being on the leading edge of an incredible idea isn't enough. Without help it will probably go nowhere. Is not the role of our most influential foundations to supply that assistance?

THE BUSINESS WORLD HELPING THE ARTS

The business world in the United States likes to think of itself as one grand collective patron. In 1967 American businesses gave $22 million to arts organizations; by 1990, more than $1 billion. This impressive level of funding—the growth figures may be misleading because of inflation—however, is not especially altruistic. Corporate image gets a great boost from association with the arts, and the billion dollar figure is only a dribble of yearly revenues. Two men who consistently lobby the business world for more arts involvement are George Weissman, the former chief executive officer of Philip Morris and present head of New York's Lincoln Center, and David Rockefeller, the retired Chase Manhattan chairman. They were both founding members in 1967 of the Business Committee for the Arts, Inc. (BCA). This national organization of chief executive officers finds ways to stimulate arts interest in the business sector. The Matching Gift Programs for the Arts encourages employees of corporations to commit funds to arts concerns of their choice. More than two hundred fifty business managements match such gifts, even from retired employees. *BCA News*, the newsletter published by the committee, is a good source of business philanthropy gossip. An arts education resource guide and other information bulletins with such titles as "Involving the Arts in Advertising: A Business Strategy" and "Building Community—Business and the Arts" are also published. But lofty as BCA sounds, arts organizations can't really go to it to ask for help. The perception by arts leaders is that chief executive officers are often more concerned with looking good and using committee dinners to network about business concerns.

Another network for business philanthropy is the Arts & Business Council, Inc. (ABC). Founded in 1964, the council has become more of a viable help to the arts than BCA. Through its national program, Business Volunteers for the Arts (BVA), started in 1975, free management consultant services are offered to arts groups. Among BVA's New York clients, sixty-seven percent have budgets under $200,000. The Bronx Arts Ensemble, for example, took good advantage of BVA by requesting assistance in marketing and audience development. An executive from a New York food concern was assigned to the case and put his company's graphic design experts at work on a new brochure. By arranging for the group to perform at a local benefit, the business volunteer created a way for the players to meet influential community leaders. Sadly, despite all the good intentions coming from various segments of the business community, well-known corporations such as Exxon have pulled back their arts support. One of oil's Seven Sisters, Exxon was a forerunner in its sponsorship of the arts. No longer. Why? According to Len Fleisher, manager of contributors coordination, "A traumatic period for the oil industry led to a review of priorities" in the corporate contributions budget. The 1985 annual U.S. giving budget of $60 million was reduced to $35.4 million by 1989. Fleisher, who was running an arts program, had his job description change dramatically. These days he has considerably less contact with the arts. The corporation took a "hard look" at the giving program and with a reduced budget, health, welfare, and community service became priorities. Over eighty percent of 1989's contributions were allocated for these causes. Exxon phased out several national programs in the arts but continues to fund local cultural institutions and a number of national service organizations. Fortunately, not all corporations have pulled support on the scale of Exxon, but funding patterns have become incredibly homogeneous— more of that Indian Chief theory. Large money givers keep dollars swirling in the same direction: education, community projects to build audiences, and helping young musicians. Although many of these causes are wonderful, such as helping music education in the public schools, how frustrating it is that often not enough money is given to be meaningful. How much money would be enough? That is a hard one to answer. But it is clear that tokenism, a little here and a little there almost like an affectionate pat on the head, trivializes the dilemma faced by the arts world.

One group supported by Consolidated Edison (Con Ed), the big New York electric utility, is New Music for Young Ensembles, Inc. (NMYE), founded by Claire Rosengarten. The reasons? Both young performers and young composers benefit from the support. Young instrumentalists, alongside established artists, perform works of composers commissioned by NMYE. Composers are encouraged to write music of moderate difficulty which will challenge but not overwhelm young musicians. A major objective of NMYE is to build audiences for new music. The goals are certainly admirable, but why not also help mid-career artists taking time off to do special projects?

Although it is not unusual for a corporation to have an in-house foundation, American Telephone and Telegraph has an atypical, decentralized funding approach. Seven regional contributions managers screen proposals. These managers help local groups facilitate activities. For example, a regional manager can provide services to communities, donate equipment, etc. Regional screening helps keep local contact in the community.

Grants generally go to major cities, where most AT&T customers are. Projects are put in a priority order for the national level, according to specific objectives laid down by the board of trustees of the AT&T Foundation. Any proposal national in scope goes directly to the vice president in charge of contributions in New York. He and his staff make recommendations to the Board of Trustees, which generally approves them. Of the $32 million per year spent by the foundation, $4.8 million goes to the arts. One project funded in 1989 was a jazz fellowship program of Meet the Composer, to which AT&T contributed $100,000.

Philip Morris, which the *Wall Street Journal* has labeled the "art world's favorite company," has worked hard to acquire a reputation connected to arts patronage. The hope is that its public image as a major producer of tobacco products will be eclipsed. Like Con Ed and AT&T, Philip Morris is interested in serving communities, particularly in places like Richmond, Virginia, where many employees live. The National Coalition for Individual Artists (mentioned in more detail in chapter 6), innovative because it offers individuals multi-year grants, is being supported by Philip Morris, which provided $75,000 to launch this effort.

The Cultural Affairs Department at Philip Morris's New York headquarters takes on about twenty projects a year. Its cultural staff is bigger than at other corporations, a sign of just how much image matters to the company. Cultivating the identity of risk-taker and maverick funder of such undertakings as the Next Wave Festival at the Brooklyn Academy of Music is a serious business. Philip Morris wants to "break new ground and test new ideas," no doubt to divert the public's attention from the company's primary enterprise.

One of the nation's largest insurance companies, Metropolitan Life (Met Life), like AT&T, funds through its foundation. The stated goals—sound familiar?—are to "build an audience for the future" and to "develop careers of young artists." New York-based Met Life supports the National Foundation for Advancement in the Arts, the New York Youth Symphony, and St. Louis Conservatory and School for the Arts, all of which aid the growth of young talent. For all of these endeavors and others, the company gives about $1 million a year.

An arts education program called Partnerships: Arts and the Schools has been announced by the Met Life Foundation. This support is desperately needed because of the grave cutbacks in arts education in public schools throughout the country. In 1988, $75,000 was given for programs linking schools to local cultural resources. For example, Tulsa Ballet was given a $15,000 grant to perform in the schools in Tulsa and outlying areas, and the Warehouse Theater in Greenville, South Carolina received the same amount to stage productions for the Greenville school system. What a good and fresh idea! But why so little money? How can these relatively small grants make a dent in the apathy plaguing this segment of our children's education?

In its contributions program, American Express seeks three major ends, virtually identical to the other major givers: community service, education, and culture. Some grants come out of national headquarters and other decisions are made regionally. Music gets less support than the visual arts and theater. Similar to Philip Morris, American Express is looking for some pizzazz in its corporate identity. It wants to be associated with the "most exciting opportunities," "firsts," and "anniversary concerts."

New performing arts centers are of particular appeal. In publicizing the opening of the Tampa Bay Performing Arts Center, subsidized by Amex, local patrons were encouraged to get involved with subscription drives. Opening activities featured local artists who were invited to test the acoustics and space of the hall in preview concerts. No one is suggesting that arts centers shouldn't get enthusiastic support from the corporate world. But why stop there? American Express has a huge international presence. Whatever happened to ideas such as sponsoring a global cultural exchange of artists?

Like AT&T, Chase Manhattan's regional locations, at least twenty, are involved in contributions, where bankers wear a "philanthropic hat." The most recent figures reflect that Chase gives $2 million to the arts every year. Examples of music support in New York City are the symphony orchestras in each of the city's five boroughs: Brooklyn Philharmonic, Queens Symphony, etc. Following the philosophy of Met Life, helping younger musicians is given a high priority. This goal is accomplished through support to such organizations as Concert Artists Guild, Young Concert Artists, and Opera Orchestra of New York. As with Philip Morris, Chase has sponsored ballet companies on tour, i.e., American Ballet Theater and the Dance Theater of Harlem.

With a grant from Chase, the 1988 New York International Festival of the Arts in New York City commissioned six pieces of music, each by a different composer. Similar to American Express, Con Ed, Met Life, and Philip Morris, Chase says it is interested in helping the creative process: not just giving to major, established institutions, but rather "nurturing the next generation of talent." What about brand new ideas like funding research about the occupational health hazards of musicians, or music and public policy? Too controversial, no doubt. Or could the problem be as simple as no one sitting down to re-evaluate programs and initiate new ideas?

Minnesota has a track record of strong arts support, not only from the state government and foundations but from business as well. Out of the total corporate-wide giving across the state of $19.4 million, more than $8 million were given to Twin Cities-area programs in 1987. Dayton-Hudson, the department store chain headquartered in Minneapolis, has made the arts a major funding category. Here is sampling of what Dayton-Hudson contributed to music that year: $69,000 for Minnesota Opera; $241,200 to the Minnesota Orchestral Association; $90,000 to Minnesota Public Radio for Cultural Programming; $100,200 to the St. Paul Chamber Orchestra; and $19,000 to the Minnesota Composers Forum. These figures do not include money given to foundations for further arts support. In 1988 some of these sums increased: The Minnesota Orchestral Association was given almost $300,000 and the St. Paul Chamber Orchestra more than $121,000. As in the Mary Flagler Cary Trust, here is an organization truly involved in the day-to-day cultural life of the community, in this case, the Minneapolis-St. Paul metropolitan area. National grants are also awarded. Among the 1988 recipients were the American Symphony Orchestra League ($12,000), Meet the Composer ($8,500), and Opera America ($8,500).

As stated often in this chapter, many of the major sources of corporate funding espouse more or less the same goals. Businesses doing the most good are giving real money to large numbers of local cultural organizations, like Dayton-Hudson. Aren't there companies out there with new views yet to be tapped? One thing is sure. The days are past where the American economy was dominated by fifty to one hundred giant organizations traditionally generous to the arts. Some executives of music associations blame this state of affairs on the latest wave of corporate mergers, raids, and takeovers, which force chief executives of target companies to pare costs and increase profitability. In this tense atmosphere, arts funding, not perceived by the stockholders as having a direct impact on earnings, is often the first to go.

Foundation guidelines have been in flux. Some of the largest institutional donors have a case of the blahs when it comes to fresh ideas about how to help the arts. Changing funding patterns, i.e., much less funding for music by both foundations and corporations, have made for depressing news in development offices of music organizations. The decline of funding by U.S. corporations to the arts from 1986 to 1987 was significant: from $550 million to $495 million, and this trend seems to be sticking. However, thousands of middle-size companies have sprung up to challenge the titans.

Also, Japanese companies are contributing more to the American nonprofit sector than ever before. Some estimates say the annual increase is thirty-five percent. "This year Toyota, Nissan, Honda, Sony, and Hitachi and other Japanese-owned firms will award grants equaling $140 million to American non-profits," the *NonProfit Times* reported in 1989. Why is this happening? Heightened interest in corporate community relations and more liberal tax treatment of overseas corporate giving provide two inducements. Clearly, arts development officers will have to look to these new funding sources to generate the business support levels of yesteryear.

On a positive note, changing trends in philanthropy, which bring withering cuts from old standbys, also present new opportunities and a stimulating challenge for those out there looking for support. Perhaps new donors will listen to new ideas from artists. A fresh outlook would be welcome indeed. On an even more positive note, there are a few foundations out there with officers who are creative, innovative thinkers. These folks are in touch with artists and care about the real needs of the arts community, rather than sticking to the boring words of stuffy, arbitrarily composed guidelines. One example of this new sensibility has been advanced by arts program officer Rachel Newton Bellow of the Mellon Foundation. After consulting musicians in the field and contemporary chamber ensembles, she proposed funding period instrument orchestras specializing in early music. Fresh ideas! The foundation approved the idea, and fourteen groups in each category were funded in 1989. Bellow's philosophy? "I can only be as good a foundation officer as the field allows by expressing to me what it needs." How wonderful it would be if this attitude started a new approach of funding what we artists consider worthy projects. We would be given a chance to influence grants policy, by offering input where it really counts. Of course, the Indian Chief theory would then be obsolete. And nothing would please me more.

CHAPTER

6

Where To Go For Help: Organizations That Serve Artists

BEING a musician can be lonely, especially when freelancing in a big city. I've worked in a number of foreign countries where I didn't know a soul, but I've never felt so alone as when I lived in New York, near family and friends, after I finished my master's degree and set out as a professional. In such a vast cultural wonderland as New York City, it is hard to feel that what you do matters. We all want to make an impact. We want to make a useful contribution. We want somehow to make a statement that is individual and genuine. We even want to make a living! Yet in a place where people easily feel anonymous, finding a means of artistic expression is frustratingly difficult.

There *is* support available to musicians—more than most of us realize. Organizations have been created whose sole purpose is to serve us; hence, they are called service organizations. They are the nonprofits with 501 (C) (3) tax status, which foundations and corporations like to fund. Unlike the giants that support them, these groups *are* allowed to give money to individuals. Some assist with career choices and others advise artists about legal and financial matters. The pamphlets and handbooks published by service organizations, usually available free, are remarkably informative. They may even trigger the odd brainstorm. Like the ideal high school guidance counselor, there are some special folks working in these places who actually enjoy comforting musicians in need. By the way, the establishments discussed in this chapter comprise just a fraction of what exists. The National Association of Artists' Organizations (NAAO) in Washington, D.C., publishes the NAAO *National Directory of Artists' Organizations,* which lists more than one thousand.

CAREER HELP FOR MUSICIANS

Some nonprofit organizations are best at serving musicians with some career experience. Others cater to younger artists. Musicians at every career stage deserve as much help as they can get. Take full advantage of what is available. Ask questions of people who can help. Send for printed material about services rendered. Don't be shy.

Most of the organizations listed here specialize in help for composers and performers. Others have broad-based artist agendas. Be ingenious about finding help. Searching for advice or fellowships from lesser-known organizations can reap rewards. For example, the American Music Center (AMC) is a superb clearinghouse of information about the arts. A discussion with one of the council's staff can provide interesting career leads. Composers can apply for AMC fellowships as well as the more competitive grants offered by the National Endowment for the Arts. A violinist living in Maine can benefit handsomely from the resources of the Minnesota Composers Forum in the following way: A Minnesota composer could be commissioned to write a violin piece for the performer's Minneapolis concert. By hooking up with a local composer, the Maine violinist might well be eligible for funding by Minnesota philanthropies. This state has a wonderful attitude toward artists. The maxim here is "look beyond the obvious." Let your imagination go. Squeeze the maximum you can out of every agency serving artists. On the other hand, in some cases a pursuit for opportunities is a waste of time. Even well-intentioned helping associations can give misleading impressions of what they can offer the artist.

AFFILIATE ARTISTS

Since 1966, New York-based Affiliate Artists has successfully matched promising artists with corporate sponsors. Richard Clark, himself once an operatic baritone, founded a nonprofit vehicle to help young singers gain exposure and income. It soon grew to include a diverse lot of performers—instrumentalists, dancers, mimes, and actors. Today, Affiliate Artists is one of the most successful ventures around for helping mid-career performers. The competition to become an Affiliate Artist is fierce. Only

about three to five percent of applicants are accepted into the program. In 1989 there were thirty-six instrumentalists and eight conductors on the Affiliate Artists roster. This is how it works: In residencies underwritten by corporate sponsors, a performer on the roster goes to a city where a corporation has factories or offices. The performer gives two presentations, called informances, each day for a week. The places for performance range from factories to parks to corporate offices. All of this is organized by Affiliate Artists in working with the community to present performing arts in the most professional way. The artist gains lots of performing experience in addition to earning a respectable salary, about $1,000 plus expenses for a week's residency. As reported in *The Wall Street Journal*, one saxophone player described playing a "horrendously difficult" piece two hundred fifty times while an Affiliate Artist. It allowed her more chances to play the piece than most performers get. "Money can't buy confidence like that," she observed.

While artists gain experience in the field, audiences are built in the most unlikely places. Richard Clark's motto is, "If you give people an opportunity to participate in the action, a fair number will come." Any problem with audiences of ex-convicts listening to avant-garde music? According to Clark, "It doesn't matter what music you perform. Your passion in the material will be communicated. It will come through. People are curious. You can make them more so."

Affiliate Artists has taken a genuine interest in career development of American artists. Their alumni include pianist Jeffrey Kahane, flutist Carol Wincenc, and conductors Hugh Wolff and Myung-Whun Chung. Long-term sponsorships like the Xerox program for pianists and Exxon orchestral residencies for young conductors have given young artists valuable exposure. Exxon has pulled out in recent years, but Clark has managed to find new patronage. The Xerox program gives young solo pianists a chance to do concerto repertoire with orchestras, an experience difficult to come by without a major career. On the other hand, without such experience, you can't have a major career. A Catch-22 of sorts. The same type of circular reasoning applies to young conductors, who gain invaluable experience working with major orchestras as resident assistant conductors and learn how to be music directors, as well.

AMERICAN COUNCIL FOR THE ARTS

The American Council for the Arts (ACA), based in New York City, works to inform, educate, and lobby for the arts, with the objective of improving this country's cultural climate. Funders of ACA have been such corporate entities as American Telephone and Telegraph Company, the Gannett

Foundation, and Southwestern Bell. Energies at the council are focused on particular subjects: arts education, the originating artist, private sector support of the arts, and international cultural relations. Books published by ACA, including *The Modern Muse: The Support and Condition of Artists, Money for Artists, The Art of Filing, Our Government and the Arts, Who's to Pay for the Arts?*, and *National Directory of Art Internships*, are all exceptional information tools for artists. An individual membership to ACA includes subscriptions to *Vantage Point* and ACA *Update*, access to ACA's reference library, and discounts on all ACA books.

AMERICAN MUSIC CENTER

In March 1939, five composers—Aaron Copland, Marion Bauer, Otto Luening, Howard Hanson, and Quincy Porter—met in Copland's New York apartment to lay plans for the American Music Center (AMC). In November of that year the AMC office opened its doors. The center maintains a large circulating library of twenty-six thousand scores of American music, of which about one-third are published. The library is located in New York City at the center's office. Scores are sent anywhere in the world free of charge. The center sponsors the Margaret Fairbank Jory Copying Assistance Program of grants to defray music copying—computer or hand copying—costs. The lifetime maximum for a composer is $3,500. Of that sum, no more than $2,000 will be given out at any one time. Usually the award is only a portion of what a composer has requested.

The AMC *Newsletter* and monthly *Opportunity Update* are available to members, but for most of what AMC offers membership is not a requirement. The AMC staff answers hundreds of questions each week pertaining to issues on publishing, copyright, royalties, and grants and fellowships.

AMERICAN SYMPHONY ORCHESTRA LEAGUE

The American Symphony Orchestra League, based in Washington, D.C., serves as a research, education, and information clearinghouse for symphony orchestras in the United States and Canada. The ASOL has established a system of categorizing symphony orchestras according to annual budget: There are seven groups of professional orchestras, with annual expenses ranging from $8 million for Group I to $240-399 thousand for Group VII. Other categories of orchestras studied are urban, community, college and youth. Individuals, as well as orchestras, can join. Workshops are sponsored by ASOL. Among them are a week-long seminar in orchestral

management and an institute of orchestral studies for young conductors. The ASOL publishes *Symphony Magazine*, which has all the latest orchestral news. A listing of available positions in orchestral management, the *Administrative Service Announcement*, is published bi-monthly. Job listings for conductors and orchestral members are also announced.

CHAMBER MUSIC AMERICA

Chamber Music America (CMA) was founded in 1977 to provide a unified voice for professional chamber ensembles. The New York-based organization, headed by executive director Dean Stein, exists to improve the professional lives of American ensembles. Lobbying has paid off. With CMA urging, in 1980 the National Endowment for the Arts established a direct funding program in chamber music. Since then, the NEA has given more than $2 million in direct grants to ensembles and presenters. Through CMA, grants are sponsored for residencies and commissions, instrument insurance is available under a group plan, and even credit cards with terms helpful to the fragile finances of musicians are offered. *Chamber Music Magazine*, a quarterly review, has articles like "East Meets West in Chamber Music" and "Living on Air: The New Challenge of Radio." Other CMA publications include *Directory of Summer Workshops, Schools & Festivals* and *Organization Manual for Chamber Music Ensembles*.

Chamber Music America wants to see its five hundred and eighty member ensembles get concerts. One deterrent is the often haphazard operating methods of community concert administrators. In an effort to bring basic management skills to these folks, CMA has organized workshops for presenters. CMA annual conferences for its membership, which besides ensembles includes twenty-seven hundred individuals and businesses, focus on topics like repertoire, funding, touring, and presenter development.

MEET THE COMPOSER

John Duffy, a composer living in New York, has had a great impact on the lives of American composers. He had a vision and in 1974 turned it into a reality, Meet the Composer, shaping the organization according to his own values. He wanted to get away from the "ivory tower syndrome." Duffy believes that "people in the arts shouldn't alienate themselves from the middle and working classes in life." Meet the Composer creates a setting for the composer's assimilation.

The organization supports about eight thousand events a year nation-wide, including those sponsored by the eight regional Meet the Composer affiliate organizations. Through the Meet the Composer/Orchestra Residencies Program, which ends in 1992, twenty-eight composers have had residencies with nineteen major orchestras. The Meet the Composer/Reader's Digest Commissioning Program, in partnership with the Lila Wallace–Reader's Digest Fund, Inc., and the National Endowment for the Arts, was initiated in 1988 as a three-year commissioning program for concert music, opera music, music theater, and jazz. More than $400,000 in commission fees are awarded annually. The Composer/Choreographer Project, also launched in 1988, supports collaborations between American composers and choreographers by American dance companies. The three-year project was established with funding commitments of $1.3 million from the Ford Foundation and the Pew Charitable Trusts. First year grants ranging from $10,000 to $60,000 were awarded to nineteen ballet and modern dance companies for commissioning new works. In the third year, the awards were expanded to include ethnic and tap dance. The Meet the Composer Jazz Program, funded by AT&T, the Rockefeller Foundation, and the National Endowment for the Arts, awards commissions to jazz composers and supports residencies with the ensembles for which the composers are writing. In the first year of the program, eighteen jazz composers received commissions that totaled $300,000.

Meet the Composer has published two valuable handbooks. The little booklet called *Commissioning Music* gives a clear explanation of how a performer or patron engages a composer to write a work. *Composers in the Marketplace: How to Earn a Living Composing Music* is a must for every composer. It covers everything from self-publishing to demo tapes to press kits to film and television. Also, there is an excellent resource section in the back.

THE MINNESOTA COMPOSERS FORUM

In 1973 two young Minnesota composers, Libby Larsen and Stephen Paulus, founded the Minnesota Composers Forum. The pair, who met as graduate students at the University of Minnesota and later became composers in residence with the Minnesota Orchestra, established a means for composers to help each other. The forum became a model for similar support groups around the country, such as the Wisconsin Composers Alliance and Connecticut Composers Alliance. Activities include producing concerts, offering fellowships, administering a recording series, and providing legal aid negotiating and writing contracts. It all boils down to helping composers make a living writing and then getting their music off the page and into the concert hall.

NATIONAL FOUNDATION FOR ADVANCEMENT IN THE ARTS

The National Foundation for Advancement in the Arts (NFAA), under President Grant Beglarian, former dean of the University of Southern California's School of the Performing Arts, provides opportunities for artists starting out. Each year the Arts Recognition and Talent Search (ARTS) awards cash grants to gifted seventeen- and eighteen-year-old artists. In 1990 ninety-three cash grants were given totaling $144,500, in amounts of $3,000, $1,500, and $500. Every year up to twenty ARTS awardees are designated as Presidential Scholars in the Arts, each receiving a $1,000 award from the Geraldine R. Dodge Foundation. Even ARTS applicants who don't qualify for grants are eligible for scholarships. Through NFAA's Scholarship List Service about $3 million in scholarships are earmarked for ARTS applicants annually. Approximately one hundred and fifty institutions of higher education participate in this service.

The New World Symphony (See chapter 3) was initiated by NFAA in 1986 to support young orchestral musicians in their developing years. Based in Miami, the symphony is now an independent organization.

NEW YORK FOUNDATION FOR THE ARTS

On the face of it the New York Foundation for the Arts, created in 1971 to facilitate the development of artists and arts audiences throughout New York State, looks awfully good. In fact, a fair number of New York artists have benefited by the grants, fellowships, and programs the foundation administers. But the focus here is on the creative or originating artist, not the performer. Perhaps for a good reason. Theodore S. Berger, the Executive Director, quoted an expert in the field as saying "Nineteenth-century composers keep re-creators employed." So to balance the scales, the composer in this society needs more help than the performer. But the performer, hungry for opportunities, may get a false sense of expectation from the foundation's literature.

The Artists in Residence Program is a great idea. Professional artists are placed in a variety of educational, cultural, and community settings. But quite a bit of paperwork goes into getting on the Artists-in-Residence roster. And paper work isn't all. The next step is a five-to-ten-minute interview in front of a panel to give the artist a chance to demonstrate communications skills. The literature informs participants that acceptance onto the roster is no guarantee of getting work. No guarantee is right. Approved artists are sent a list of sponsors with grants earmarked for NYFA artists. It is up to the artist to do the rest. Fine. But the problem comes when all the effort of getting on the roster is rewarded with a rather sparse sponsor list. During five years on the roster, I have never seen more than a few sponsors for music, as opposed to ten to twenty for other disciplines. Through NYFA, I have had one ten-day residency in the New York City Public School System, which paid about $100 per day. It was a great experience, which is why the dearth of opportunities is so exasperating.

In spite of this one criticism, the New York Foundation for the Arts does much admirable work. It administers four statewide programs. The Artist's Fellowship provides cash awards to creative artists for use in career development. Artists' New Works sponsors advisory and fiscal services to professional artists for individual projects. Revolving Loans is a short-term loan service for nonprofit cultural organizations and Information and Communications Services offers conferences, seminars, workshops, and publications for artists and cultural organizations.

FYI (For Your Information), previously published by the now-defunct Center for Arts Information, has been saved by the foundation. It is a little gem, full of useful tidbits about new publications, work space, new grants, and residencies.

Berger sees one of the primary problems for artists as the continuation of funding: making a one-time grant a more substantive income opportunity. To this end, The National Coalition for Individual Artists, a seven-state consortium administered by the foundation, comprising the arts councils of Arizona, California, Massachusetts, Minnesota, New York, North Carolina, and Ohio, has been formed to provide multi-year support for individual originating artists. The National Endowment for the Arts gave a challenge grant of $800,000 to the seven state arts councils. Each state will handle the money differently; for example, California will parcel out its $150,000 share out over three years in $5,000 Artist Fellowships to established artists. Like the MacArthur Grant, the consortium's awards are based on recognition of past work. Berger notes that "it is harder to raise money for this type of fellowship because nothing is expected back in return for the payment." This will satisfy one great need for artists because, as he explains, "Artists want and need cash, a way of making a living. They often have to do something else in order to keep it their profession." He stressed that artists must do their homework before applying for help. "People must understand the differences among project support versus individual commission versus fellowships," he says. "They need to know about deadlines and funding cycles to be in the running for the limited amount of money around. This is all part of one's professional life."

UNITED ARTS RESOURCES AND COUNSELING

United Arts, a Minnesota service organization, was founded in 1954. The Resources and Counseling Division, which was added in 1978, provides assistance to Minnesota artists and arts organizations. Assistance is available on a broad range of issues, either through individual consultations or through workshops. The Artlaw Referral Service is a low-cost, specialized legal service jointly sponsored by United Arts Resources and Counseling Division and the Minnesota State Bar Association. United Arts publishes *Basic Guide to Grants for Minnesota Artists*, which is helpful to artists in and out of Minnesota. The bibliography and national grants list in that publication give a number of ideas for support.

LEGAL AND FINANCIAL PROTECTION FOR MUSICIANS

Artists are so busy creating they often don't take the time to look after themselves. At least this is the folklore about the struggling artist. We are reputed to be deficient in business skills. For these reasons organizations have sprung up that attend to our various needs, whether it be protecting composers through music licensing, or offering legal and financial services at minimal cost.

AMERICAN SOCIETY OF COMPOSERS, AUTHORS, AND PUBLISHERS

Frances Richard is head of the symphony and concert department at the American Society of Composers, Authors, and Publishers (ASCAP). As I waited to interview her at 5:30 P.M., several young composers filed past me. Their appointments were scheduled before mine. I wasn't exactly eavesdropping, but the door wasn't exactly closed. Lots of caring advice was dispensed. Here is another helping professional to whom young musicians can turn. She is responsible for the professional welfare of about four thousand concert composers, out of a total ASCAP membership of around thirty-seven thousand. The American Society of Composers, Authors, and Publishers, founded in 1914, is the oldest performing rights licensing organization in the United States. Composer Morton Gould is currently its president. ASCAP protects thousands of composers, lyricists, and publishers against unauthorized public performances by unlicensed users. It licenses all radio stations (about ten thousand) and most television stations (about one thousand) in addition to one hundred thousand other establishments where music is played. Only a small percentage of its dealings has to do with classical music: Approximately ninety-eight percent of its $200 million annual income comes from the pop field. ASCAP offers such workshops as "The Marriage of Music and Film," where three known composers scored an identical film sequence, and the audience evaluated the results. Educational programs include the ASCAP Foundation Max Dreyfus Scholarship, created to encourage the study of music theater; the ASCAP Founsation/ Boosey & Hawkes Young Composer Award, honoring the composer Aaron Copland; and ASCAP Foundation grants to young composers. ASCAP is one of three performing rights agencies for composers in the United States, the others being Broadcast Music Inc. (BMI) and the Society of European Stage Authors and Composers, Inc. (SESAC).

BROADCAST MUSIC INCORPORATED

Unlike ASCAP, Broadcast Music Inc. (BMI), founded in 1940, is owned by its stockholders. While ASCAP's management is handled by a board of directors elected by its full membership, the BMI board is composed of its principal stockholders, the broadcasters, who set policy. BMI has a membership about a third larger than its main competitor, representing more than sixty thousand songwriters and composers and thirty-five thousand publishers.

Like her counterpart at ASCAP, Barbara A. Petersen of the concert division spends a good deal of her time giving advice to young composers. Many of them want to know how to send scores to conductors, how to get into writing film music, and just how to get one's music played in the first place. Where ASCAP has members, BMI has writer and publisher affiliates, and licenses all sorts of music users, from hotels to skating rinks to symphony orchestras.

BMI offers special awards to young composers, such as the Pete Carpenter Fellowship for young composers of film and television music. Music business workshops and seminars offered in conjunction with universities—an example of which was "Making American Music" held at New York University—and the Musical Theater Workshop are sponsored by BMI. Publications like *The Performance of Copyrighted Music: Questions and Answers* and *Handbook for Writers and Publishers* are issued free.

VOLUNTEER LAWYERS FOR THE ARTS

There are about thirty-seven independent offices of Volunteer Lawyers for the Arts (VLA) throughout the United States. The oldest of them is in New York City. The different offices vary greatly as to services provided, fees, and methods of serving artists and arts organizations. Legal advice is given on such matters as copyright law, contract law, real estate, and insurance as they pertain to arts issues.

Some VLA programs are housed in arts councils or commissions, while others function in conjunction with their local bar associations. Many of them operate resource libraries open to the general public and publish books about legal issues, as well as newsletters such as *The Working Arts*, which is produced by California Lawyers for the Arts (formerly Bay Area Lawyers for the Arts).

AMERICAN FEDERATION OF MUSICIANS

An international umbrella association of over five hundred local affiliates in the United States and Canada, with a membership of about two hundred thousand, the American Federation of Musicians (AFM) is the world's largest union of performing artists. The AFM protects the rights of professional musicians. Each local is autonomous and regulates its own schedule of fees and dues. Members of all locals receive the monthly *International Musician*, the AFM newspaper. Most major orchestras advertise openings on its back pages. A number of services are offered by AFM; for example, "Roadgig" is an emergency service for the travelling musician, a sort of musician's AAA. If a musician is stranded on the road by an employer who refuses to pay, a union troubleshooter will show up, arrange for legal assistance, advance money, and arrange for travel home. If you should need this service, call 1-800-ROADGIG. There is a computerized job referral service. The Professional Musicians Club is a program open to AFM members, aimed at offering discounts on various goods, services, and benefits such as instrument insurance, and a free copy of *Music Matters: The Performer and the American Federation of Musicians*.

AMERICAN GUILD OF MUSICAL ARTISTS

The American Guild of Musical Artists (AGMA), founded in 1936, has jurisdiction over performers in opera, ballet, oratorio, and chamber choruses. The services offered to members are life insurance, medical, dental, and optical health plans, a welfare and pension fund, legal and professional advice, and an AGMA relief fund.

CHAPTER

7

Government and the Arts

COMPARED to many countries, the U.S. government pales in its record of arts support. To put it another way, there are few industrial nations that give less support from the central government to the arts. Representative Mary Rose Oakar from Cleveland has introduced a bill to create a Secretary of Arts and Humanities in the Cabinet. Such a move could give the arts more national visibility, but so far few in government seem much interested in the proposal. The fifty state arts councils, which distributed $270 million in 1988, certainly help take up the slack, but even this support is in jeopardy. Legislators in several states have proposed eliminating their arts councils. The complex censorship issues that surfaced in the 1989 controversy surrounding the National Endowment for the Arts, Robert Mapplethorpe, and Andres Serrano add even more strain to the relationship between government and artists. With all the current pessimism about that relationship, federal programs already in place to assist arts organizations and artists seem insignificant. Still, help *is* available. A number of government programs benefit individual artists. Are you an avant-garde composer or performance artist with a project defying established guidelines? Contact the National Endowment for the Arts Inter-Arts Program. Want to get government assistance with a recital overseas? The United States Information Agency has programs, albeit somewhat limited, to help musicians. Trying to find money for a research project in music education? Don't overlook grants sponsored by the Department of Education. Looking for a playing job immediately after college? Believe it or not, the U.S.

government is the largest single employer of performing musicians in the country. Individuals can respond to government policy. Dissatisfied with the National Endowment for the Arts' application procedure? There is a public forum where you can voice complaints.

Government bureaucracy is exhausting to wade through. Sometimes you have to call five different numbers only to end up with a vague idea of who it was that you should have talked to in the first place! Telephone numbers and names of program officers change frequently. What did not exist a month ago in the U.S. Department of Education, such as a new gifted and talented program, may suddenly be announced tomorrow.

Program officers in every government agency are paid to advise you, the taxpayer. They can be enormously helpful. You can save a lot of time and energy by getting information and pointers from the right people. There is also a public liaison office for each government department which can provide names of individuals in specific programs. If you get someone on the phone who is unfamiliar with your situation, don't stop there. Keep at it until you have the answers you need.

NATIONAL ENDOWMENT FOR THE ARTS

In 1983 the American choreographer Martha Graham lobbied Congress to appropriate a large sum of money for the dance company bearing her name. She was fed up with not getting more help from the National Endowment for the Arts. Many thought this action audacious and downright tasteless. It surely wasn't the first time the grand dame of modern dance had veered into uncharted territory. What this move demonstrated clearly is that even famous arts organizations like Martha Graham's company are riddled with severe financial problems and need more money than the National Endowment can possibly provide with a modest budget, which was $17.9 million for fiscal year 1990. The overall picture is not exactly uplifting: Federal spending for the arts has decreased by about twenty-four percent over the last eight years.

We can lament the deplorably small sum spent by our government on the arts, or we can be grateful that we have arts endowments at all, beset with problems as they may be. The original stated purpose of the National Endowment for the Arts and the National Endowment for the Humanities, both created by Congress in 1965, was to encourage and support American artists and cultural institutions. Explains Bill Vickery, former head of the National Endowment for the Arts' music program, "The NEA was never conceived as a financial Rock of Gibraltar. Its main job has been to reward high quality and excellence of the leading arts organizations." Livingston Biddle, the former head of the NEA, says in his book *Our Government and the Arts* that when the endowment budget went up, so did the dollars coming from the corporation and foundation world and the private sector. Vickery points to the high level of scrutiny that goes into every application for money to the NEA, whose crucial function is to offer a "national forum for evaluation," a "litmus test" of an applicant's worth on a national level. When a small regional group is chosen for a grant, it has survived the test and been designated worthy of support. Local private and corporate sponsors take note and are inclined to contribute more.

There are at least four programs at the National Endowment for the Arts that fund music projects. The music program is the obvious one. It is the largest single-discipline program, with the largest staff. Fellowships are awarded in a number of categories: to composers, solo recitalists, presenters and festivals, music ensembles, career development organizations, centers for new music resources, and for professional training and music recording. Every year, the fellowships are offered in a different selection of these categories. Jazz performance, composition, study, and management are part of the music program.

In 1980 opera and music theater broke off into a separate division. In this program, grants categories are professional companies, regional touring, services to the art, new American works, and special projects. Individuals with strong track records as producers are eligible for funding in the "individuals as producers" subdivision of new American works. A musician recently received a grant from special projects for the reorchestration of a lost John Philip Sousa opera. Two of the NEA's interdisciplinary programs also support music endeavors: Media-Arts and Inter-Arts. Media-Arts funds film, video, radio, and television endeavors focusing on music topics. The Inter-Arts Program awards grants to presenting organizations and for "New Forms," or art that transcends the traditional boundaries. Individuals can get help from Inter-Arts. A composer or performance artist has only to find a fiscal agent to submit the proposal, that is, a sponsor with tax-exempt status.

All programs in the NEA use the peer review panel system to evaluate applications. The music program, for example, administers about a dozen different panels each year. Each panel member's one-year term is renewable by the NEA to create a certain amount of continuity, but there is usually about a thirty percent turnover of panel members each year in the music program. Once the panels have made their choices, these grant recommendations are given to the National Council on the Arts for final ratification. The council, a body whose job is to advise the NEA, is composed of twenty-six distinguished individuals in the arts appointed by the President of the United States. If a fellowship application to any program in the NEA is unsuccessful, the applicant can obtain a report of the panelists' comments through the Freedom of Information Act. Depressing news can be transformed into a valuable learning experience. Occasionally, misconceptions can be corrected. In one case, a very prominent composer was turned down for a fellowship. Feeling defeated, he wasn't going to inquire about what happened. But friends urged him to call the program officer. It turned out that his music had nothing to do with the decision. Because the correct number of scores had not been sent, his application had never even made it to the panel!

After the panels have made their decisions, a public forum, announced in the Federal Register, is held in Washington, D.C., at which the application process is reviewed. Criteria for the fellowships are discussed. The public can suggest ideas for changes in the next year's application book. In other words, if you have been unsuccessful in getting an NEA grant and are adamant that some part of the application was ambiguous or unfair, it's time to speak up. Your words may be a catalyst for change.

NATIONAL ENDOWMENT FOR THE HUMANITIES

At the National Endowment for the Humanities (NEH), with a total appropriated budget for fiscal year 1990 of about $157 million, no one program is specifically earmarked for music. But such music disciplines as musicology, ethnomusicology, music criticism, and music theory are considered in virtually all categories. The endowment's divisions cover a wide spectrum. The Division of Education Programs includes Elementary and Secondary Education in the Humanities, Higher Education in the Humanities, and a History Center. The Division of Fellowships and Seminars includes the following: Fellowships for University and College Teachers and Independent Scholars, Summer Stipends, Travel to Collections, Younger Scholars Program, Faculty Graduate Study Program, and Summer Seminars for College Teachers and School Teachers. The Division of General Programs includes Humanities Projects in Media, Museums, and Historical Organizations; Public Humanities Projects; and Humanities Projects in Libraries. The Division of Research Programs relates to Texts-Editions, Texts-Translations, Texts-Publication Subvention, Reference

Materials-Tools, Reference Materials-Access, Interpretive Research-Projects, and Regrants-Conferences.

Here are some examples of grants NEH has awarded to music projects: Fellowships and Seminars' Summer Stipend, for full-time independent study and research for two consecutive months, granted $3,500 for a Comparison of Fanny Mendelssohn Hensel's Piano Works and Her Brother, Felix Mendelssohn's "Songs Without Words." The Public Humanities Project, to increase public understanding of the humanities, allocated $40,295 to support development of a program book, symposium, public master class, and gallery exhibition to explore the work and contextual history of the composer Franz Schubert. Within the Division of Research Programs Texts-Editions category, for the preparation of authoritative and annotated editions of significant texts and documents, $106,690 was awarded to support a coordinated national series of scholarly editions of American music.

Like the National Endowment for the Arts, peer review panels scrutinize grant applications. A National Council on the Humanities, the counterpart of the National Council of the Arts, ratifies panel recommendations.

UNITED STATES INFORMATION AGENCY

The United States Information Agency (USIA), headquartered in Washington, D.C., is responsible for the U.S. government's overseas information and cultural programs. Domestically, over five thousand civil servants, including those in the Voice of America, support the program. Foreign service officers are assigned to 205 American posts in 127 countries grouped in five geographical areas: Africa, Europe, East Asia and the Pacific, American Republics, and North Africa/Near East/South Asia. Overseas the agency is known as USIS—the United States Information Service. One of the agency's missions is to spread American culture worldwide. Not surprisingly, a number of foreign service officers are former practitioners in the arts. It is not unusual for the foreign service to be a second career for its personnel. The average age of those taking the foreign service exam keeps rising. Some enter the field in their forties.

The Arts America program, within the Bureau of Educational and Cultural Affairs of USIA, was created in 1979. The same year, the National Endowment for the Arts' panels became the USIA's artistic advisors. Performing artists who have indicated an interest in traveling overseas can be screened by panels of experts from the NEA. For musicians, the two positive ratings given by the NEA are "recommended" and "highly recommended." Activities such as recital appearances or visits to foreign cultural institutions usually happen in response to requests from posts abroad, but USIA sends only highly recommended artists on Arts America tours. Names of artists touring privately are circulated four times a year to U.S. embassies. In other words, a post can "pick up" an artist touring in a particular part of the world. Embassies can also furnish an artist information about cultural resources, concert halls, and musical contacts. Even when USIS posts have no budget to sponsor recitals, the "America Houses," local binational centers, provide another option. With separate budgets, these cultural centers frequently organize appearances of visiting Americans.

There are three regional offices of USIA that help facilitate Americans once they are overseas: the African Regional Service (ARS) in Paris, the Regional Project Office (RPO) in New Delhi, and the Regional Resources Unit (RRU) in London. For instance, if a musicologist teaching at a university in Pakistan would like to do research in Jordan and Syria, the RPO in New Delhi would contact the Middle Eastern posts and act as the professor's liaison in the line of communications.

Speakers or lecturers sent abroad by Arts America usually visit two countries during a two-week period. Speaking engagements could entail anything from a film maker speaking at a foreign film festival to a music critic addressing a symposium on arts criticism. These appearances are organized in response to requests from overseas.

Likewise, the American Cultural Specialists (ACS) program responds to requests from USIA posts abroad. ACS participants are teachers or coaches such as theater directors, choreographers, or instrumentalists who are sent to assist with a project or performance of a foreign arts organization. A specialist usually goes abroad for two to six weeks to work with one institution. For example, an American trombone player was recently dispatched to Warsaw to coach orchestral brass players there. Language skills are understandably an important asset, although the trombonist in Warsaw wasn't required to speak Polish. Latin America is an area frequently requesting cultural specialists, so Spanish comes in handy. Although one can't really apply to be a cultural specialist, curriculum vitae are accepted for future consideration. However, the director of this program warns against an overzealous approach by the applicant. It is not appreciated. The theme of this book is taking the initiative, but it is important to know when to lay off. This is one of those times.

The Artistic Ambassadors Program was founded several years ago by

John Robilette specifically to promote the careers of young American instrumentalists. As wonderful as this program is, it is limited to musicians just starting out. What about the thousands of mid-career American musicians who surely have a lot to offer? What a good bunch of cultural envoys America has waiting in the wings! Let's hope a new creative way of actively promoting our artists abroad, and not just the handful of superstars who go on world tours as a matter of course, or the facilitation or "picking up" of artists already engaged overseas, will be used by USIA as we approach the twenty-first century.

One of the truly grand programs administered by the USIA is the Fulbright Teacher Exchange Program and summer seminars for educators, which has been in place for more than forty years and operating in more than one hundred and twenty countries. About sixty-two hundred grants are awarded each year for American students and teachers to go abroad and for foreign nationals to come to the United States. Fulbright opportunities for Americans in the arts are plentiful all over the globe. Refer to chapter 10, "The International Musician," for more detail about the Fulbright programs and the agencies administering them.

I have been "facilitated" several times by USIA when I was planning a tour abroad. The tour wasn't planned by the agency, but as I was going anyway, help was offered. Here is a story of one of my USIA adventures:

"Thank you for the Rochberg," he said, clasping both my hands warmly as we chatted over cake and coffee. The time was April 1986. The place was Warsaw, Poland. The professor, head of the electronic music studio at Kracow's Academy of Music, had come to Warsaw to hear my recital. He particularly liked the *Sonata for Viola and Piano* by George Rochberg. The recital had been sponsored by the cultural officer of the American Embassy in Warsaw.

I had decided to go to Poland to collect material for my reference book on music schools. Lot Polish Airlines, the national airline, promised me free air fare. I let the Arts America program of USIA know of my plans. Since I had already been screened as an endorsed artist by the NEA, the Washington office sent a cable and cassette of my performance to the cultural attaché in Warsaw. The cultural affairs officer in Warsaw, James Hutcheson, was interested in the American repertoire I sent. In the interest of furthering cultural ties between Poland and the United States, he agreed to facilitate my visit. He cabled Washington to offer accommodation in Warsaw and a modest honorarium for a viola and piano recital sponsored by the American Embassy. I was thrilled. It was just the opportunity I was seeking to balance the research part of the trip. Assistance from the USIA made many aspects of the trip easier. For starters, it was quite nice to be met at the airport! All transportation arrangements and research meetings at the various schools were accomplished with ease. An unexpected recital at the Academy in Katowice popped up at the invitation of my pianist for the Warsaw recital. Not even the tragic Chernobyl disaster, which occurred while I was in Poland, could put a damper on this memorable experience.

DEPARTMENT OF EDUCATION

If music education is your interest, it is good to be aware of activities in the Department of Education. Under the umbrella of the School Improvement Program, the National Programs and Activities branch has an Arts in Education Division. (See what I mean about bureaucracy?) This division gives two direct grants, renewed annually, to the Kennedy Center for programs administered there: Alliance for Arts Education (AAE) and Very Special Arts.

The Jacob K. Javits Gifted and Talented Program is administered by the Office for Improvement of Practice, a division of the Office of Educational Research and Improvements. Passed under the Elementary and Secondary Educational Amendment of 1988, the legislation defines the gifted and talented as "children and youth who give evidence of high performance capability in areas such as intellectual, creative, artistic, or leadership capacities, or in specific academic fields and who require services or activities not ordinarily provided by the school, in order to develop such capacities." The government provides funds appropriated by Congress to give opportunities to America's youth. Money is not given exclusively for the arts, but since the arts disciplines are often badly neglected in school curricula, they would seem to be likely recipients. It is hoped that in the competitive awarding of the grants, arts proposals will be strong enough to do well.

The Department of Education and the National Endowment for the Arts have sponsored projects together, such as the Arts Education Research Center. This center had two sites, New York University and the University of Illinois at Urbana-Champaign, for a three-year research study that terminated in 1990. In each site, different aspects of teaching arts in classrooms throughout the United States were examined. Conclusions obtained from the study are available from each of these universities upon request.

The Department of Education's Office of Educational Research and Improvement (OERI) invites applications for new projects under the Field-

Initiated Studies Program, encouraging individuals and groups to develop fresh ideas that will advance educational theory and practice. The guidelines are broad enough to include a variety of music education projects.

THE FULBRIGHT-HAYS SEMINARS

The Fulbright-Hays Seminars Abroad program takes place under the auspices of the Department of Education's Center for International Education. The center is responsible for deciding on seminar topics and locations—which change each year—as well as how many people will go, and through a panel process, the selection of attendees. The purpose of the program is to help United States educators increase their understanding of other cultures through study abroad. The seminars are then administered by organizations such as the Institute of International Education's Arts International. Some have a specific arts focus. For example, in the China Arts in Transition program, arts curriculum specialists and undergraduate faculty are selected to explore the different regional responses to Chinese arts through travel to Beijing, Shanghai, Guilin, Hong Kong, and Taipei. However, this program is obviously affected by the continuing developments in the political relationship between the United States and China.

MILITARY BANDS

Just imagine: a music career with a decent beginning salary, increasing through promotions; medical, dental, and pension benefits; possible tours of duty abroad; and, best of all, a free education. Not bad for a full-time life as a performing or conducting musician. This is the job description for a career in one of the United States military organizations—the Army, Navy, Marines, Air Force, or Coast Guard. Together they serve as the biggest employer of professional musicians in the country. Over the years, many musicians have taken jobs in military ensembles while earning undergraduate and graduate degrees in music at little or no cost. Many positions are in Washington, D.C., conveniently located near learning institutions like Catholic University and George Mason University, which have good graduate programs in music. Positions in military musical ensembles are advertised in much the same way as the symphony orchestra jobs, most notably in the *International Musician*. Candidates usually audition in Washington, D.C. Like symphony auditions, there are usually preliminary and final rounds. Often auditions are held behind a screen.

One downside of life in the military music world is that players need to be on call for everything in case extra personnel are required for a particular event—twenty-four hours a day, seven days a week, excluding about four paid weeks of yearly vacation.

A large percentage of today's military musicians are women. For example, 31 out of 169 in the Navy Band are women. Gail Ascione is one of them. She has been a clarinetist in the U.S. Navy Band since 1977. Growing up in Annapolis, Maryland, near the U.S. Naval Academy, she had band members for her early teachers and musical role models. During her high school years there were no women in the bands—the first were hired in 1972—but she already knew she wanted to play in a military ensemble. When women first joined, "a lot of men resented them," she recalls. "It wasn't easy to be a woman in the band back then. They had to play better than anyone." But times have changed. "Younger men have a different attitude toward women. The old resentments are gone. Men assume ensembles will be coed—for example, one of the Navy choral groups is fifty/fifty." With the rank of senior chief musician, Ascione has a secure position. In addition, she has taken on collateral duties, unpaid extra projects on the side, such as being in charge of uniform lockers and acting as the enlisted women's representative. She describes a feeling of contentment many musicians struggle for: "I like to play. There aren't many jobs where I could make a steady living playing rather than teaching. I am doing what I want to be doing."

An overview of the armed forces musical world follows. All addresses for applications and more information are listed in the Resource Guide.

ARMY

The U.S. Army has more than twenty-five hundred enlisted musicians and about eighty musicians who are officers, some ranking as high as colonel. They play and conduct in fifty-two musical organizations comprising the Active Army Bands Program. Fifteen of these are in Europe, Panama, the Orient, Alaska, and Hawaii. In addition, seventy-four Army Reserve and Army National Guard bands use musicians on a part-time basis. The Army's premiere organization, the U.S. Army Band, was founded in 1922 when General John J. Pershing gave the order, "You will organize and equip the Army Band." The ensemble serves as the official music group for most diplomatic and state functions in Washington, D.C. Opportunities to perform abroad are not infrequent. In 1988 alone, the Band performed at the International Marching Band Pageant in Tokyo and Osaka, Japan, and at the Army Tattoo '88 in Brisbane, Australia.

Since Pershing's memorandum, the band has added a number of Washington, D.C.–based organizations to its overall operation. These include the U.S. Army Ceremonial Band (for funerals and parades), The Army Blues, The U.S. Army Brass Quintet, The U.S. Army Herald Trumpets, The U.S. Army Chorus (all male) and The U.S. Army Chorale (male and female, a pop group). The Washington Army Band personnel need White House access clearance, which is the same as top security clearance. If clearance is denied, a member is transferred, without further audition, to another band such as the U.S. Military Academy Band in residence at West Point, the Fife and Drum Corps in Atlanta, or the U.S. Army Field Band in Fort Meade, Maryland.

Training after the audition includes Basic Training, and Advanced Individual Training at the Armed Forces School of Music near Norfolk, Virginia. The School of Music is used to train musicians for the Army, Navy, and Marine Corps musical organizations. Its basic curriculum is structured within twenty-three weeks, but can be shortened for advanced performers. The curriculum includes special techniques for marching bands and showmanship.

NAVY

The Navy Music Program employs about eight hundred musicians in seventeen official navy bands, located in the continental United States, Hawaii, Guam, Italy, and Japan. The Navy's top-flight Washington-based band and its specialty groups give about twelve thousand presentations annually. Small groups include the Sea Chanters chorus; Commodores Jazz Ensemble; and Country Current, a seven-piece country bluegrass group that accompanied President Bush on his 1989 trip to China. The Navy's counterpart to the U.S. Military Academy Band at West Point is the U.S. Naval Academy Band, based at the Naval Academy in Annapolis.

AIR FORCE

It wasn't long after the 1947 formation of the Air Force—the newest branch of the Armed Forces—that its bands began playing. Activities are focused around the U.S. Air Force Band at Bolling Air Force Base in Washington, the U.S. Air Force Academy Band in Colorado Springs, Colorado, and forty-five other groups in the United States, West Germany, and Japan. The Air Force specialty ensembles include the Show/Dance Band, Popular Music Combo, and Protocol Combo. Air Force musicians get on-the-job training rather than attend the School of Music used by the other branches of the Armed Forces.

MARINES

The U.S. Marine Band, called "The President's Own" because of its strong White House presence, is the only service band whose members are not required to go through basic training. They are also exempt from Physical Fitness Tests required by other armed forces branches, although they are expected to maintain proper weight and personal appearance. Another departure from other branches is that the Marine Band doesn't have separate concert and ceremonial units. The entire pool of musicians can be called to perform anything from a chamber concert to funerals and outdoor ceremonies. Small ensembles such as the Marine String Quartet and the Bugle Corps, often featured as White House entertainment, maintain distinct identities.

COAST GUARD

John Philip Sousa helped the Coast Guard Band get started in 1925. Forty years later an Act of Congress, signed by President Lyndon B. Johnson, proclaimed the permanence of the band, including it as one of the country's five premier service bands. The forty-two-member Coast Guard Band has within its ranks a Combo, Brass and Woodwind Quintets, and the Dixieland Jazz Band, all located in New London, Connecticut. An annual series of concerts is presented at the Coast Guard Academy's Leamy Hall Auditorium, in addition to chamber music and summer concerts. A 1989 tour to the USSR marked the first time a U.S. Armed Forces band had been there in decades.

MAKING YOUR WAY IN
THE WORLD

INTRODUCTION: THE LIFE JOURNEY OF THE MUSICIAN CONTINUES . . .

What a sense of accomplishment it is to have your education behind you and to become savvy about music resources, audition procedures, recital opportunities, and all sorts of career matters. While asserting our musical identities, it is consoling to know there are organizations out there that are set up specifically to help out struggling musicians. Even our government lends a hand in creating career opportunities.

Now comes the fun and scary part! Going out into the world as a musician in this society presents a distinctive combination of challenges and frustrations. But the possibilities of interesting career niches are wide open. Mixing good, original ideas and hard work together can translate into enormous career satisfaction. Use your imagination and take initiative. Chances are that the rewards will overcome the frustrations and disappointments when you take on an exciting project, whether it be commissioning a special new work, making a record, arranging a world tour, or taking an orchestral position. Go ahead, take that plunge! Read on, and take note of those who did.

CHAPTER

8

Hustling:
Taking the Initiative
Stories from the Field

THE COMPOSER WHO DIDN'T WAIT FOR A COMMISSION

WHILE teaching composition at Lawrence University in Wisconsin, Steven Stucky went to the university orchestra conductor and declared (didn't ask) "I would like to write an orchestra piece for you." This is not always how such things are done, but no one, least of all Stucky, was waiting around for the almighty orchestra commission. OK, the conductor said. So the piece, *Transparent Things*, got written and was performed by the Lawrence University Orchestra. But that was only the beginning. Stucky sent the work *unsolicited* to the Minnesota Orchestra. In other words, the Minnesota Orchestra did not ask to see the work. By chance, the orchestra had just gotten a grant from the Jerome Foundation to do an informal reading of scores. Stucky's score was in the "slush" pile up for consideration. It made the cut and was read by the orchestra. On the basis of that reading, the Minnesota Orchestra commissioned Stucky to write another orchestral work, *Dreamwaltzes*.

Dreamwaltzes was performed by the orchestra and Stucky sent a tape of it to Pulitzer Prize-winning composer John Harbison. At the time Harbison was composer-in-residence of the Los Angeles Philharmonic. He told music director André Previn about Steven Stucky's score and played him the tape. Previn liked the piece, and presumably on the basis of what he heard, invited Stucky to become the Philharmonic's next composer-in-residence. So on the basis of a non-commissioned piece written for the little-known Lawrence University Orchestra, Steven Stucky was commissioned to write another piece that eventually got him the position of composer-in-residence for the Los Angeles Philharmonic. Stucky tells his students at Cornell University, "Write for your friends. Take the initiative. Your composition is its own reward. Other rewards will come. Have enough *chutzpah* to send your works around. Write the best music you're capable of. If it's a good piece people will know it."

A VIOLINIST WITH A BIT OF CURIOSITY

One day Stanley Kurtis, a New York violinist, was walking down Broadway. At West 72nd Street, he ran into a violinist colleague. "Do you play the mandolin?" the friend asked. He explained that he had been approached about a new Broadway musical which required the violinist to play mandolin. He would need a substitute who could play both instruments. Kurtis, who had never played the mandolin, was intrigued. He did research about repertoire, read *Mandolin World News*, found a teacher and learned to play the instrument. After hearing recordings of mandolin concerti, he hunted down the respective performers in Germany and Italy, and went to Europe to study with them.

Kurtis realized that if one show used mandolin, there might be other performance opportunities. Maybe there was a need for mandolin players. He let contractors, those that hire freelance musicians, know of his newly acquired skill. Within two years, he was playing mandolin in the Prokofiev ballet score *Romeo and Juliet* at New York's Metropolitan Opera House. Soon after that he doubled on violin and mandolin in the musical *Brigadoon*. He was the featured soloist at Washington, D.C.'s Kennedy Center in Hummel's *Concerto for Mandolin and Orchestra*. In looking back on what happened, Kurtis reflects: "Things can go so way beyond where your brain could conceive they can go. For every action there are more reactions than you can imagine." By the way, the Broadway show offer which had kicked off his interest in the first place never materialized!

*A*TTEND A MUSIC CONFERENCE AND GET FREE TRIPS TO EUROPE?

In November 1985, while attending a conference of the College Music Society in Vancouver, British Columbia, I had a fateful conversation. From the discussion emerged a simple idea that opened up a whole new world to me. The little tidbit of advice I received translated into thousands of dollars of airplane tickets during the next three years.

Meeting pianist Michael Smith was unremarkable, although I probably never would have met him had there not been a Vancouver conference. It cost a lot to attend; the meeting was definitely beyond my means at the time. But the reasons to go outweighed the reasons not to and off I went.

One evening there was an informal get-together of American musicians who lived out of the United States. Having recently returned from a six-year stint in Israel, I joined the gathering. Discussion got around to the topic of my research and a subject that had been troubling me: How was I going to get to the Eastern European countries to visit the famous music academies to be included in my reference book? Smith, a pianist who lived in Sweden, sat across from me. "Oh, it should be fairly easy to get to Poland," he said. "Contact Lot Polish Airlines in New York. They will be happy to give you a round-trip ticket. Just tell them you'll acknowledge their help in your book."

The outcome was just as Michael Smith had predicted. Lot is a national airline and proud of its country's cultural resources. Without much effort, the round-trip ticket was secured. Ditto for Malev, the Hungarian airline; Finnair, the Finnish airline; and SAS, the Scandinavian airline. With the luxury of free travel to Poland, Hungary, Finland, and Norway, I was able to arrange recitals in these countries without having to ask for exorbitant fees, undertook some exciting research for my book, and was able to enrich my life in the process. All because an original thinker with a fresh perspective was generous enough to share an idea with me.

*F*ROM MONTANA TO ALASKA

A few years ago I joined the roster of artists-in-residence for the state of Montana. Late in the summer of 1986, I got a letter inviting me, along with the other fifteen or so members of the roster—writers, actors, visual artists, and dancers—to come to Helena for a weekend, no salary but with expenses paid, to share our artistic endeavors with one another. As the coordinator of the event put it to us, there wasn't enough money in the budget to give any one of us a residency, but there was enough to get us all there. Why not? It provided an ideal environment for building some new contacts and relationships with artists who weren't musicans (for a change!). Montana is a pretty place. Perhaps an idea from someone in another art form would provide a fresh career catalyst. That is exactly what happened. While walking to one of the seminars, a poet with whom I'd struck up a conversation described a great experience he'd had teaching at an arts camp in Sitka, Alaska. I asked about the music program and discovered there was a person in charge of stringed instruments. I made my interest known to the Alaska camp, and two years later the teacher for stringed instruments resigned. I was hired for the position. What started as an off-hand conversation in Helena, Montana, resulted in a wonderful Alaskan adventure.

A TOUR TO DOWN UNDER, NEW ZEALAND, AND FIJI

Sometimes it is just a matter of writing letters. That is how my five-week lecture and recital tour to Australia, New Zealand, and the South Pacific got organized. I am always in the process of updating research on Music Schools. The *Chronicle of Higher Education* is on my "must read" list each week. It provides information about institutions all over the world. The *Chronicle* first introduced me to the existence of many universities in the Southern Hemisphere such as the University of Canterbury in Christ-church, New Zealand. For years I had wanted to visit universities in that part of the globe. My first batch of letters, announcing a hypothetical tour, included one to pianist Maurice Till at the University of Canterbury. Luckily for me there was no violist on the university's staff. A concert of piano quartets (needing a viola) had been tentatively scheduled. Within a couple of months I received a substantial invitation from Christchurch: to participate in a Town Hall concert (including the piano quartets), to give a recital at the university, and to deliver a lecture. Once this invitation was confirmed, I immediately let other universities and performance or-ganizations know I would be in the area within a specific period of time. Six months of preparation plus many letters, faxes, and telephone calls generated engagements at seven universities in the Southern Hemisphere. The cost of my airplane ticket was covered with the fees I earned. Usually

I had fine accommodations and hospitality from gracious colleagues. Recording solo recitals for the Australian Broadcasting Commission and New Zealand Radio, as well as presenting the first viola recital ever at the University of the South Pacific in Fiji, were part of the experience. Sounds like a dream? It was. The beautiful letters I've gotten from students across the world help remind me that it actually happened.

*A*N OBOIST WITH A VISION

In a world where classical music soloists are usually pianists and violinists, oboe player Bert Lucarelli has done admirably. He hasn't let playing a nontraditional solo instrument stand in the way of a rich and creative career. In fact, an adage that has inspired Lucarelli is: "You must always take what is a perceived disadvantage and turn it into an advantage." He explains, "That is what I have done with the oboe." Many works have been written for him. Lucarelli's discography includes a recording that has sold more than seventy-five thousand copies. As he was carving out his solo career, no one came to him and said, "I decided to write you a major concerto for the oboe, arrange a performance in Carnegie Hall, and get the piece recorded by RCA." Yet all these events came to pass. It took simply a creative mind, a clear vision, and three telephone calls.

First, Lucarelli phoned the composer John Corigliano, a friend, and asked him if he'd like to write an oboe concerto. Then he phoned the American Symphony Orchestra and asked if it would present the premiere of John Corigliano's *Concerto for Oboe and Orchestra* at Carnegie Hall. Then he phoned the New York State Council on the Arts (NYSCA) and asked about its interest in funding the American Symphony Orchestra's project to premiere the Corigliano work. Lucarelli knew if NYSCA provided funding, the American Symphony could get a matching grant from the National Endowment for the Arts as well. Altogether, about $25,000 was raised. Virtually none of it went to Bert Lucarelli. In fact, he had to ask Corigliano to buy him a $125 set of tails out of his commission fee to wear for the Carnegie Hall performance! The concerto proved to be a tremendous career vehicle for Lucarelli and an important addition to the oboe repertoire. RCA Records heard a tape of the concerto and wanted to record it. But more money needed to be raised for the project: $20,000. Without delay, Lucarelli went back to NYSCA, which had already made an investment in the work's premiere, and to a prominent music patron. The money was secured and the recording was made. Since that time, there have been many more records and premieres for Lucarelli. Martha Graham chose the Corigliano work as the featured new music of her 1989 New York season, accompanying the dance American Document. Of course, Bert Lucarelli was the soloist. He is no longer a starving musician. Today he can no longer fit into those $125 tails, but he has no trouble affording new ones.

CHAPTER

9

A Record Can Be Your Calling Card

IS it really possible for a young musician or seasoned professional without a world-class solo career to make a solo record or compact disc? Yes. Many of the fine records and compact discs available today have been made by musicians who aren't household names. No one promises that the big record companies will come knocking at the door of musicians without international careers, but there are smaller companies around that a musician can contact. Some musicians simply put out and distribute records on their own using their own funds. Anyone can create a record or compact disc label. No need even to incorporate. Like so much else in this book, it is up to the musician who wants to be recorded to get going and take steps to initiate a project. Here are the stories of some who did just that.

RECORDING SUCCESS STORIES

The Cleveland Duo, composed of Cleveland Orchestra violinists Carolyn Gadiel Warner and Stephen Warner, recently came out with its first compact disc. The duo has an active recital career, performing violin duo repertoire and violin and piano works (Carolyn doubles as pianist). The Duo had thought about making a record so was ready to seize the chance when it was offered. A new classical label, Cappella Records, had been created in Columbus, Ohio. Russ Nagy, who helped originate the idea

111

for Cappella, is in charge of Artists and Repertoire. He wanted the folks in the Cleveland Orchestra to know about the label, so he met with about thirty interested members of the orchestra after a rehearsal. Nagy recalls: "Some of the musicians were shocked that we couldn't advance artists' fees before the record was out, but the Warners had the right attitude." They were willing to discuss a recording project with the understanding that Cappella would pay for producing the record, but fees would come later out of shared royalty profits. With an impressive track record of concerts, the duo got funding from the Ohio Arts Council to pay expenses and honorarium. The recital compact disc of the duo features the Warners in twelve Bartok *Duos for Two Violins*, Brahms *Sonatensatz*, Debussy *Sonata for Violin and Piano*, Milhaud *Sonata No 2 for Violin and Piano*, and a work by the Czech-born Canadian composer Oskar Morawetz for violin and piano. Many companies would not go for the idea of a one-hour recital record of largely standard recital pieces, especially played by a group without name recognition. But Cappella did and is delighted with the results. So are the Warners, who manage their duo without the help of an impresario. The compact disc, now also available on cassette and distributed throughout the United States and Canada, has received good reviews and will no doubt help boost the duo's recital career.

While walking down the street in Paris, oboist Bert Lucarelli paused at a store of the music publishers Billaudet. On a whim, he entered and asked "Do you possibly have any old oboe music—like opera fantasy pieces arranged for the oboe?" The man disappeared and returned with a musty old box filled with sheets. Lucarelli was all set to buy the lot. "Oh, you can just have it!" said the shopkeeper. Given his penchant for singers and operatic literature, Lucarelli knew there was a future record in all of this. He applied for a sabbatical from the Hartt School of Music to undertake the necessary research. Part of that 1985 sabbatical year was spent in the Paris Bibliothèque and the British Museum. Photocopies and microfilm were obtained, and the record to be called the Bel Canto Oboe was now on its way.

Meanwhile, back in the United States, the late record executive and producer George Mendelssohn, founder of Vox Records, had sold his business but was finding retirement rather boring. So he started a new classical record company, Pantheon Records. Lucarelli had previously recorded for Vox, and proposed the new project idea to Mendelssohn and Pantheon Records. He sensed that Mendelssohn could contribute a great deal to the project. "A good A & R [artists & repertoire] man wants to have an impact on the product. If you go with an ironclad idea you're almost usurping that role. Better to go with a loose proposal and benefit by a record professional's participation. These people know all about old recordings, market strategy, and audience." Sure enough, Mendelssohn introduced the idea of varied textures and instrumentation to replace the sound of only oboe and piano. Strings and harp accompaniment were eventually included on the Bel Canto Oboe compact disc, which was released by Pantheon's Priceless label.

Lucarelli recorded the CD at Mastersound Studios in Astoria, Queens, New York. The sound there reminds him of the "natural wood resonance" of the old 30th Street Studio once used by Columbia Records. He prefers recording in this studio rather than in churches because "you have control over temperature and humidity conditions. Under stressful, long recording hours, this is a particularly welcome attribute." He also enjoys working with recording engineer Ben Rizzi, in residence at the studio. Lucarelli gives the ultimate compliment: "I trust him with my sound."

Violinist Stan Kurtis is rather atypical among average New York free-lance classical musicians. He is also a jazz artist and his taste in periodicals reflects this diversity. Kurtis found his record contact in *Billboard* magazine. A column on new record companies contained an item announcing that a Canadian company, Fanfare Records, was interested in crossover projects (classical musicians performing jazz and vice versa). Like the Cleveland Duo, Kurtis already had an idea for a record when he became aware of the potential for a recording opportunity. Reading the notice in *Billboard* provided a catalyst to get going on it. The idea had started to germinate years before when he purchased a "bright orange" piece of used sheet music from Joseph Patelson's Music House in New York. It was a popular tune done by Joe Venuti, the great jazz violinist. Somehow that orange music stuck in Kurtis's mind and he became aware that Venuti's legacy was largely unrecorded. Why not find a pianist suited to such repertoire and record it? Lots of research had to be done in order to bring this project to fruition. The process created an exciting search for Stan Kurtis, but was painstakingly slow. He found that "you get excited at the early stages but then it becomes harder to stick with it." Just finding the Venuti tunes from the 1920s and 1930s was a project in itself. After months of combing everything from the Library of Congress to used sheet music stores to the libraries of older club date violinists, Kurtis finally came up with all sixteen tunes in the Venuti portfolio. Along the way, he contacted Dick Hyman, the distinguished jazz pianist whom he greatly admired, who saw "there may be a project in this." Kurtis and Hyman made a demo tape of one of the Venuti works. What had begun in glimpsing an announcement in *Billboard* led not only to a record but also a new, rather thrilling professional association for Stan Kurtis. "Dick Hyman allowed me to learn along the way, while being partners." Eventually the demo blossomed into a compact disc and cassette made for Fanfare, produced and packaged by Pro-Jazz and distributed by its parent company, Intersound Inc. The reviews have been good and new projects are in the wind.

Ron Barron, the principal trombone player of the Boston Symphony Orchestra, made his first solo record in 1975. "At the time there wasn't much trombone music recorded. I had recently come back with the second prize from the Munich International Competition, and wanted to record some solo works." Barron was teaching at the Boston Conservatory at the time, so the conservatory auditorium during the quiet of late night hours became his studio. John Newton, a well-known Boston-based recording professional, served as engineer and Barron himself helped produce the record. Today he would do it differently and hire a producer. "Better to have someone else there to listen and bounce your ideas off of." After the recording sessions, Newton got Barron in touch with a company to re-master the tape, and with other companies to print record labels, design the jacket, print the jacket, and ship the record. Barron himself took care of distribution, by putting advertisements in music publications and hiring an organization to get libraries to buy it, many of which did. The record, *Le Trombone Francais*, was the first to be made on his own label: the Boston Brass series. The record opened doors for Ron Barron, one of them into Nonesuch, for whom he recorded *Cousins*, which features trombone with cornet played by Gerard Schwarz.

Other brass players have initiated their own recordings in the last several years. The Dallas Brass, founded by trombonist Michael Levine, is a flourishing young ensemble that plays about one hundred and twenty-five concerts a year. The group's first compact disc/cassette was made in the simplest way. The ensemble chose a Dallas church as the recording space, and an engineer recorded using only one very high quality stereo microphone. The Dallas Brass philosophy: "Record the way you perform." All production, packaging, and distribution was done exclusively by the group. Cassettes and compact discs have been sold at concerts. Levine deems the project a financial success. "We've sold fifteen thousand cassettes and fifteen hundred compact discs and we've made back our money several times over."

Trombonist Don Lucas made a record, in cassette form, to use as a business card, demo tape, and introduction to his solo work. As a result of his experience, he now presents a clinic called "The Making of a Custom Studio Recording" for young musicians. The project wasn't cheap: it cost Lucas about $43,000 to produce *Hymns for Trombone*, on which he performs trombone solos with different background orchestrations. The logistics of his project were much more complicated, thus more costly, than the making of a recital record. He used the Houston studio Rivendell Recorders, run by Chuck Sugar, and flew a number of the musicians participating in the recording to Houston. The Lucas project involved four weeks of recording and two additional weeks to mix and remix the multi-track recording. The tape was mastered by the Nashville company Mastermix, run by Hank Williams, Jr., which specializes in country and commercial music. This mastered tape was transferred to digital format on videotape, which was then sent to a cassette company. Another master tape was made from the digital video cassette. One thousand cassettes were produced, covers designed and the final product wrapped. The price for compact discs would have been considerably more expensive. For his purposes, Don Lucas finds the cassettes satisfactory as "small showcases and demos for record companies."

CREATIVE RECORD PRODUCERS AND COMPANIES

One step toward making a demo or complete tape is becoming familiar with the names of freelance classical record producers. If you decide to pursue a project, chances are you'll be hiring one of them. Tim Martyn is one of the corps of sought-after freelance classical record producers in New York City. His company, Classic Sound, maintains post-production and editing facilities in New York's popular recital hall, Merkin Hall. From his considerable experience recording concerts in Merkin, Martyn recommends it as a site for making a demo, and notes that the hall houses a beautiful nine-foot Hamburg Steinway piano. Among other New York recording locations used by Martyn and his distinguished producer-colleagues Max Wilcox, Judith Sherman, Elizabeth Ostrow, Joanna Nikrenz, and Marc Aubort are the auditorium of the American Academy of Arts and Letters, Manhattan Center, and Sommer Center at Bronxville's Concordia College.

Before embarking on a project, do a little homework about the classical record companies out there, both famous and lesser-known. Learn about repertoire recorded by the various companies. And find out where, as well as where not to send unsolicited demos and master tapes.

Everyone has heard of CBS Masterworks, now Sony Classical, and RCA, now part of BMG. But unless you've just won a major competition or have one of the music industry superstars backing you, chances of getting recorded by these labels are slim. The biggies are looking for international artists who sell their own records through busy globetrotting careers. If someone is unknown to them, the stock line is, "We rarely rely on tapes." A debut label was started for young artists some years ago at CBS. Unfortunately, it was an experiment that did not continue. The major record companies, CBS Masterworks, RCA, EMI, and Deutsche Grammophon, may not be in the cards for the up-and-comers, but there is a lot of information which can be gleaned from these companies to build one's recording savvy.

Steve Epstein, one of the record producers at Sony Classical, tries to locate the best places to record. New York's CBS 30th Street Studio, originally a church built in 1850 on 30th Street between Second and Third Avenues, used to be a favorite recording spot. But it had a fate that occurs too often: the property was sold in the early 1980s to a developer who tore it down. These days Epstein favors Alexander Hall at Princeton University for chamber music and chamber orchestra recording and the Manhattan Center for full-sized orchestras. He explains, "The hall where an orchestra performs is not always the best place to record." Because of the sensitivity of the digital medium, according to Epstein, "Microphones don't have to be placed as close to the musical source as in the pre-digital era, particularly in the 1960s. The quality of the recording environment has therefore become more critical with digital recording." One of the challenges of his career is taking an active role in the technical, as well as musical, decisions in records he produces, "whether it be something as conventional as a Mahler Symphony, with five to seven microphones to capture the entire ensemble, or in a Baroque recording of Wynton Marsalis playing all three trumpet parts simultaneously."

Among the smaller companies, Arabesque Records has been highly acclaimed for its quality recordings. Ward Botsford, who founded the company in 1979, says he is one of the few people in his field who "always wanted to get into the classical record business since I was sixteen years old." He described one of the differences between his company and CBS Masterworks (now Sony Classical). "It is easy for CBS to decide on repertoire. They look in the catalogue, see what record is most recorded, and make one more of it. There is always room for another *Nutcracker Suite*. It is a function of the size of their company. That could not work for us. We don't have the advertising and promotion budget. We do things that have never been done before—unique projects. I love to do oddball things."

Does Arabesque take unsolicited tapes from unknown artists? "We don't buy out. We have on occasion, but they very often don't work out. Even if we receive a good master or demo tape and a good idea for a project, rather than use that tape we'll record the artist again. An example of this is Steve Lubin on Arabesque's fortepiano recordings." When Botsford receives suggestions of repertoire and artists, "I never throw anything out. The vast majority is garbage. Generally things are wrong. Only about one-tenth of one percent goes somewhere. You need a certain type of artist for unusual repertoire. Big artists often won't learn new works. I must find artists who are willing to learn unknown repertoire." He cites the case of pianist Ian Hobson. "Hobson wanted to record standard repertoire. I told him I'd like to work with him but wanted to record the Leopold Godowsky Etudes. He learned them and five months later we recorded them." The outcome? "The Godowsky, because it is so unusual, was reviewed. It didn't sell for one year—this music is an acquired taste, it takes time—until Hobson came out with another record. Then it started selling well. It is important for Arabesque and for the artist to do unusual repertoire."

In the United States, Arabesque records at the Sommer Center for Worship and the Performing Arts at Concordia College in Bronxville, New York. Botsford explains how the hall came to be built: "The President of Concordia College, Dr. Ralph C. Schultz, an organist, wanted to create a recital facility with great acoustics. We were the first to use this chapel and now other people do also, including CBS."

Two-thirds of Arabesque's instrumental recording is done in the United States. Orchestral recording, however, is mainly done abroad. Arabesque projects include a Polish venture with the Cracow Philharmonic and American conductor Gilbert Levine doing Shostakovich's *Symphony No. 1, Concerto for Piano and Orchestra* with pianist Garrick Ohlsson, and the *Age of Gold Ballet Suite*; a record of works by Benjamin Britten with the English Chamber Orchestra and Elizabeth Söderström; and a record of pianist Jerome Lowenthal performing the Tschaikovsky *Piano Concert No. 1* in its original version with the London Symphony Orchestra and conductor Sergiu Comissiona, finishing a set of all the piano concerti; and a premiere recording of Rossini repertoire with the tenor Rockwell Blake.

The general Arabesque philosophy? "If you're in the classical music business, you need to take a long view of things. It takes time to make good wine. In music taste must be acquired in the same way. Listeners must have adventuresome taste to listen to what we do."

New World Records, another maverick smaller company, was the first record company started as a not-for-profit venture. Specializing only in American music, it began with an initial grant from the Rockefeller Foundation to produce a one hundred-record Anthology of American Music. Elizabeth Ostrow, Vice President, Artists and Repertoire of New World Records, which produces about eighteen discs annually, talks about how the company has continued after the initial project. "Off-shoots of the original anthology that didn't make it into the first one hundred records, such as our American cowboy music set, continue to be made. Project ideas come from the original editorial committee, staff, board—and then there are unsolicited ideas."

What about unsolicited projects? Ostrow says, "We listen to everything we receive. A small number of projects do make it to release, such as a record of Charles Griffes' piano music. Some years ago a musicologist contacted us with the idea of recording the collected piano works of Charles Griffes. We are now developing a record of the music of the composer Leo Sowerby, which was also an unsolicited project. Ostrow adds, "We pride ourselves on recording both established name artists and the bright unknown upcoming talent. An unknown artist is helped with a recommendation of a colleague known to us. As in all walks of life, recommendations open doors." If you're making a demo tape, Ostrow has some advice: "Make the tape with good supervision, using a good producer and an engineer who knows about equipment and halls. If you proceed blindly or with poor advice, you will have wasted your time and money."

Contrary to Cappella's concept that recital records work, Ostrow cautions, "What makes a good concert may not necessarily work as a record, although I don't rule out a recording of a live recital. In a concert a certain eclecticism works. But it won't necessarily make good programming for a record."

Among the New York recording locations used by New World Records are the auditorium of the American Academy and Institute of Arts and Letters, the Manhattan Center, and RCA Studio A. Ostrow advises, "Before you try a hall, ask to hear a recording made there. Often halls sound different to the naked ear than they do through a microphone over speakers."

Telarc International Corporation, based in Cleveland, Ohio, has a fine reputation among record enthusiasts. This small company concentrates on classical crossover and jazz recordings. For example, it has produced over twenty-five records with the Cincinnati Pops Orchestra under the direction of Erich Kunzel and at the same time has recorded the Vienna Philharmonic with Andre Previn. Obscure works are not the fare of this label. Co-founder and Grammy Award-winning record producer Robert Woods cautions musicians against sending his company unsolicited tapes. He receives hundreds of tapes every month and tries to listen to everything. Woods advises young musicians not to "waste time and money making a tape without management." Instead, "make a demo of a live recital. Talk to managements." He is much more inclined to listen to a tape sent by management but will listen to a live performance tape. What interests him is "a hot talent who will be touring and having a management behind him to help promote records."

Woods says he is always on the lookout for a good classical record producer. What qualities are necessary? "A personality to work with diverse sorts of people, psychological insight in understanding individuals, a performance background, performance skills, and above all, great ears." He adds the surprising view that "there is more opportunity in classical record production than in pop music."

Nonesuch Records has long been committed, though not exclusively, to recording twentieth-century works. Recent releases of music by the likes of Steve Reich, Philip Glass, John Adams, George Perle, John Harbison, and John Zorn reaffirm the philosophy expressed by Nonesuch head Robert Hurwitz: "Music should be reflective of its time." One Nonesuch project has the opera diva Teresa Stratas singing Kurt Weill theater music, and another features the World Saxophone Quartet playing the music of Duke Ellington. Are these jazz or classical? Nonesuch is attempting to do away with such barriers. The label's Explorer series has introduced the field of ethnomusicology, with instruments and music from various world cultures, to the general public, while period music on original instruments performed by artists such as Malcolm Bilson and Anner Bylsma has also been presented. Nonesuch has carved out a successful niche for itself as a company for maverick repertories, proving Hurwitz's contention that "small labels have a better chance to make interesting music."

Dorian Recordings is a new compact disc-only label that does most of its recording at a 1875 concert hall built atop a savings bank building in Troy, New York. The late conductor George Szell once called this hall "the finest in the United States." Recording engineer Craig Dory, one of the founders of the Dorian label, remarks that "this hall allows the artist to play more freely than anywhere I've been in the world." It is the "true pianissimo" possible at the Troy Savings Bank Music Hall that led to the success of one of Dorian's first discs, *The English Lute Song*. Other compact discs on the Dorian label include *Organ Encores*; Tschaikovsky's suite of miniature tone poems for piano, *The Seasons*; opera arias arranged for brass, *Solid Brass at the Opera*; harpsichordist Colin Tilney playing Scarlatti sonatas; and the complete organ works of Cesar Franck, performed by Jean Guillou. Because Craig Dory and Dorian's co-founder Brian Levine have created a label that features the recording space as much as it does artist and repertoire, musicians are advised to send Dorian demo tapes and repertoire ideas, rather than finished master tapes on speculation.

One label that does consider completed master tapes for production is the Musical Heritage Society (MHS) and its affiliated Music Masters label. A decade ago I sent a master tape to MHS's head of artists and repertoire Jeffrey Nissim. Within a year the record was out on both MHS and Music Masters labels. The tape had been recorded in Jerusalem at the Jerusalem Music Center solely as an audition tape for European radio stations. It was only after the recording was completed that I realized the music was a suitable length for an LP disc and that there was a cohesive record logic to the repertoire: Shostakovich's *Sonata for Viola and Piano*, Hindemith's *Trauermusik*, and Partos's *Yiskor*. A major reason MHS accepted the tape was Nissim's enthusiasm for the special quality of the Jerusalem Music Center. This point emphasizes that location for a master tape is as important as the artist and repertory.

Remember that recital record made by the Cleveland Duo? Cappella Records is a new company open to new ideas. Along with the Rushmore Jazz label, it was created under the auspices of a parent company, Discovery Systems. Russ Nagy, the newly created label's head of artists and repertoire, is happy to receive demos and unsolicited master tapes. "I need ideas to be in business," he says. For example, he sees a dearth of recorded music for chamber choir and hopes to fill that void. He is also interested in recording works which would have a "long shelf life." Two composers of particular interest to him are Hugo Wolff and Paul Hindemith. "Cappella can cater to a specialty market because it has Discovery Systems to fall back on." He calls the new label a "long-term investment" for the parent company.

Once you have a tape or idea for a project, don't stop at the companies mentioned in this chapter. There are others—Bridge Records, Harmonia Mundi U.S.A., Newport Classics, Northeastern Records, and Composers Recordings Inc.—to name a few. They are listed in the annual *Billboard's International Buyer's Guide*. Who knows if there aren't other labels being created by adventurous record buffs as I write. Keep aware of new developments. Like Stanley Kurtis, you may find out about companies by reading *Billboard* or other periodicals, or like Ron Barron you may choose to come up with your own label. If expenses of the new era of digital seem daunting, look for grants to defray the costs. The National Endowment for the Arts, in particular, has special recording grants. Don't underestimate the value a solo record will have for your career. Even more important, don't underestimate the thrill of coming up with a good project and bringing it to fruition.

CHAPTER 10

The International
Musician

STUDYING ABROAD

THERE is absolutely no substitute for leaving one's home culture to study in another. Even in this age of technological wizardry, neither computers nor fax machines can teach us about the cultural fabric of another society. You have to be there, preferably on a day-to-day basis, for at least several months. A year of study at London's Royal College of Music changed the course of my musical life. After that experience, I was intoxicated with the excitement of being abroad and travelled to play in numerous European festivals. Familiarity with career patterns and opportunities in other countries enabled me to arrange performances and recordings in many parts of the world. Eventually I took a six-year appointment in a foreign orchestra.

Because of the universality of music, our profession lends itself naturally to study in other countries. Being exposed to different styles of playing, unfamiliar contemporary composers, and attitudes of performers and scholars in other places helps ward off the false impression that any one country is the musical center of the universe. In fact, each country has its own kind of cultural provincialism. Not that anything is wrong with cultural patriotism, but greater exposure to other environments will lead to a broader perspective for the performer. Naturally, it will not happen in the practice room or library. One can have that experience without leaving home.

INTERNATIONAL FELLOWSHIPS

Travel is expensive. On the other hand, few foreign countries have higher tuition costs than the United States. Here is a list of agencies which assist American students with study abroad.

ARTS INTERNATIONAL

Arts International administers programs developed by the Institute of International Education (IIE), the largest U.S. higher educational exchange agency. This arts branch of IIE encourages increased international collaboration in all the arts, with targeted interests in grants, advocacy, exchange, and information. Arts International sponsors programs for curriculum specialists, young professionals, graduate students, and faculty at higher education institutions.

MUSICA: MUSICIANS FROM THE UNITED STATES AS INTERNATIONAL CULTURAL AMBASSADORS

Through this program, American classical musicians are given up to $1,000 to participate in international competitions abroad. From eight to fifteen grants are awarded annually. MUSICA strives to keep an American presence at these competitions and at the same time to create an international context for musicians' career development. The program, founded in 1952, has sent approximately six hundred contestants abroad. Over half have returned with prizes.

An expanded use of MUSICA's funds is now in the experimental phase. This change of guidelines makes travel grants available to musicians attending workshops and masterclasses abroad and to composers so that they can hear the premieres of their own new works overseas.

CINTAS FOUNDATION FELLOWSHIPS

These fellowships are open to creative artists of Cuban citizenship or direct lineage living outside of Cuba. The program promotes the development of professionals in the various arts fields, including music composition. Fellowships of $10,000 are awarded annually.

THE FUND FOR U.S. ARTISTS AT INTERNATIONAL FESTIVALS AND EXHIBITIONS

This fund provides support for U.S. artists and arts organizations who have been invited to performing arts festivals, and artists' representation at exhibitions. The program was initiated by the National Endowment for the Arts and the United States Information Agency, with the Rockefeller Foundation as private partner. The 1988 disbursement was $600,000.

New programs and activities of Arts International are announced on a special page of *FYI*, the newsletter published by the New York Foundation for the Arts. (See chapters 2 and 6.)

INSTITUTE OF INTERNATIONAL EDUCATION (IIE) U.S. STUDENT PROGRAMS DIVISION

IIE is one of the agencies administering grant competitions under the Fulbright Program. The U.S. Student Programs Division awards Fulbright Fellowships to undergraduate and graduate students who are American citizens.

FULBRIGHT SCHOLAR PROGRAM

The Fulbright Scholar Program came into existence with the Mutual Educational and Cultural Exchange Act of 1961. The primary source of funding is an annual appropriation made by Congress to the United States Information Agency. Grants are made to U.S. citizens and nationals of other countries for activities including university teaching, advanced research, graduate study, and teaching in elementary and secondary schools.

In 1947, following passage of the Fulbright Act, the Conference Board of Associated Research Councils established the Council for International Exchange of Scholars (CIES), a private organization, to cooperate with the government in the administration of the Fulbright Scholar Program. The CIES also administers the Indo-American Fellowship Program, Spain Research Fellowships, and the NATO Research Fellowship Program.

Each spring CIES publishes a booklet listing one thousand teaching and research opportunities for American faculty and professionals in approximately one hundred countries. About thirty lecturing and research grants are offered in music. Most awards require a doctorate and/or the appropriate professional experience.

INTERNATIONAL RESEARCH AND EXCHANGES BOARD

The International Research & Exchanges Board (IREX) offers research awards for music scholars in a number of Eastern European countries.

For example, for American performers and composers, awards offered in cooperation with the USSR Ministry of Culture include a nine-month stay at a conservatory in the Soviet Union and two one-month stays for advanced students in performance or composition.

THE JAPAN FOUNDATION

The Japan Foundation has a Professional Fellowship Program and a Visiting Professorship Grant Program. For the Visiting Professorship plan, an institution in Japan must request a particular artist from the foundation. In this program, the foundation's support will not exceed three-fourths of the total costs. Dissertation Fellowships and Study Tour to Japan grants are also available.

ROTHMANS FOUNDATION

Rothmans Foundation Fellowships are awarded by the Rothmans Foundation-Education Division for postdoctoral research at an Australian university. Applicants must have held a doctoral degree for no longer than three years to qualify. The annual value of the award is approximately $30,000 (Australian).

PROFESSIONAL OPPORTUNITIES FOR AMERICAN MUSICIANS TO TEACH OVERSEAS

In a profession flooded with the unemployed, here is *finally* a job market where opportunities abound: teaching in private and Department of Defense schools located throughout Africa, Asia, Central and South America, Europe, and the Middle East. "We just don't have enough people to fill the music positions we're notified about," says an officer at the Princeton, New Jersey, International Schools Services, which recruits staff for schools abroad. She wishes ISS had more music candidates on file for teaching positions.

This is the story. There are about six hundred and fifty private American and international schools around the world. Most are independent schools governed by boards of directors drawn from the communities they represent. A small number are company- or church-sponsored. The student bodies at these schools are usually multinational, populated by the children of government officials, diplomats, journalists, and professionals living out of their home countries. English is the language of instruction and the curriculum is based on a standard U.S. program.

Different types of organizations help find teachers for these schools. Some are employment firms working to help a teaching candidate get placed. Others, like International Schools Services, set up active files for candidates who have completed application forms.

INTERNATIONAL SCHOOLS SERVICES, INC.

International Schools Services, Inc. (ISS) is a private not-for-profit organization founded in 1955 to advance the education of American children attending schools overseas. ISS services to overseas schools include recruitment and recommendation of personnel, curricular and administrative guidance, getting materials, school management, financial management, consulting services, and publications. *The ISS Directory of Overseas Schools* provides information about hundreds of institutions.

Administrators make recruitment trips during February and March of each year. During this time ISS sponsors two International Recruitment Centers (IRCs) in the United States and one overseas. These IRCs provide ISS candidates the opportunity to interview with overseas school heads. About five hundred and fifty teaching and administrative positions are listed at the IRCs each year. Only active ISS candidates may register and schedule interviews. In addition to the placement opportunities offered through IRCs, ISS recruits staff for vacancies that occur in the late spring, summer, and midyear. Approximately two hundred such vacancies are listed with ISS annually. Candidates are notified of job openings at the time schools are sent their dossiers. There is a $50 registration fee for each candidate. Files of candidates must be updated yearly, at no additional cost, although a $25 fee is charged to update an inactive file. Files not updated for five years are considered closed. Prospective teachers must have at least a bachelor's degree, two years of experience. Certification is usually required. The dossiers are then sent by ISS to the appropriate schools and the rest of the review process is left to them. A $600 placement fee is charged when a candidate accepts a position at a school contacted by ISS. Sometimes the school will pay the fee.

OFFICE OF OVERSEAS SCHOOLS,
U.S. DEPARTMENT OF STATE

The Office of Overseas Schools of the U.S. Department of State is an umbrella organization for all the government agencies finding staff for the international schools network. This office issues useful materials such as the booklet *Overseas American-Sponsored Elementary and Secondary Schools Assisted by the U.S. Department of State.*

DEPARTMENT OF DEFENSE

The Department of Defense has its own schools located in different regions of the globe and its own method of recruitment. A list of DOD schools is published in the booklet *Overseas Employment Opportunities for Educators.* Deborah South, who teaches drama and music in the Department of Defense's Heidelberg American High School in West Germany, enthusiastically recommends the experience. Her salary has doubled from what it was as a teacher in the Texas public school system.

AMERICAN FIELD SERVICES EDUCATORS PROGRAM

Another way of going abroad to teach is through the American Field Service Educators Programs. Teachers are placed in Latin American (Spanish is a requirement here), China, and Thailand.

THE PEACE CORPS

The Peace Corps has limited opportunities for musicians, but music can be combined with other programs. For instance, one music teacher who was accepted into the Peace Corps taught English in Liberia, while at the same time serving as a choir conductor.

UNIVERSITY OF PITTSBURGH

The University of Pittsburgh sponsors a program called Semester at Sea: Institute of Shipboard Education. Students receive college credit while sailing the world. Ethnomusicology is a part of the curriculum, and in a recent semester the courses Gamelan Anklung of Indonesia, Introduction to World Music, and Music in the Middle East and India were offered. Obviously the opportunities here are few, but they do exist for the adventurous. Ethnomusicologists with backgrounds in Asian and Mediterranean music are encouraged to apply. Finding a professional niche overseas will put you in close proximity to an abundance of interesting opportunities. Graduates with music degrees from American universities, preferably with teaching credentials (K–12), can use a teaching job as a vehicle for extensive traveling and expansion of career outlets.

Radio engagements

Most countries in Europe and some other parts of the world have national radio stations of which they are proud. Citizens of these countries often pay special taxes to keep the stations operating at a high cultural level. It is not unusual for the larger systems, like Radio France, to have separate departments for chamber music, symphonic music, and contemporary music. Often there is a radio orchestra—sometimes more than one— which is part of the radio system. Records and compact discs are used for broadcast, but these radio stations look for innovative programming and take pride in hiring their own artists. Many are interested in presenting twentieth-century American music. All it takes is sending a record or a tape and repertoire suggestions. Even if an artist is not well-known, a producer impressed with the tape and repertoire suggestions may well offer an invitation to record a program, usually thirty to fifty minutes. Recording schedules are often drawn up a year in advance. Payment for one such booking can range from $300 to $800. Be sure to be familiar with all rules about work permits, visas, and prior musicians' union approval in the countries where you will be working to avoid unpleasant surprises after you arrive.

Orchestral positions

There are several ways to keep informed about positions abroad. The easiest is to read the American Federation of Musicians newspaper, *International Musician*, regularly, as well as the German magazine *Das Orchestra*. On the next page is an example of an Australian orchestral position advertised in the *International Musician*.

Even if you are not interested in the particular horn position listed, you have been informed about a center for information. A talk with this ABC staff member may yield news of other orchestral opportunities in Australia.

HELP WANTED

SYMPHONY
ORCHESTRA

Principal Conductor:
Dobbs Franks
Concertmaster:
Barbara Jane Gilby

The Tasmanian Symphony Orchestra, which enjoys the highest reputation in Australia, and beyond, under the direction of the Australian Broadcasting Corporation, wishes to engage a:

PRINCIPAL 3RD HORN

Auditions will be held in Hobart on Monday, 17th July, 1989.

The salary is within the range of $29,323-$30,971 for a 96 hour, 4 week roster.

AUDITION REQUIREMENTS: Strauss Horn Concerto No. 1 (complete). In addition orchestral excerpts will be made available 72 hours before your audition.

Those who are unable to audition live will need to make their own arrangements to record their audition and submit, with their tape, a statutory declaration or a signed statement that the work is their own, that the tape was not edited at all and that the excerpts were not opened earlier than the prescribed time. Audition tapes will need to reach this office by 5.00pm Friday, 14th July, 1989.

If you want to live in one of the most beautiful places on earth and enjoy a rich musical lifestyle, please send a written application quoting reference number TC9H14 including a curriculum vitae and contact telephone number to Employment Officer, ABC, GPO Box 9994, Hobart 7001, Australia by Friday 23rd June, 1989. If you are unable to appear live or would like more information on the Tasmanian Symphony Orchestra please contact John O'Carroll, as soon as possible, c/- Tasmanian Symphony Orchestra, 163 Liverpool Street, Hobart 7001, Australia. Telephone (002) 35 3635.

AUSTRALIAN BROADCASTING CORPORATION

THE ABC IS AN EQUAL OPPORTUNITY EMPLOYER

INTERNATIONAL CAREER AIDS

INTERNATIONAL SOCIETY FOR MUSIC EDUCATION

The International Society for Music Education (ISME) was formed in 1953. Prior to ISME, there were other attempts to establish international networks for music educators. The first, in Lausanne, Switzerland, was a conference of music teachers organized by Percy Scholes. Prague, Czechoslovakia, was the site of a 1936 conference entitled First Congress for Music Education. The Paris conference followed in 1937, and the next year's meeting in Switzerland focused on the music education of handicapped children. Charles Seeger, often looked upon as the father of ethnomusicology, formally submitted the ISME proposal at the Brussels International Conference attended by 40 countries. ISME became a member body of the International Music Council. The *International Journal of Music Education* is published twice a year, the *ISME Yearbook* annually. Special interest groups, called commissions, hold seminars in seven areas: Research; Education of the Professional Musician; Music in Schools and Teacher Training; Music Therapy and Music in Special Education; Community Music Activity; Music in Cultural, Educational, and Mass Media Policies; and Early Childhood Music Education.

INTERNATIONAL ASSOCIATION OF MUSIC LIBRARIES

This association can provide useful information on the music research tools available in the libraries of its member countries. For example, the New Zealand Division publishes the newsletter *Crescendo* three times a year, providing valuable information on the music resources and current events in New Zealand.

COMPOSERS' SOCIETIES AND MUSIC CENTERS

Composers' societies and music centers around the world can provide important information about musical matters. For example, upon request, the Canadian Music Centre/Centre de Musique Canadienne (CMC) can send a computer printout of cello compositions by Canadian composers. The Australian Music Centre can provide information about performance locations and regulations for foreigners performing in Australia, as well as information about Australian composers. See the Resource Guide for a list of these international music organizations.

CAREER LITERATURE

BOOKS

There is ample resource material about professional musical life in the United Kingdom. The *British Music Yearbook* is endlessly useful. Leave it to the British to be downright practical and fill a musician's every need for information. It lists literally hundreds of societies and associations in the United Kingdom. The publisher of the yearbook, Rhinegold Publishing Ltd., has produced an array of helpful materials. *The British Music Education Yearbook* is just as packed with information but with more advice and ideas for music students and teachers who are in the United Kingdom. *The Students Guide to Graduate Studies in the UK* is self-explanatory. *Musician's Handbook*, edited by Trevor Ford, is a superb all-around guide for classical musicians. Though geared to a British audience, it is worthwhile reading for all musicians. The chapter "Finding Your Way Round the Associations," by Susan Alcock, offers good, short descriptions of them. *Arts Festivals in Britain and Ireland* gives many ideas about performance opportunities in the United Kingdom. There are many other festivals besides the world–renowned Edinburgh Festival, and here you'll find a comprehensive listing of them. *Who's Who in Arts Management* will tell a performer the credentials and background of managements being considered as presenters in the United Kingdom. The same is true, with an international perspective, in *Who's Who in International Arts Management*. *Guide to Arts Marketing* will have particular interest for arts administrators, but also offers ideas for anyone trying to fill a concert hall. Speaking of arts administration tools, The Arts Council of Great Britain has an Information Service for Arts Administrators and a specialist reference library with over five thousand books, reports, and papers on cultural policy, arts administration, and social and economic questions related to the arts. The library is in London and is open by appointment to arts administrators and researchers.

Books on other parts of the world include: *Scholarships, Fellowships, and Grants for Programs Abroad; Funding for Research, Study, and Travel: Latin America and the Caribbean*; and *Funding for Research, Study, Travel: The People's Republic of China, Academic Year Abroad* and *The Insider's Guide to Foreign Study. The Schirmer Guide to Music Schools* and Conservatories Throughout the World, International Handbook of Universities, World of Learning, the Commonwealth Universities Yearbook and the reference section of Musical America offer a global view of schools.

PERIODICALS

The monthly magazine Music Teacher deals with the British system of education and the different opportunities available to music teachers in the United Kingdom. Classical Music, a bimonthly magazine, presents news of music and the arts. Other British publications include Early Music, The Gramophone, International Arts Manager, Musical Opinion, The Musical Times, The Strad, Opera, and Tempo. Musical America lists most of the important music periodicals, by country, under the heading "International Music Magazines."

MUSICAL PORTRAITS

INTRODUCTION

Interviewing people for this section was utterly inspiring. At some point I had to say to myself "STOP! YOU'VE INTERVIEWED ENOUGH PEOPLE ALREADY!" It took willpower like turning off a movie that has you hooked. I was fascinated at the amazing lives people have made for themselves. The diversity of fields connected to music is astonishing.

In this part of the book I attempt to fulfill two goals. First, to chart a wide variety of music career options and give some background and resource information about them. Some categories have introductions, where I felt an explanation would shed light on a particular career. Second, to show how people in assorted music-related careers have carved out interesting and useful lives. I have profiled those in traditional music disciplines and those who have created career slots for themselves. Some have changed tracks in mid-career. A number of artists trained as performers find stunningly original ways to use their gifts later in life. There are those who had no formal training in music but with innate talents managed to find a place for themselves.

The best lesson I have learned from those I've interviewed is: Be aware of your gifts, even the ones you didn't know that you had, and always have an adventurous spirit about finding a professional niche which suits you. Love what you do.

11

Getting to Be the Boss: Arts Administration

"HEADHUNTER" is a term well known in the world of big business. Not usually associated with the nonprofit sector, right? Wrong. Placing professionals in the nonprofit sector is now often handled by executive search firms. It can be pretty rough. As one headhunter puts it, "There is a shoot-out among the major firms to get the work." Development and executive positions in the arts are serious business. Not every arts administrator is placed by a headhunter, of course. But the world is changing. Musicians should be savvy about how their bosses get chosen. Some may very well decide to defect to management themselves.

Korn/Ferry International, one of the best-known executive search companies, has found executive directors for the New York City Ballet and the San Francisco Opera. A principal of the firm explained why the company began working with nonprofit organizations: "The boards of arts organizations are often made up of corporate executives. They know their own companies use executive search firms, so why not the arts organization they are serving?" Korn/Ferry conducts searches only for jobs with salaries of at least about $65,000. Like all such firms, it works as part of a team with the organization's board of directors and search committee to fill a particular position.

What qualities were needed in the executive director of the New York City Ballet? "We looked for a good manager, someone with fund-raising experience, a good representative for the institution, sensitivity to the art, someone who would be a good partner with the artistic director. We cast a wide net beyond the world of the arts and sat down with the search committee, the board of directors, and representatives of neighboring organizations at Lincoln Center to see what the job was, what the cultural environment was, and what personality would fit. We aggressively go after potential candidates." In the case of the New York City Ballet, which has a $25 million-a-year budget, those who might have been considered included number two people from big organizations, executive directors from small ones, people from the corporate world, and even college presidents thinking of early retirement. A search usually takes three to four months, sometimes longer. The short list of three to seven candidates is drawn up in about four to six weeks. Leads are found from "sourcing calls" to prominent people in many professions, colleagues in the particular one, and those who have been finalists for other searches. Korn/Ferry does have a data bank of resumes submitted by job-seekers. However, executive search firms are retained by the employer organizations and are *not* employment services.

Another firm describes the consummate arts executive. "The more diverse and entrepreneurial the person is the better . . . arts executives understand accountability. Many people don't understand the accountability factor: as the executive director you must be accountable both to the staff *and* to the board, the body of governance. The candidate for an executive position must be a good inside *and* outside person. Arts organizations are bottom-line oriented . . . the head of it must have internal and external expertise."

Erich Fuchs, head of Erich Fuchs Enterprises in New York, specializes in recruitment of mid- and high-level executive positions of cultural organizations. His advice to performing musicians thinking of a career in arts administration? "Become an administrative assistant in development at an arts organization while you are performing. . . . Even a clerical job in an organization instead of waitressing will bring you some experience in the field."

What about getting a master's degree in business administration? Korn/Ferry says it is desirable. A consultant from another firm says, "The M.B.A. helps people to think strategically: where the company will be in five years, how to run a capital campaign, what is needed in the long term, how to deal with internal problems." Erich Fuchs recommends three schools that offer an M.B.A. with a special focus in arts administration (not to be confused with a master's in arts administration): University of California at Los Angeles, State University of New York at Binghamton, and University of Wisconsin at Madison. Even if graduates of these programs begin at low level positions, Fuchs says they accelerate faster.

Another credential has gained credibility in this job market. The National Society of Fund Raising Executives grants a Certificate of Fund Raising Executives on the basis of an examination.

Looking for more information about this career? There are job listings: the National Arts Jobbank, published by Westaf, is updated and mailed every two weeks. It advertises not-for-profit, government and academic positions. Art SEARCH, The National Employment Service Bulletin for the Arts, advertises administrative positions and arts internships. The College Music Society offers a monthly listing of jobs in the academic music world, such as dean of a music department or development officer of a conservatory of music. Orchestral administrators can find employment listings at the American Symphony Orchestra League.

Source material? A trade publication on the subject is *Fundraising Management.* The book *Jobs in Arts and Media Management: What They Are and How to Get One!* offers a good overview of the subject. The career kit at the back of the book is a good reference guide. *Careers for Dreamers and Doers: A Guide to Management Careers in the Nonprofit Sector,* published by The Foundation Center, and the quarterly publication *International Arts Manager* also contain useful material.

Performers who change careers and join the ranks of management are not a rare breed. Those profiled in this chapter, Jerry McCathern, executive director of the Brooklyn Philharmonic Orchestra; William Vickery, president of the St. Paul Chamber Orchestra; and Judith Arron, executive director of Carnegie Hall, are three performers who found creative outlets in administrative positions. None of them ever received a management degree.

JERRY MCCATHERN, executive director of the Brooklyn Philharmonic Orchestra, was a celebrated cornet player in his hometown of Hereford, Texas, by the time he entered high school. As a University of Houston freshman, he was on the fast track of the music profession, playing trumpet at age eighteen in the Houston Symphony Orchestra. The conductor at the time was Sir John Barbirolli. Success had come to McCathern so young; however, by the early 1970s, after a disappointing experience at the Juilliard School and a stint as principal trumpet in the Orchestra Filharmonica de Sao Paulo in Brazil, his life took an abrupt turn.

McCathern left the music profession, working briefly in a meat-packing plant in Texas and then later for four years at the international desk of Braniff Airlines in Kansas City, Missouri and Houston, Texas. Why the sudden switch in careers? "The fire in my playing went out. I wanted to give the real world a chance, and I thought there must be an easier way to make a living." But while taking a break from the music world, McCathern learned some valuable job skills. In a nutshell? He recalls, "I learned about humility, computers, marketing, sales, and how to get along with the boss."

After this interlude away from music, he was ready to make a fresh go of it, and started playing all over again. McCathern decided to try his fortunes in the free-lance music world of Houston. But this existence was precarious and insecure, and he wanted to regain control of his own life. With other colleagues and the advice of a lawyer, he founded the Texas Chamber Orchestra (TCO).

The Cultural Arts Council in Houston at the time was, in fact, looking for groups to support. The TCO incorporated and formed a board of directors. McCathern was involved with all aspects of the group: fundraising, publicity, contracting, and playing. He was president of the board, manager of the orchestra, and principal trumpet, all at once. It was a great hands-on experience, but far too much responsibility for one person. At an American Symphony Orchestra League Conference, he was given this advice: No organization should have to rely on one person. It should be able to exist without you. Get out. The TCO board at first refused his resignation, but after much resistance to the idea, his resignation was finally accepted. His career in arts management, whether or not he realized it at the time, had begun.

He had learned the basics from the Texas Chamber Orchestra, and went on to become performing arts manager of the Houston Festival Foundation, which produced New Music America 1986. Then McCathern made his way to New York, recruited by an executive search firm to become Director of Development of the Staten Island Children's Museum. From there he went to his current job at the Brooklyn Philharmonic Orchestra.

McCathern sits hunched over his desk in a cozy office on the sixth floor of the Brooklyn Academy of Music, surrounded by orchestra programs, budget proposals, coffee cups, and tea bags. He discusses the state of arts funding in New York, some aspects of which he finds particularly unfair. "Why doesn't the Department of Cultural Affairs do more for the arts? According to the Alliance for the Arts, eighty percent of the money goes to thirty-two cultural institutions in city-owned buildings." In other words, an institution situated in the wrong building will be out of luck. Another perennial struggle facing arts administrators is that "the arts are competing against other nonprofits. Education gets the most, social services are next, and the arts get leftovers."

Sure, there are frustrations in every career, but watching the orchestra's boss hard at work crunching numbers in Brooklyn, this writer has a hunch Jerry McCathern has found his calling.

WILLIAM VICKERY, president and managing director of the Saint Paul Chamber Orchestra, was a trombone student at Juilliard working in the school's orchestra library when the chief librarian left in his senior year. Vickery told the Dean *he* could run the library. This self-proclamation would prove to be a turning point. Unbeknownst to Vickery, a future career track in music management had already begun. He managed to juggle the chief orchestra library position with school activities, receiving both his bachelor's (1971) and master's degrees (1972) in trombone. Juggling would prove to be a skill worth having.

After short stints in a Mexican orchestra and as a free-lance musician in New York, he was back on the administration track. From head of the orchestra library at the Aspen Music Festival, he became an assistant in the personnel manager's department. On he went up the ladder of administrative positions: first orchestra manager at Juilliard, then assistant dean of the Aspen Music School where he had "indoctrination by fire." Suddenly an enormous amount of responsibility fell upon him. "In my first month on the job Gordon Hardy, President and Dean, was in Europe, the other assistant dean, Robert Biddlecome, was in South America on tour with the American Brass Quintet, the music director Jorge Mester was in Louisville, and I had to put the music festival and the school together." Then the concertmaster was unable to return to Aspen! "It [concertmaster] is a sensitive position. You need a many-faceted individual. The concertmaster must teach, play chamber music, and lead the orchestra. Suddenly the board said: 'Come to Colorado and put together a budget.' The whole first year was like that!" What skills could he bring to this new position? Vickery says an affinity for mathematics helped. "But I had never made a budget. It was a hands-on experience. I got a feel for every facet of the organization, saw the process through from beginning to end. As librarian and personnel manager, I had always received the schedule. Now I had to create it!" In planning the schedule for the Aspen Music Festival, he learned to juggle concerts, a summer music school, and all logistical arrangements for one hundred six contracted artist/faculty members. He had to make sure one person wasn't expected to show up at two simultaneous rehearsals. "Decisions had to be made and then you had to take responsibility for them." How did he cope? "You roll up your sleeves and do it!"

Finally, he recalls, "The summer arrived. Kids came to register. The first concert happened and I had had a lot to do with it. I felt an enormous sense of pride at having helped put it together." He worked for the Aspen Music Festival for eleven years, leaving as Executive Vice President in 1987.

Did he miss playing? "When I joined the Aspen Music Festival, there was no more time for playing. But I stopped playing in a gradual way. I was so absorbed by management tasks there was no time to look back. I had transferred the satisfaction of playing into doing something else. In putting all the pieces together, problem-solving—a great amount of creativity goes into all of that. Creative juices are caused to flow. Creative needs are being satisfied." He defines administration as "a creative process to get everything happening."

Vickery became head of the music program of the National Endowment for the Arts in 1987, and two years later assumed the top administrative position at the Saint Paul Chamber Orchestra. The orchestra's board of directors recruited him.

For Vickery, Aspen and the National Endowment for the Arts had served as management school. "At Aspen I had to coordinate activities of the orchestra, chorus, chamber music, opera, conference on contemporary music, school, assist in making the programs—put it all together. Now in Saint Paul we have an Artistic Commission made up of three music directors. I work with all of them to coordinate different series of concerts. It is not a foreign thing for me. It is an interesting programmatic and intellectual exercise, putting together a season as well as a budget."

The most important thing to tell someone interested in going into management? "You have to love music, love the process of making music happen. I could not imagine *not* going to our concerts. I love listening to them."

In a big, comfortable office at 881 Seventh Avenue, an address better known as the Carnegie Hall building, sits JUDITH ARRON, executive director of Carnegie Hall since 1986. She comes across as a diplomatic person, yet with dignity, firm resolve, and strong opinions; a fitting profile for someone whose job entails frequent contact and negotiation with some of the biggest temperaments and egos around. Running one of the world's great halls is no doubt the most visible position Arron has had in her rich career. While it was never part of a career master plan, she actually spent years honing the skills needed in this demanding job.

Although Arron was trained as a cellist and pianist at the University of Puget Sound in her native Washington State, she never intended to play professionally. Even during college, she knew she wanted to go into arts management. But she maintains that a performance background has been an invaluable asset, helping her to empathize with the artist. "Everyone is nervous when they walk onto the stage of Carnegie Hall, no matter how many times they have played here. I try to help the artists however I can." This, she feels, is one of her most important responsibilities.

Immediately after graduating from college in the late 1960s, she began working at the American Orchestra League in Washington, D.C. While organizing special training projects and national conferences, she made many important contacts among conductors and orchestra managements. She put orchestras together for special seminars and was associate editor of what is now *Symphony Magazine*. One of her most challenging assignments was to conduct a nationwide survey for the U.S. Office of Education Study of Youth Concerts Throughout America. She traveled widely to hear concerts. One of these trips led to a job offer by the Cincinnati Symphony Orchestra to develop a community outreach program for young people. She accepted.

During a seventeen-year tenure in Cincinnati, Arron built an outreach program for youth that became a model for educational programming in other parts of the country. She eventually became artistic administrator of the orchestra. The job included budgeting, negotiating contracts, engaging artists, and having a major role in programming repertoire for concerts. This gave her the background and qualifications for her next, totally unexpected, career opportunity.

Arron was recruited by an executive search firm for Carnegie Hall. After several rounds of interviews and final approval by Carnegie Hall officers Isaac Stern, James D. Wolfensohn, and the board of directors, she was formally offered her current position.

At Carnegie Hall, Arron works long days, filled with such tasks as programming for two halls (both Carnegie Hall and Weill Recital Hall), hiring artists, administering a $17 million annual budget, fundraising, traveling the globe to "get to know firsthand what we're bringing here," and even handling the leasing out of offices in the Carnegie Hall building. She also tries to attend as many evening concerts at the hall as possible and, amazingly, manages to be there most of the time. Although staff can represent her, "I feel guilty when I miss concerts." It is no wonder she describes her job as "a commitment to a lifestyle more than to a profession."

Unlike most major concert venues, such as Lincoln Center's Avery Fisher Hall, Carnegie Hall has no one resident ensemble. That means there is usually a different group or soloist performing on the Carnegie Hall stage each night. Arron is ultimately responsible for what is presented at every concert. To help with this enormous responsibility, she obviously needs to keep current with goings-on in the music world. I asked which publications help her keep informed. Her list includes *International Arts Manager*, *Musical America*, *Symphony Magazine* and especially the Sunday *New York Times*, which she calls "must reading for people anywhere in the world."

Arron's overall concern about the profession of arts administration? "People look at it like a business, but what we put on the stage is music. My position looks very glamorous, but it entails long hours and a huge commitment. It can all fall by the wayside without a deep commitment to music. But then, if you don't love music, what are you doing in this business?"

12

Creating and Recreating Music

INSTRUMENTS are the vocal chords of non-singing musicians. The concert hall is where it all gets heard. In the twentieth century even chamber music has evolved from a living room sport into fare for a larger audience. Musicians have been known to fill professional roles as both instrument makers and experts in acoustics. Here are a few examples.

ACOUSTICIAN

Acoustics research and consulting is a considerably important profession these days. A $108-million concert hall in Dallas is all the rage. New concert halls are being planned for Philadelphia and Birmingham, England. The firm undertaking the acoustics consulting for these projects is New York-based Artec Consultants Inc. Not surprisingly, a high percentage of employees at Artec and in the field at large have some sort of music background. Meet two of them.

DAVID GREENBERG attended Indiana University in Bloomington, Indiana, as a French horn performance major, studying with the renowned teacher Philip Farkas. Since his early teens, he assumed that his life's work would be playing in the horn section of an orchestra. It was while preparing for his senior recital that he realized "this was not the career for me . . . the pressure of the moment was not pleasant." Greenberg had many interests outside of music; he excelled in physics. "I wrote to thirty to forty acousticians to find out about their career paths and to ask what training and preparation they might advise for me." This career research led him to Purdue University's "design your own program" interdisciplinary engineering (IDE) program to catch up on engineering requirements, from which he received a second B.S. degree. Greenberg then entered masters programs at Penn State University in both acoustics and architectural engineering.

What is his role at Artec? "We work closely with architects on the design—shape, size and finishes of a new hall. We also give engineers and architects guidelines about acoustic isolation and noise control issues." Greenberg's orchestral music background makes him sensitive to how performers hear each other on stage and sight lines to the conductor. Nice to have someone looking out for the musicians, isn't it?

CAMERON FRUIT works with computers at Artec. He found out about the firm at the University of Wisconsin at Platteville, where he completed a double major in music and electrical engineering in the early 1980s. Artec was the acoustics and theater consultant for a new fine arts center being built. The company's president, Robert Wolff, came to speak to a music class and mentioned the firm's interest in hiring people with both musical and technical backgrounds. When Fruit graduated, the professor who had arranged the acoustics presentation urged him to contact the firm. He did. His letter was answered with two telephone interviews and then the job itself. "My work started in Tampa, Florida, where a new hall had just opened. I learned that, while part of the job was in the office, the other part was on-site work at the halls." He has helped devise computer programs for acoustics design, showing such phenomena as sound rays in a room, paths of sound, and the time it takes sound to get from the source to the receiver. But Cameron Fruit is also looking out for musicians' concerns. "As a violinist, I know how important it is for musicians to have enough space to play. I consider this when working with platform design."

INSTRUMENT MAKER AND RESTORER

Violin maker and restorer WILLIAM MONICAL, whose shop is located in Staten Island, New York, has a novel approach to training young colleagues. He sends them to a toy store to buy jigsaw puzzles of ten to twelve pieces. "I get them to look at the curves and shapes, positive and negative sides of the puzzle, and put it together upside down—without looking at

the picture. Training the eye in a particular way, developing an optical aptitude, and retaining information about shapes is essential in our profession." Along with memory of shapes, he cites "judgment of how to use tools" to be another crucial skill. "You must know how to sharpen tools in a correct shape to do the cutting. It takes a long time to learn how to do it. Surgically sharp is not good enough." Knowing different woods and understanding them, he says, is another essential for the profession.

Monical is clearly passionate about his work. "You find something so engrossing, so interesting, that you can imagine working with that subject twenty hours a day—authenticating instruments, researching objects, trail blazing in new directions."

Starting out as a violist with interests in musicology, he "became interested in the instruments themselves and wanted to know how they were made." He studied for three years at the violin-making school in Mittenwald, West Germany, with Aloys Hornsteiner and Karl Roy. Roy was interested in early instruments, which was helpful for Monical, who wanted "to get both sides," i.e., to learn both modern and early instrument making and restoration. Studies followed in London with Dietrich M. Kessler, who is "among the finest makers of viols." He returned to America and worked in the shop of Jacques Francais in New York. Today, Monical has a business in which he works on both early and modern stringed instruments.

Most people who become violin makers have played violin or another stringed instrument. Monical feels a playing background helps a maker "understand the physical needs of the player." But how does a candidate for the profession first become acquainted with the demands of the career? "Meet violin makers, see what their job entails, what their occupation involves." Becoming a professional is no quick process. Monical stresses the fact that "fifteen to twenty years are needed to begin to have the knowledge necessary to work as a professional."

He lauds the training available in the United States. "Europeans now come here to study," he says. Three American schools that teach violin making are the Violin School of America in Salt Lake City, the Chicago School of Violin Making in Chicago, and the North Bennet Street School in Boston. Schools in Europe include those of Mittenwald in Bavaria; Cremona, Italy; and Newark, England. Formal training in a school "is an absolutely critical prerequisite" because "time and financial demands on experienced professionals make the apprenticeship system virtually impossible these days." After the formal training, the journeyman stage begins "much like a medical internship," the young maker working in a shop at

an entry level salary under the supervision of an experienced colleague. Here repair and restoration skills will be learned. This may be the first opportunity for the young maker to see instruments of the great luthiers. Monical remarks, "One needs this period to define a specialty and focus on specific interests."

The American Federation of Violin and Bow Makers, the professional association of violin makers in the United States, was founded in 1980. Its original membership of twenty has expanded to seventy plus fourteen associate members, those in the learning stages of the violin-making business. Monical stresses the important function of the federation as a national career resource. "We are devoted to helping train the next generation of violin makers. To obtain information," he advises, "write a letter, or contact the member of the federation closest to your locality." A list of federation members is available from the organization. (See Resource Guide.)

What about career prospects? Monical is encouraging. "Horizons are limitless for well-trained and dedicated violin makers. We are short on violin–making professionals to serve our country's musicians."

BOW MAKER

While playing the violin as a student, YUNG CHIN became fascinated by his instrument and bow. Today, as a bow maker, he makes, repairs and rehairs bows, and buys and sells them. Bow making is a less formalized profession than violin making. But like violin making, professional bow makers usually learn their craft under the guidance of one particular individual. After almost eight years of working in the shop of New York bow maker William Salchow, Chin went into business for himself. It is a competitive business, even in areas like New York and London, where there is quite a large market of musicians to be served. A bow business's most secure income comes from bow rehairing, a service all string players need periodically.

The only institutionalized bow making programs in the United States are summer courses. William Salchow teaches bow making at the University of New Hampshire, while Vahakn Nigogosian teaches bow repair at Oberlin College's summer school. Resource material on bows? Recommended texts are *Bows for Musical Instruments* by Joseph Roda, Vatelot's *Le Archet Francais*, and John Bolander's *Violin Bow Making*. The latter is the only source which describes the actual making of a bow. Chin reads *The Strad, Strings*, and the *Journal of the Violin Society of America* to keep current on what is happening in the business.

CREATING MUSIC

CLASSICAL COMPOSER

LIBBY LARSEN is very successful. She is one of a small group of American composers who actually makes a living writing so-called "serious" music. But she has gone beyond the business of just helping herself. With colleague Stephen Paulus, she founded the Minnesota Composers Forum in 1973, one of the nation's most valuable service organizations for composers. The forum sponsors concerts of American composers, offers fellowships, runs a recording series, provides legal assistance for composers, publishes a newsletter, and has become a model for other composers' support groups in the United States. "When we set up the commissioning program, we went around to other existing programs like the NEA and Rockefeller Foundation and found that there was no commitment to performance. We were the first to create a program tied directly to performance of the works commissioned. I feel that music can't live unless it is performed.

"I never particularly wanted to teach. And Steve Paulus felt the same way. We had something else in common—all of our parents came from business backgrounds. We learned about long-range planning." The forum was founded on the premise that "contemporary classical music is really a declining market and the standard repertoire is an expanding market. The goal is to have your own music heard—to make it a reality—creating a new market for the contemporary classical market. The optimum goal is to create a large, active, competitive field. Then you can do your best work."

Larsen has her hands full for the immediate future. New commissions include *Frankenstein*, commissioned by the Minnesota Opera, a piano concerto for Janina Filkowska, a symphony for the Albany Symphony Orchestra, and a piece for singer Arlene Auger based on Elizabeth Barrett Browning's *Sonnets from the Portuguese*.

Useful tips for young composers? The booklet published by Meet the Composer called *Composers in the Marketplace* (see chapter 6), which gives suggestions about money transactions in commissioning, "codifies the field" and is "a wonderful tool." Libby Larsen reads technical articles on negotiation. "Negotiation is not adversarial, it is just an art, and can be a real support to us. I respect the art of doing business. There is a myth that combining business skills with artistic skills is a sellout. But we are on the point of crisis. Unless we start addressing business issues in the fine music schools, we will be in trouble. There is emphasis on creativity but not on the need to balance that creativity with the reality of society. There is no understanding of how the artist can be part of our society. Artists must learn to speak the language of business. Mutual respect of each other's worlds—art and business—is needed."

ELECTRONIC MUSIC COMPOSER

MIKE SANSONIA has carved out a varied career as an electronic composer and general electronic specialist. Sansonia became curious about music at an early age. He would try any instrument, and was in fact surprised when at one point someone called him a "good guitarist," because he didn't associate himself with any one instrument. "I was just a musician." Sansonia was later trained as a pianist and as an arranger/orchestrator. He explains, "The one thing I'd like to get across is that access to the technology does not guarantee good music. What's more important is the good ol' stuff like ear training and counterpoint."

His work in the electronic studio started out with demo production for songwriters and singers. This was a service to singers and songwriters needing a good representation of their work for auditions. At first he rented an eight-track recording studio and hired a drummer, and using his musical knowledge produced the session, "putting it all together" for the client.

Then Sansonia bought his own equipment. To let people know about his new studio, he advertised in New York's *Village Voice*, sent out printed flyers, and joined songwriter's organizations. Over the years his work in the electronic media has gotten much more diversified. He does everything from demos for music publishers—"new demos for old songs"—to work with a children's theater company, to writing songs about traffic safety and arranging choral numbers on the subject of nutrition. He also produces electronic entertainment at tradeshows, provides the runway music that accompanies models for fashion designers' presentations, and has written music for cable television and most recently for dance. In accepting commissions from choreographers, Sansonia is experimenting with a new floor control for the electronic instruments, activated by the physical gestures and movement of the dancers. "If you saw the movie *Big* with Tom Hanks, it's similar to the 'piano' he was dancing on. My design is somewhat more flexible, in that it doesn't have to be laid out like a keyboard, and it isn't limited to piano sounds."

Some classically trained instrumentalists have mixed feelings of fear and contempt for the electronic age. There is no question that synthesizers have already replaced live musicians in the commercial arena of television and radio jingles. What does Sansonia have to say about all of this? "Electronic equipment shouldn't be used to replace acoustic instruments. Electronics is simply a tool to create new sounds and ideas. As live musicians playing acoustic instruments try to be more perfect and technically precise, so I strive electronically to be more human, the highest ideal of which is the human voice and sound of the violin." To orchestrate electronically with success, one must know about real instruments.

The technology is changing fast. I asked Sansonia if he was sorry today's equipment wasn't around years ago. He explained, "I'm glad this equipment didn't exist when I learned to play—I learned much more without shortcuts." What does the future hold? "Already there has been a backlash in folk and popular music against the overuse of electronics." Sansonia looks forward to work in psychoacoustics and the use of acoustic instruments with electronics. His newest passion is the trombone, exploring its acoustic characteristics and researching possible electronic controls in woodwind and brass instruments. The impressive aspect about the work of Mike Sansonia is that, however mechanical the workings of his world may appear at first glance, music and its ideals come first.

MIDI, an acronym for musical instrument digital interface, is a communications tool that has revolutionized the possibilities of electronic equipment. It helps put sounds together in infinite textures and combinations. In Sansonia's studio, the computer controls the electronic equipment through MIDI. The studio includes an eight-track tape machine, mixing board, stereo machine to make copies, separate drum machine with specific sounds including finger snaps, and synthesizer activated by keyboard controls. The synthesizer produces sounds electronically without outside input. The current vibrates in a manner roughly analogous to the vibration of a string, or a drum head. A sampler digitally records sounds and then plays them back at different pitches. Sansonia describes his equipment: "Most of the synthesizers and samplers I have in my studio do not have their own keyboard. They are controlled by the 'master' keyboard or the computer. They can also be controlled by a guitar controller, which plays like a guitar but puts out MIDI information, or a wind controller, or my MIDI foot controller."

Sansonia, like any conscientious professional, keeps fully informed about current trends. Looking for contacts in the songwriters' world to let people know about his studio's services, he goes to song swaps and informal get-togethers of songwriters and singers. The National Association of Music Merchandisers has biannual tradeshows for retailers taking place at Disneyland in Anaheim, California, and in Chicago, where new equipment is unveiled. Here he gets ideas for new acquisitions for his studio. Music

Net, calling itself "The Electronic Information Network for Musicians," is accessible to subscribers by computer modem. MIT publishes the quarterly *Journal of Computer Music*. *Backstage*, a weekly newspaper, has a section devoted to the commercial/production side of the theater world. Other periodicals helpful to the musician involved with electronics are *Music Technology Magazine*, *Electronic Musician*, *Billboard*, *Keyboard*, and *Guitar Player*. For information about guitar and string jazz developments he reads the newsletter *Fiddle and Dance Workshop*, which deals primarily with the folk string idiom.

RE-CREATING MUSIC

Instruments are built, halls are constructed, and composers create, but all of this is for naught without performers to bring the music to life.

What about the profession of conducting? Despite the importance of the conductor's physical image as the primary focal point for the audience, the *real* substance of the conductor is his/her ability to unify the musical interpretation of the group being led. The sum total of musical background and knowledge and life experience the conductor brings to the music is all-important. I've always thought of great conductors as the most inspired and poetic of chamber music coaches. The ones who succeed in bringing the music to life have the special gift—not specifically in conducting, which is no more than a tool—of being great musicians. Not surprisingly, many of the most eloquent of them are not *just* conductors, but rather, very well-rounded musicians—accomplished composers, writers, and instrumentalists. Leonard Bernstein, Erich Leinsdorf, and Lukas Foss all embody this quality of versatility.

In the following letter, Lukas Foss speaks of his philosophy of conducting to a young colleague. In it we gain insights into his own musical sphere.

Letter to A Young Conductor
Dear . . . .,

You are courageous: anyone who wants to start his career conducting 20th century music has musical curiosity, idealism and courage. Bravo! You are not motivated by the glamour-lure of the "Maestro image." You are not the stereotype, brought up on recordings of 19th century masterpieces, practicing charisma in front of a mirror, memorizing gestures. That aspiring hopeful is lost to the cause. Only a crash course with the Italian police-traffic department can cure him. How elegantly functional are the Roman traffic conductor's gestures. Functional = beautiful. That's true of the shape of a violin or a piano, and I believe it's true of a conductor's movements.

Your first question is the unanswerable question: "How can I get a chance to conduct so I can learn my job?" I'll attempt to answer: "In the 1980's the mark of a conducting talent is the ability to get a group together and conduct it." Well—it's not that simple. No group, nor orchestra will put up with a student conductor, least of all a student group. In order to be allowed to stand up there and learn how to conduct, you have to know how to conduct. That means: you have to pretend that you can do it as you learn how to do it. I'm afraid I did just that, age 17 at Tanglewood. For my audition with the great Serge Koussevitsky I had to conduct *Til Eulenspeigel*. I had never conducted a real symphony orchestra before. Of course, I was not ready. Of course I did not realize that what I was doing was pretending, acting out the business of conducting, going through the motions. I thought I was doing the real thing. Perhaps my naivete was the reason I got away with it. After ten years of pretending (or should I say pretense), I began to understand how difficult it is to get others to play something the way you think it should be played.

This brings me to your question about conducting psychology: neither threats nor flattery work with professionals. Don't manipulate your fellow musicians. All you need is the natural authority that stems from your knowledge of the score. That knowledge is the prerequisite. It gives you the right to teach the music to them.

Yes, a conductor is a teacher; he is also a doctor: detection—diagnosis—correction—is his daily task. An experienced conductor is one who, as he detects an imperfection, diagnoses the trouble and at the same moment thinks of the corrective measure.

On to your technical problem. "How to listen carefully and at the same time beat clearly." You have defined "conducting technique" with that question. A young conductor's beat goes to pieces at rehearsals as he listens to the orchestra play. Comes to the concert and concentrates on his beat and stops listening. In order to beat clearly and listen as well, you must divorce your arms from your ears. Your arms are ahead of the music, since your movements precede, invite the sound. (Every beat is an upbeat.) On the other hand, your critical faculties *react* to the sound. In a word: your beat is ahead of the music—your ear follows it. Again, it takes years until that schizoid situation becomes natural.

My rehearsal methods? Just a few simple rules: No lectures. No sarcasm. No time-wasting jokes. You want cooperation, not popularity. Don't start and stop, over and over. Orchestra musicians are a patient lot, but there is a limit. How annoyed they get if a conductor asks for one thing, then changes his mind. To you, to me this may be the moment of truth, an idea, a discovery. Forget it. Rehearsals are for them to learn the music, not for you. (Doesn't he know what he wants?)

Next on your list: Interpretation. A bad word on *my* list. The composer does not want his music interpreted. If interpretation means anything at all, it would be a searchlight on the score through which you rediscover the composer's intention so that you can distinguish it from that form of mental laziness which passes for tradition (Toscannini's definition of tradition: "the last bad performance"). In a word: play an old symphony as if the ink were not yet dry. All good music is new.

The very last thing in a conductor's development is "leadership." Contrary to the popular notion, no one is born a leader. There has never been a child-prodigy executive. A leader must be mature. He must understand those he leads, identify with their lot and their problems, and yet—this is a mysterious thing—he cannot be "one of them," he is alone because he bears the ultimate responsibility for the music. When the musicians sense this human and musical concern in the conductor, they will follow him, play for him, give their all.

What a strange profession is the conductor's. Consider this: he does work with his back turned to the audience; and that work is conveyed through a sign language which the musicians learn to understand. At rehearsal he tells them how to play on instruments they know better than he; he has the power to demand, to insist; but at the performance he is powerless should the French horn (or anyone else) enter a bar too early. What can he do? Glare? There he stands, a symbol of impotence. Indeed, a leader is in command as well as at the mercy of the led. Are you sure you want to be a conductor?

Yes, you do. You should. And you don't need more counsel; you need an orchestra. Let me tell you how to get one. Oh—so sorry—I'm running out of space.

Good luck,
Lukas Foss

*I*NSTRUMENTAL PERFORMERS

Performers wear many hats. The road to becoming an orchestral musician is discussed in chapter 3, and ideas about recitals are thrashed around in chapter 4. Career soloists, the select few who trek from city to city and around the globe, have careers which are pretty much spelled out by tradition. I have chosen to describe performers whom I believe need some explaining: free-lance musicians and performers of early music. The first, unsung heroes in my opinion, are the rank and file musicians who have an important role in the urban cultural life of the United States.

THE FREE-LANCE MUSIC WORLD

New York is one of the major centers for free-lance musicians in America. The work described by this label can mean anything from playing in Radio City Music Hall to playing a Broadway show to making a television jingle to substituting in the New York Philharmonic.

A study tracking a year in the life of New York freelancers showed a huge range of salaries: $7,200 to $72,000. The study was conducted by Robert Lindsay, professor of finance and economics at New York University's Stern School of Business. Professor Lindsay is an avid trombone player. Over the years, while attending trombone and brass conventions, he became intrigued watching professional musicians take out their datebooks. What were they so busy scribbling in them? Curiosity led to the study called "Concert Free-Lancers in New York City." The working lives of forty-four of the busiest New York musicians in the "single engagement concert field" were scrutinized during 1986. All of the musicians had bachelor's degrees, and two-thirds of the musicians had advanced degrees. The median income of the group was $28,900, far less than the minimum wage earned by a member of the New York Philharmonic ($52,000) or the Metropolitan Opera Orchestra ($47,736) (1987–88 figures). The musicians in Lindsay's study were versatile in their musical skills. They worked for a total of 451 separate employers, performing no less than 15,900 services for the year. Reports Lindsay, "The most significant pattern to emerge . . . is that more years of professional experience do not guarantee more services."

Job security is almost nonexistent in freelancing. There is no absolute assurance of being hired unless there is a contract, although many contractors, those delegated by orchestral managements to hire musicians, are extremely loyal to those who have proved themselves over the years. Yes, there is freedom to turn jobs down, which one doesn't often have in full-time symphony positions, but there is also the freedom to starve. Lindsay points out, "Many hundreds of musicians barely make a living at this kind of work."

In spite of all the pitfalls of a freelancer's life, there are times when freelancing is convenient. While in school, jobs without long-term contracts bring in extra money on a flexible schedule. After living and working overseas, freelancing can help a musician renew former contacts and re-enter the American job market. Many find the varied array of musical opportunities stimulating. In fact, some of the best musicians in the United States thrive on the challenges of the free-lance life, performing in ensembles with the highest musical standards. They, of course, are the lucky ones.

FREE-LANCE MUSICIAN AND CONTRACTOR FOR ORCHESTRAS

In 1988 the *New York Times* published an article entitled "A Freelancer's Lot is Filled With Allegros." Many thought it left a false impression that the average salary among freelancers was much higher than it actually is. JONATHAN TAYLOR, New York free-lance trombone player, contractor, and personnel manager of a number of New York orchestras, responded with a letter to the editor of the *Times* to set the record straight. "The sad truth is that most musicians would probably be thrilled to earn $15,000 (a year) from performing." He supports Lindsay's findings and Gunther Schuller's contention about the numbers being wrong. "I receive hundreds of calls and resumes from musicians soliciting work. Unfortunately I have few opportunities to hire most of them . . . there are large numbers of capable musicians who are severely underemployed, in spite of their abilities, because the economy of the arts in the U.S. cannot support them."

When Taylor is not writing letters to newspapers or fulfilling his job as personnel manager of the American Composer's Orchestra, the New Orchestra of Westchester, and the Paul Taylor Dance Company, he is busy playing trombone in a variety of New York ensembles.

Throughout his youth Taylor had played trombone in orchestras, including summers at Interlochen, the national music camp in Michigan. But he did not plan to make music his profession. As a Harvard undergraduate, Taylor decided to become a child psychologist; he had almost no academic background in music. It was Leonard Bernstein's *Candide* that had a deciding hand in changing his fate. Through Harvard and on into Yale graduate school he played in university orchestras. At Yale, the conductor was John Mauceri, who at the time also happened to be conducting *Candide* in New York's off-Broadway circuit. The year was 1973.

He offered Taylor a position. "At the time I was playing *Candide,* I was still planning to finish graduate school. Actually, I was writing exams and papers during my rests in the pit! In retrospect, it worked as a career vehicle, but the decision had made itself." Unlike many musicians, Taylor was able to break into the free-lance world with a decent income. He played in *Candide* for two years.

Taylor learned early that freelancing required "being flexible with roles and having a unique gift for versatility." Advice for young musicians looking for free-lance work? "Don't expect too much too soon. Be realistic about your expectations and be patient." On the positive side, Taylor remarks, "If people are good at what they do and have a responsible and professional attitude, they should eventually attain some degree of satis-faction, as long as expectations are not out of line." What *not* to do with a contractor? "Calling multiple times after sending a resume doesn't help and can be an annoyance. It can keep me from eating dinner! I do un-derstand people are eager, but sending a resume and making one followup call are enough." The single most important help? "I like to get references of colleagues who know the person's playing. It is helpful for me to speak to someone who has worked with or heard the new kid on the block."

EARLY MUSIC PERFORMERS

The early music movement took off in the United States in the late 1980s and is likely to continue growing in the 1990s. There are bound to be new professional opportunities for instrumentalists. But perhaps even more importantly, players and listeners alike are learning about performance practice and experiencing well known works in a new/old context. Here are profiles of two early music performers.

LAURA JEPPESEN is a Boston-based viola da gamba player and a well-known personality in the ever-growing early music movement that is taking root in the United States. As a graduate violin student at the Yale School of Music in the 1960s, she remembers being influenced by the spirit of the times, a climate of taking risks and trying out new ideas. At Yale, "students were encouraged to become adventuresome. I made my own curriculum and was told to define my professional goals. I had to sit down and soul search: decide what I liked, what I didn't like, what I wanted to do with my future. I realized I loved history." How did she come to play the viola da gamba? "I had a course with the musicologist Leeman Perkins and was assigned to realize the string parts in a collection of French songs. I went to see the Yale Collection of Instruments, which included two gambas. They were available for anyone to play. I sat down with a gamba and realized this was an area of music which was connected to history, where I could make my own contribution. I was being asked to forge my own destiny and was looking for something to identify with."

As it happened, she had found it. She spent the next three years in Europe, studying viola da gamba with Wieland Kuijken and other well known players. "I had a lesson with every professional gambist I had ever heard of." Boston, with its history of early music performance by the Boston Camerata, and with resources such as the instrument collection at the Museum of Fine Arts and the school of harpsichord-making, was a logical base after studies abroad.

Jeppesen marvels at how instrument collections can encourage early music activity, since the one at Yale certainly influenced hers. She calls her generation of American early music performers the second. "Harpsichordist Wanda Landowska and the Dolmetsch family rediscovered the instruments, but with a nineteenth-century stylistic approach. Our generation has been on the cutting edge of scholarship. Disciplines have intersected, musicology has made performance more informed."

"Makers of early instruments have come a long way. As the professional level of playing has improved, makers have been influenced and inspired to make modern instruments. Since the gamba is less durable than the violin family of instruments, these new reproductions are needed." The interest in amateur playing of gambas has also increased. "This view of music for pleasure goes back to the original function of the instruments. A typical view of wealthy English homes in art works often showed a corner of the living room with viols on the wall." English consort music emerged from this tradition. "The music is accessible to amateurs—it was written to be easy to play." Amateur gamba players today have organized the Viola da Gamba Society of America, which promotes consort playing among its members, and publishes a yearly journal. It is not surprising that the New England chapter, given the history of the area, is very active. Workshops given by professionals are sponsored, with master classes to raise the level of playing. The ranks are swelling, going back to the authentic setting of making music at home.

Besides the society, Early Music America is a support group for early music performers. The British publication *Early Music Magazine* is the major scholarly resource for both scholars and amateurs, with reviews and information about auctions and current activities. It gives an accurate glimpse of the early music worlds of both Europe and the United States, and is the most successful example of a journal which caters to professionals, scholars, and music lovers.

Violinist DAN STEPNER keeps active as both modern violinist and baroque player. He describes this balanced existence as "musically healthy." Although many musicians specialize in one world or the other, he sees doing both as natural. "I think there has been a continuity of violin playing through history—more than with keyboard instruments—the same basic technique with different parameters." He is the first violinist of the Lydian String Quartet, which is in residence at Brandeis University. With gambist-wife Laura Jeppesen and harpsichordist John Gibbons, he founded the Boston Museum Trio. String quartet playing opens up an enormous and beautiful repertoire. Baroque playing offers a different sort of challenge. "I try to get away from doctrine, and use musical instincts. For example, instead of following a tradition of no vibrato, I use it selectively, expressively. Because of the work of musicologists, there is now a growing seventeenth-century violin repertoire available. Playing baroque violin invites a performer to become more historically aware." He recommends three method books for budding baroque players: The Francesco Geminiani Method (1751) (a facsimile of the first edition is available); Leopold Mozart's treatise; and Giuseppe Tartini's method book. "These books give a lot of insight into the times, as well as into string playing. I have found Tartini to be an interesting figure and have discovered Mozart and Haydn borrowed ideas from him. Haydn's violin writing shows his influence." Other sources of note are David Boyden's *The History of Violin Playing* and the J. J. Quantz treatise *On Playing the Flute.*

As early music performance proliferates, the debate about period performance versus modern performance becomes more heated. For Stepner the real test of whether a performance works is not only dependent upon the instruments used. "The intelligence of the musical mind guiding the interpretation is most important. Playing Bach's *Mass in B Minor* with Robert Shaw on modern instruments, for example, opened the piece up for me." At the same time, he extols the "sumptuous colors and the different moods which can be brought out" on period instruments.

CHAPTER

13

Music and Scholarship

CURATOR

A summer internship at the Smithsonian Institution turned life around for CYNTHIA ADAMS HOOVER, at the time a budding musicologist. Two weeks after her arrival in 1961, the curator of the collection of instruments left. Plans were in process for a new building, to be called the National Museum of History and Technology. A museum career, something she would never have imagined, was laid out before her. Hoover loved research and was particularly interested in American music, one of the interests of the new museum's division of musical instruments. She had no training as an curator. Graduate work in musicology at Brandeis and Harvard Universities had followed her undergraduate studies at Wellesley College. After her undergraduate studies were completed, Hoover served as director of student and social activities at Harvard Summer School and discovered a talent for administration.

At the Smithsonian she was called upon to put all of her skills together. Hoover is most enthusiastic about the museum curator's career track for musicologists. "Although there aren't a lot of big collections in the U.S., there are many small ones in regional museums. Museums are good performance venues and collections can inspire ideas for concerts." About thirty years later, Hoover reflects on how she came to her career as a curator. "Life is what happens when you have planned something else," she muses.

* * *

LAURENCE LIBIN is curator of musical instruments at New York's Metropolitan Museum of Art. He never had any idea it would be his life's work. As a harpsichordist with a background in musicology, he had taught music at New Jersey's Ramapo College. While Libin worked on his Ph.D. dissertation at the University of Chicago, his predecessor at the museum, Emanuel Winternitz, retired. One of Libin's professors at Chicago recommended Libin for the position, which he got. "I never thought I would work in a museum," he says. He thought he would take a "leave of absence" from the college. It has lasted eighteen years.

As museum curator he has taught courses through Columbia University, New York University's Institute of Fine Arts, and the City University of New York.

*E*THNOMUSICOLOGIST

ANTHONY SEEGER grew up in a distinguished musical family (his uncle is Pete Seeger, his great uncle Charles Seeger), nurtured by folk music and world music from an early age. Striving to maintain individuality, he distanced himself from a formal music program in college. His Harvard B.A. was in the interdisciplinary major Social Relations, a combination of sociology, social psychology, and social anthropology.

For his Ph.D. research in anthropology at the University of Chicago, he undertook field work in Brazil's Amazon region, studying the social groups among the Suya Indians and the ways in which they perform music. Those he was studying liked the fact that he was a musician and taught him their music. He, in turn, taught them some American folk music. Brazil was home for more than a decade. Seeger then taught anthropology at the National Museum of Rio de Janeiro from 1978 to 1982. He helped establish a master's program in musicology at the Brazilian Conservatory of Music in Rio de Janeiro, one of the first degree programs in ethnomusicology in South America. In Brazil, where culture can be an important tool for realizing social goals, he participated in the "political arm" of anthropology. Active in the Indian rights movement, Seeger was president of a pro-Indian Commission, a movement using music as its tool. He helped to organize a Seeger family concert in Cambridge in 1981 to raise money for Indian groups.

Returning from Brazil, Seeger joined the faculty of Indiana University's department of anthropology and assumed the directorship of the Indiana

University Archives of Traditional Music. The archives serve as an invaluable repository of folk traditions of the world for scholars. But just as importantly, they can actually help cultures recapture their histories. In one instance, an American Indian tribe had lost some of its songs, but they were located in the archives.

Seeger became involved with the question of how to make music available to people and found himself getting away from anthropology and back into ethnomusicology. His concern with the dissemination of music to the public brought him to his present position as head of Folkways Records at the Smithsonian Institution. This turn of events brought Seeger full circle: As a child he had been affected by music from India he had heard on a Folkways recording.

Founded by Moses Asch in 1947, Folkways was a small, independent record company with a generally liberal and international focus. When Asch decided to sell the company, he considered it imperative to find a way to keep the company's historically valuable twenty-two hundred titles available. The Smithsonian Institution agreed and in 1987 Folkways came under the umbrella of the institution. In 1988 Seeger joined as director. "We do projects no one else is doing," he notes, citing these recent examples: music from the USSR, a Hawaiian album, and French music from the Caribbean.

He has some advice about studying ethnomusicology. "There is a dual approach to ethnomusicology: First, the sounds of music from peoples around the world is the subject of analysis. Second, is the anthropological emphasis: the *groups* producing the sound are subjects of inquiry. The two contexts are different. The ideal is to mix them. Indiana University, University of Illinois, and University of Washington in Seattle go the way of social sciences. UCLA is trying to change its emphasis on sound, opting for the center course."

How do you make decisions about which schools to attend? "Each school has something different to offer. Read articles in the field. Decide whose work you like. Start a dialogue with a chosen scholar at a particular graduate school. That professor can help find funding, advise you on field study, and provide support. Graduate study is more like an apprenticeship than a continuation of college."

Ethnomusicologist R. ANDERSON SUTTON spent his undergraduate years at Wesleyan University, which is known for its strong curriculum in world music. But Sutton had not chosen Wesleyan for that reason. As a freshman he had not yet decided on a major, let alone a career. However, exposure to the resources of Wesleyan—hearing gamelan music, studying Indian music, and receiving a general background in world music—fed his interest in ethnomusicology. After college, he decided either to go to law school or pursue graduate study in ethnomusicology. Sutton recalls, "By the time of the law boards, I had already decided on ethnomusicology." He received a teaching assistantship at the University of Hawaii at Manoa.

His major interest emerged as the music of central Java, Indonesia, which also entailed learning to play the gamelan. "I liked the sound, I liked to play, and there was a nice camaraderie among members of the group at the University. This social aspect was important." Ethnomusicology faculty members Hardja Susilo and Ricardo Trimillos were two important influences for Anderson. Susilo ran the gamelan ensemble and built a sizable following of students. Sutton credits learning from him "how to introduce a piece and teach gamelan performance." With Trimillos, he remembers having "inspiring long chats" about the larger questions of world music cultures. While still a graduate student in Hawaii, Sutton made his first field trip to Indonesia, followed by a ten-month research trip on a fellowship from Hawaii's East-West Center.

Sutton chose the University of Michigan for his doctoral studies, which proved to be a good balance to the work done in Hawaii. "We worked hard in Hawaii in gamelan performance, while University of Michigan was more of a think tank, a good intellectual atmosphere with visiting scholars from Indonesia." His Ph.D. dissertation, which brought him back to Indonesia for further field work, was a study of how gamelan music fits into Javanese culture and interacts with other aspects of the culture. Sutton went directly from graduate school to his first job at the University of Wisconsin at Madison, where he has remained. Sutton feels that the university has been very supportive of his research, which has enabled him to return to Asia a number of times. His forthcoming book, *Traditions of Javanese Gamelan Music*, discusses different regional styles of gamelan music in central and east Java.

How does Sutton perceive current trends in ethnomusicology? "I see young ethnomusicologists becoming less technical and going more toward the social sciences. There is a growing acceptance among young ethnoscholars to be more concerned with context and related aspects of culture. Journal articles reflect this strong ethnographic sophistication." But then, he adds, "trends are at least somewhat determined by the marketplace, and I see job advertisements asking for ethnomusicologists with a background in anthropology theory." Sutton comments on "a lingering identity crisis of ethnomusicologists." He explains: "We tend to look up to, and quote, scholars in the social sciences rather than other ethnomusicologists." The ideal, he suggests, is to strike a balance between musical and anthropological intellectual sophistication. "It may be easier to become a musician first, for which formal training is a lengthy process, and then grapple with anthropological intellectual theory later." In the end, "it doesn't matter which comes first, but an ethnomusicologist must have sophistication in both."

To give insight into the world of ethnomusicology, Sutton recommends three books: *Worlds of Music* by Jeff Titon, of which "the first and last chapters, thoroughly untechnical," offer a good overview on the discipline; *The Ethnomusicologist* by Mantle Hood; and *The Study of Ethnomusicology* by Bruno Nettl, which is "sophisticated and at times tongue in cheek. The first chapter includes informal explanations of the field which can be used at a cocktail party. On the other hand, unless the reader already knows something about ethnomusicology, the humor may be lost."

MARCIA HERNDON describes herself as a "music addict." She was a professional organist at age ten, and before long she also conducted the church choir. After studying ethnomusicology at Tulane University, she did field work with the Cherokee Indians and then went on to study the music of the Maltese, mainly their fighting songs. With a Ph.D. from Tulane, she taught at the University of Texas and at the University of California at Berkeley, publishing seven books and numerous articles.

But the traditional university career was not for her at that point in her life. "I've always had the habit of dreaming about something and letting my heart lead." With several colleagues she took the risk of opening an independent Music Research Institute near Berkeley, where she could take on projects of special interest. She has worked on practical problems, for example, why American orchestras are going out of business; music and health, specifically, how young children are turning up the volume on their radios and losing their hearing; and political issues, such as how music and public policy in different countries intersect, and music censorship. She copes on a shoe-string budget. Her work force? Convicted criminals doing their hours of community service, research interns, and associates and foreign graduate fellows in ethnomusicology who get credit for working at the Institute. Ideas for the future? Says Herndon, "I have a wooden box of 5 x 8 index cards full of them."

The future also brings a new chapter in Herndon's career. She is ready to re-enter academe, having accepted an invitation to become a full professor at the University of Maryland in 1990. The institute will continue to make its distinctive contribution, with Herndon in a lesser role.

MUSIC LIBRARIAN

Work for a music librarian exists in the music division of a municipal library, in a university or conservatory, at a radio station, or for an orchestra. There are several associations relevant to the music librarian's career: The Music Library Association (MLA), which publishes the journal *Notes*, the American Library Association (ALA), and the Special Libraries Association (SLA). The Education Committee of MLA compiles the *Directory of Library Offerings in Music Librarianship*, a most useful tool for those interested in training for the discipline.

LIBRARY OF CONGRESS LIBRARIAN

GILLIAN ANDERSON is a music specialist/librarian at the Library of Congress in Washington. She is also active as a conductor, musicologist, and radio producer, and has become expert in an unusual skill: reconstructing music for silent films. In 1989 Anderson conducted the premiere of the reconstructed version of D.W. Griffith's *Intolerance* (1916) as part of the New York Film Festival, the first time live music had ever been presented as part of the festival. Preparation included the tedious activity of beating time silently for four months and memorizing no less than 250 tempo changes.

"I love the intersections between music and history," says Anderson, whose dream was always to become a scholar/conductor. After getting a biology degree at Bryn Mawr—her parents were against a music major— she found a way to get the training necessary to pursue her goals. A summer choral conducting institute at Harvard University with Iva Dee Hyatt and the encouragement of scholar/librarian Isabelle Cazeaux at Bryn Mawr provided the inspiration and role models she badly needed. Next, she went to the University of Illinois to pursue a master's degree in musicology. She felt it was a "homecoming" finally to be studying music. "I found the place to be open intellectually and artistically stimulating. Very nutritious." The Ph.D. program required that she choose between performing (conducting) and history. She wanted both, so she left academe at that point. Washington, D.C., was the next stop. The year was 1971. The American bicentennial was approaching and Anderson steeped herself in political music of the revolutionary period. After a lot of persistent knocking on doors at the National Endowment for the Humanities, she secured $170,000 in grants from them for bicentennial music projects. Anderson wrote a book, *Freedom's Voice in Poetry and Song*, produced radio documentaries, gave speeches, made three recordings, conducted a number of performances (White House, Kennedy Center, etc.), and suddenly the bicentennial celebration was over and with it, her employment.

Enter the library career. She joined the staff at the Library of Congress as a reference librarian, an entry level "GS-4" position, without any library credentials. But Anderson knew how to undertake research and was aware of the gold mine of resources at her new place of employment. In 1978 she was promoted to reference librarian. Her interest in music for silent films has continued during the library career. Her *Music for Silent Films (1894–1929): A Guide* outlines her work. Among her accomplishments as a librarian was convincing the Museum of Modern Art to loan film scores and cue sheets to the Library of Congress to preserve them on microfilm.

"I was very lucky to make a place for myself without the requisite degrees. But to move further, I knew I must have a library degree." She went back to school after a decade at the Library of Congress and completed a Master of Library Science at the University of Maryland. The next step may be back to academe, this time perhaps as head of a university's music library.

*M*USICOLOGIST

Musicology was officially defined as a profession in the United States with the founding of the American Musicological Society (AMS) in 1934. Musicologists Oliver Strunk and Gustave Reese in association with Charles Seeger, Joseph Schillinger, and Joseph Yasser were the early proponents of the organization. According to Lewis Lockwood, professor of musicology at Harvard University, in the middle part of this century musicology "became more deeply anchored as a branch of the humanities and firmly established itself in its natural home, the American university." He writes of the "running debate about the nature of the discipline." As the end of the century nears, Lockwood and other music scholars note that the boundaries among the scholarly music disciplines of musicology, music theory, and ethnomusicology are rapidly becoming less defined. Concerns of the three disciplines overlap, supporting Lockwood's contention that "we are all part of a very complex and highly rarefied but fundamentally unitary discipline."

AMS publishes a booklet entitled *The Ph.D. and Your Career: A Guide for Musicologists*, containing a good career bibliography. The society's

Committee on Career Options has put together a list of musicologists employed in music-related nonacademic positions who are available to answer inquiries from students interested in similar careers. Likewise, the book *Humanities Ph.D.'s and Nonacademic Careers* presents alternative careers for young scholars.

LEO TREITLER, who teaches doctoral students in musicology at the Graduate Center of the City University of New York, encourages his students to write about their scholarly pursuits in the first person. "I went on a campaign to encourage students to speak for themselves and take responsibility for what they say. I will be their critic, as will their fellow students." Why the first person? "It is an admission that what we scholars produce is an interpretation. We are, after all, performing interpretive acts." He has found that "a student doesn't become a scholar until he or she gets hooked on a particular historical problem. The alert teacher has to find out what historical problems really engage students, engage their imaginative thought. I am not in favor of a structured program of study in musicology."

Treitler, who has previously taught historical musicology at the University of Chicago, Brandeis University, the State University of New York at Stony Brook, New York University, and Columbia University, never set out to become a musicologist. "I don't think most undergraduate students think of studying historical musicology. The truth of the matter is that people get into musicology from different places. Some learn disciplines of classics or history first, but almost all musicologists have played at one time and want to study music." In Treitler's case he started with the piano from an early age and at sixteen went to the University of Chicago, where he earned a bachelor's degree in liberal arts. After graduate work in science and psychology, and a stint in the army as a clinical psychologist, he returned to music and did his master's work at the University of Chicago in composition, followed by a year of composition study in Berlin on a Fulbright. The next stop was Princeton University, for what Treitler thought would be further study in composition and theory. But he discovered the eminent musicologist Oliver Strunk and he got "swung in the direction" of a Ph.D. in musicology.

Strunk was surprised to see his student take to the field of medieval studies. Treitler explains, "This field was so fascinating from an intellectual point of view . . . distant and hard. It takes a great deal of imagination, you are reconstructing to an enormous degree. Someone has said 'you have to knit your own middle ages.' Scholarship is synthesizing knowledge rather than plucking it ready made." Medieval studies "forces you to be conscious of how you are putting things together. You feel yourself working at it. For me, at Princeton, that was the attraction."

What about the intersection of the scholarly disciplines? "There is a paradoxical situation: musicology, music theory, and ethnomusicology are all increasingly professionalized and therefore isolated from each other. At the same time the three subdisciplines have become more aware of each other's methodologies, and there is crossover because the scholarly problems overlap."

How have these developments become apparent in the field? Treitler's experience is an example: "I was invited by the Society for Ethnomusicology to run a workshop on history, because ethnomusicologists are now interested in a historical perspective on other cultures. There was once a time that anthropology was hostile to history. No longer. Likewise, historians are now interested in anthropology." Another indication of change is in the writing of young musicologists. "There are signs in scholarly literature that historical musicologists are more sophisticated in music theory than in the past—there are more sophisticated analyses." Regardless of the crossover of disciplines, it is essential for a scholar to "declare an identity in one of the subdisciplines." Once that is clear, the road is open for a strong interchange of ideas.

As a graduate student in musicology at Columbia University, RICHARD TARUSKIN had an ulterior motive in mind when he decided on a dissertation topic. He figured that a study on Russian Opera in the 1860s would get him a fellowship to the USSR, where he could meet his Russian family members. It did, and he went for a year in the early 1970s. Several years before the Russian trip Professor Paul Henry Lang had assigned Taruskin a project dealing with the historical transition from cello, Taruskin's own instrument, to viola da gamba. He was eventually given the task of running the Columbia Collegium, one of the university's major early music ensembles.

"Life has all kinds of surprises," says Taruskin, who is now Professor of Musicology at the University of California at Berkeley. After writing his dissertation he fell in love with Russian opera, and after researching the viola da gamba he became a noted performer on the instrument as well as director of the Renaissance choir Cappella Nova, with which he made a number of recordings. Today he is a distinguished authority on both Russian opera and early music performance. A forthcoming book, *Stravinsky and the Russian Traditions*, will be published by the University of California Press.

In 1981, Taruskin made a presentation to the American Musicological Society, voicing skepticism about the early music movement. It caused a bit of an uproar. He liked that. The speech was eventually printed in three different journals. It led to more provocative writing, more backlash, and, not surprisingly, more recognition. "The scholarly life is not just a contemplative, monastic existence. For me, controversy is one of the joys of this life. I don't distinguish between scholarship and criticism. But I wouldn't want to be a professional critic because I don't want the deadlines. Although I am a prolific writer, I write slowly." Does he enjoy writing? He quotes the writer Dorothy Parker. "I hate to write, but I love to have written."

Career is a word that is foreign to Taruskin. "When I think of the word 'career' I think of someone who's already dead." For him, career is nothing more than what he's doing from day to day. Characteristics that describe Taruskin's life work (so far) are versatility, the gift of articulating profound concepts to the general public and musicians alike, and an open-minded attitude to new influences. "I am against rigidity and preconceived methodologies. In fact, I'm terribly opposed to rigidity of any kind." Who knows what new interests will capture this scholar? He ponders the question. "I don't know. They could change anytime."

*M*USIC THEORIST

RICHARD COHN, a music theorist teaching at the University of Chicago, is aware of the pitfalls of a scholarly life. The son of two literature professors, he has been aware of them since childhood. "The life encourages isolation and taking yourself too seriously." For Cohn, the best part is the teaching. As a doctoral student at Eastman, he was given the opportunity to teach undergraduate theory courses and realized the experience "was the most important part of my education. I learned as much about music from teaching as I ever did from my professors. Teaching made me internalize what I was learning in my own classes."

How did someone who claims "I wasn't naturally musical but I loved music" and "I resist anyone telling me how to do anything" get into the field of music theory in the first place? With a background of piano, guitar, and harmonica, he entered Brown University as a freshman, not having a clue as to what role music would play in his studies. But a charismatic music professor provided some inspiration, and after two years at Brown, Cohn took some time off to study, practice piano seriously, and catch up on what he considered a late start in music. When he returned to Brown, he was steered toward musicology and in his senior year even presented a paper at a local American Musicological Society conference. The subject was how the Italian madrigal found its way to sixteenth-century England. "But I wasn't interested in historical problems in the way they had been defined." Piano continued to be important and he presented a senior recital, but the question of what was he going to do with his life did not disappear. "I wasn't at all career-oriented."

After graduation, Cohn taught piano in Providence and built up a successful studio. "I loved teaching piano. I loved teaching students to think about the music and project that understanding. I realized I was most interested in the structure of music, so I applied to graduate school in music theory. Eastman seemed a good choice because they were going to make it possible for me to teach immediately."

Cohn's own research interests were spurred on by the composer-theorist at Eastman, Robert Morris. "Robert Morris was a twentieth-century scholar and with him I got interested in atonal pitch theory of early twentieth-century music such as Bartok and Webern. Initially, as a concert-goer I found twentieth-century music difficult to appreciate. Bob Morris showed me all kinds of interesting paths inside the music, and soon it became very fascinating to me. At the same time I was pulled deeply into the challenge of theorizing about the structure of this music. The process of studying the structure can become quite abstract and symbolic. You have to learn how to manipulate the symbols and then apply the knowledge you have attained when going back to listen to the music and study the score."

Cohn enjoys exploring music theory's relationship to the other scholarly disciplines. With an ethnomusicologist at the University of Chicago he runs a music and language workshop for faculty and graduate students, and he writes articles for musicology journals. "I want to communicate to a much broader audience than most music theorists. Theorists have a perspective that musicologists can learn from—we should meet them half way—but theorists have not been able or willing to direct their work so that it will be inviting for musicologists and other scholars to read."

Cohn recommends several books that "shed light on the kinds of questions music theorists are trying to deal with. These are relatively informal approaches to problems that music theorists deal with from a more technical point of view." They are *Emotion and Meaning in Music* by Leonard Meyer; Leonard Bernstein's *Norton Lectures: The Unanswered Question*, which Cohn describes as suggestive rather than scholarly; and *Musical Form and Musical Performance* by Edward Cone.

V. KOFI AGAWU is primarily a music theorist but his diverse musical background renders career labels quite useless. Born in Ghana, Agawu grew up without the opportunity to hear much live Western music. Nevertheless, he made good use of records while also participating in African music-making, both as performer and composer. He played bamboo flute and composed for a local bamboo flute ensemble. "My father was a minister and felt jam sessions of African traditional music were not serious and would take time away from preparing for exams. Because of that, I had to be secretive about my music activities."

His university study began in England, where BBC Radio 3 provided extensive opportunity to catch up on listening to music. "Each new piece was very exciting. With scores in hand, I listened to all the Beethoven Symphonies and Mozart Piano Concerti—much of it for the first time." At the University of Reading he received his first degree as a composition major. As a student at Kings College, University of London, he concentrated on analysis. For a master's thesis, he did a theoretical analysis of Igor Stravinsky's *Mass*. He proceeded to Stanford University to earn a Ph.D. in historical musicology, specializing in the study of nineteenth-century music. Within this educational framework, the seeds were planted for a versatile academic career.

Agawu's first university position, at Haverford College in Pennsylvania, brought him back to African music. He taught a comparative study between African and Afro-American music and also a jazz history course. However, he had been hired primarily to teach music history and also taught courses in baroque, Renaissance, and twentieth-century music. During his next appointment at Duke University, he was hired as a music theorist, teaching undergraduate and graduate analysis courses, but also taught African music as an independent study seminar. After a stint as a lecturer back at Kings College, Agawu assumed his most recent position—teaching music theory at Cornell University. His range of interests is suitably displayed among his courses there: Mahler, music theory, and semiotics and music (the science that studies the life of signs in society).

How does he feel about teaching three scholarly disciplines in an environment where scholars are more or less expected to stick to one identity? "There is a frustration—you feel as though you don't spend enough time in any one discipline. But on the other hand, I would not want to be confined to one small corner, and I'm constantly altering the balance of my involvement with the different disciplines. As a theorist I do see a perspective: one can't ignore what the historians are doing." Agawu is the author of *Playing with Signs*, which deals with the structure and expression of music written between 1770 and 1830. Future projects include *The Music of Mahler* in the series Companions to the Great Composers for Routledge Publishers, London. He has contributed to a number of scholarly publications reflecting his interests, including *Music Theory Spectrum*, *19th-Century Music, Music Analysis, Journal of Musicology*, and *Ethnomusicology*. "Most of my published work is analytical—and I can see it is getting more theoretical in content all the time."

ORAL HISTORIAN

VIVIAN PERLIS has emerged as the foremost oral historian in music of late twentieth-century America. She is considered an expert on the lives of several eminent American composers.

In her early years, Perlis played piano and harp, later training as a concert harpist at the University of Michigan. She earned a master's of music history at Michigan and did further study in musicology at Columbia University. However, her main occupation for many years was as a concert harpist. During this period she also worked as a reference librarian at the Yale Music Library, where she was influenced by John Kirkpatrick, curator of the Charles Ives Collection. Becoming less enamored with traditional harp music, she began working more with contemporary composers at Yale. "Everything seemed to come together with my interest in contemporary music and in participating in the creation of new works."

While Perlis was working with Kirkpatrick, Charles Ives became the focus of a new career path, bringing together her training in musicology and this new-found interest in contemporary music. In 1968 Perlis visited Julian Myrick, who had been Ives' insurance partner and life-long friend. His recollections of Ives fascinated Perlis. On her next visit she brought a tape recorder to preserve stories about Ives in Myrick's own voice. She contacted others close to Ives' and interviewed them. Many were elderly and she recognized the "urgency of the situation" to get them on tape for posterity. Without realizing it, Perlis was embarking upon a new career path. At the conclusion of the Ives project, she founded Oral History, American Music, an endeavor devoted to collecting and preserving tape recorded material of American composers. Her work in Oral History has led to books, television documentaries, and seminars on American composers.

Perlis has defined the role of the oral historian in the realm of music. The most important requirement for success in this work, from her perspective, is the "research skills, dedication, discipline, and musical knowledge" one can bring to it.

CHAPTER

14

Music in Service Professions

THE ALEXANDER TECHNIQUE

MANY musicians and other artists go to Alexander lessons as part of their weekly routines. Some arts departments in universities employ Alexander teachers. Here is a capsulized history.

Early in his career, the Australian actor F. Matthias Alexander suffered from chronic hoarseness and laryngitis. Doctors couldn't solve his problems, so he undertook to solve them himself. By analyzing his mental and physical processes for nearly a decade, he cured himself. In the process he developed the technique that now bears his name. As described in *A Balanced Approach: The Alexander Technique* by Hillary Mayers and Linda Babits, the technique is a three-step process. The first is the development of an awareness of the body's physical state; second, the "inhibition" stage, the conscious decision not to respond to a situation in a habitual manner; and third, the mental directions, which teach the student how to organize the body through a series of instructions concerning the balance of its parts, most notably the head, neck, and back.

TEACHER OF THE ALEXANDER TECHNIQUE

HILLARY MAYERS and LINDA BABITS are both professional musicians and certified teachers of the Alexander Technique. They are co-directors of the New York-based Alexander Technique Affiliates for the Performing

Arts. Many of their clients are musicians. Mayers and Babits have offered seminars at institutions such as the Westminster Choir College, Hartt College of Music, Manhattan School of Music, and the American String Teachers International Workshops. Musicians find that the technique offers relief from playing with pain and improves the quality of practice time.

In "The Path to Productive Practicing: An Introduction to the Alexander Technique," Mayers and Babits write that "printed text can only partly describe the process of the Alexander Technique. The attempt would be similar to describing the scent of a rose to one who has never smelled it." Nevertheless, an explanation is offered. "In its most simple terms, the Alexander Technique is applied to bring about an integration of the head, neck and back. This physical organization of the body, which Alexander termed 'primary control,' enables a person to operate from the central core without strain or excess physical tension."

Where does the Alexander teacher come in? "By placing her hands on a student's head, neck, and back during an Alexander lesson, the teacher helps the student to observe and identify how he behaves while performing certain activities."

In their article, the authors clarify some issues. "There are many misconceptions about the Alexander Technique. It is not a system of exercises, or a relaxation technique, or a method of vocal or instrumental training. Simply, it is a *re-education of habitual movement patterns* so the body is used efficiently with the least amount of wear and tear."

Mayers graduated from the Oberlin Conservatory of Music in vocal performance. It was her desire to solve a postural problem that was seriously impeding her career. Her amazement with new-found comfort and vocal freedom led her to train as an Alexander teacher. Following a three-year training program in New York, she traveled to England to study with Patrick MacDonald, one of the top practioners. Mayers cautions people who are looking into teacher training programs, "It is wise to choose a school which is accredited by the North American Society of Teachers of the Alexander Technique (NASTAT) or Society of Teachers of the Alexander Technique (STAT) in London. Many of the new teacher training programs in the United States offer shortcuts to the standard sixteen-hundred-hour three-year course and have discouragingly low standards. Many of these courses combine Alexander Technique with other disciplines, a mixture which generally does disservice to all and confuses the basic principles of the Alexander Technique."

As the method attracts new clients, it attracts new teachers. The competition is fierce. One idea for a musician wanting to train and set up a practice of the Alexander Technique method is to settle down in a small town near a music school or college with active arts departments. Actors and dancers, as well as musicians, find the technique very helpful in forming good work habits.

CHILDREN'S MUSIC ENTREPRENEUR

The birth rate is rising significantly in the United States. This year four million babies will be born, equalling the height of the baby boom of the 1950s, although parents of newborns tend to be older than they were then. The enlightened among them want their kids to have music in their lives. Some parents start educating their kids while still in diapers. Anyone listening? There is a fresh new market out there for creative musicians. Building new audiences for the future is an important endeavor that will benefit the entire world of the arts.

TOMKAT PRODUCTIONS

ELIOT (TOMMY) BAILEN is a cellist whom I met one summer at the Grand Teton Music Festival in Wyoming. Little did I know that within the next few years he would get his Doctor of Musical Arts in cello from Yale University, get his M.B.A. from New York University, and create a successful children's music company. When I did find out, I wanted to know more.

Tomkat Productions, founded in 1986 by Bailen and Karen Prager, produces original musical products for children. The first album, *Karen and Tommy: The Dinosaur and More*, consists of ten original songs in varying styles. One of them, "Dinosaur Rap," has been a hit on children's radio nationwide. A music video series called "Live from Song City" is available, and the Karen and Tommy team is now airing on a new cable preschool television program. A book/tape collaboration with children's book author Harriet Ziefert for Harper & Row is scheduled for the future.

Regular appearances at music stores, schools, shopping malls, and concerts give the Karen and Tommy team personal contact with their young fans. Is the M.B.A. a useful tool in this music business? Bailen says he entered business school to "zero-in on the quality of my life and make a career in music financially feasible." The business was nurtured as a school project. He was awarded New York University's Frederic Slater Award for best conception and implementation of a new business plan by an M.B.A.

student. "My music business is what I plan to focus on . . . it gives me control of my time and allows space for my cello playing." So he leads a double life. While playing cello in groups such as the American Symphony Orchestra, he is busy being original and creative and a businessman. He writes music, sings these original songs while accompanying himself on guitar, records them, and now he and his colleague Karen are embarking on a television career. Could this be the best of all worlds?

TODDLERS' SONGTIME

DELORES JIJI-MORRISON has brought music into the lives of hundreds of children in the suburbs of New York City. Although she studied piano seriously until the age of fourteen, just as important in influencing her career choices were the interests of drama, dance, and college folksinging. Prior to graduating from the University of California at Berkeley with a degree in theater and teaching credentials, she spent lots of time singing folksongs with her guitar in coffee houses.

After coming to New York to teach and continue drama study, she soon had a family. Watching her own child in a music class for toddlers provided a catalyst for her own ideas about teaching music to young children. Today, in her home music studio, she sees eight small groups of children a week, each for a forty-five-minute session. Terms are eight weeks long, and the age group is children from 2½ to 3½ years old. She also performs at children's parties, in concert, and at nursery schools. Not only is there singing. The children play in rhythm instrument ensembles, choosing from among Jiji-Morrison's collection of one hundred and fifty rhythm instruments from countries all over the world. "In my classes there is constant movement to the beat, in my speech, where I try to rhyme phrases, and in the music. Each class is like a forty-five-minute ballet. I treat each instrument lovingly and try to develop the children's listening skills. I try to give them the sense that I love music and that there are sounds everywhere, including inside them."

Jiji-Morrison is often invited to speak at education conferences teaching teachers, who sometimes have no music background, how to work musically with young students. She is also music consultant to a number of nursery schools. The sixty-minute audio cassette she produced herself, *Toddlers' Songtime*, has been sold to Macmillan Publishing Company's preschool books and tapes division. More tapes are on the horizon, and more appearances. No doubt more creative ideas to keep Delores Jiji-Morrison going for a long, long time.

MOZART FOR CHILDREN

DEBBIE and SIMON SUROWICZ started their program because they couldn't find an innovative music program for their own two and one-half-year-old son. Simon Surowicz remembers, "All we could find were programs which lullaby kids to sleep. That we could do at home." Debbie Surowicz had been trained as a classical singer and her husband, who manages the program, has a theater background. The New York-based enterprise started as one or two classes in rented facilities. Within three years it has grown to ten fifteen-week sessions divided among four basic age groups, ranging from twenty months to six years of age.

The basic mission of Mozart for Children is to give young children exposure to classical music while creatively engaging them with body movement, acting out stories with hand puppets, and mime. "Especially for the youngest, it is more a play group with a classical motif." Even during snacks and rest period, music is played in the background. From the first bars of the opening "Hello Song," sung to an Italian art song, children participate without the conscious knowledge they are learning classical music. Parents of the oldest age group report that at home the youngsters continue to listen to classical music on their own. As it expands, Mozart for Children is presenting six-week residencies in the public schools, and there are plans to bring the program to groups of learning disabled children.

FELDENKREIS PRACTITIONER

Conga drummer RICHARD ADELMAN was teaching drums for a living when he had his first lesson with Israeli Moshe Feldenkreis in 1973. Adelman recalls, "I came home and played better than I'd ever played in my life. There was more fluidity of movement. I had played for fifteen years, yet it was as if I was feeling the drums for the first time." This experience led Adelman to become an authorized Feldenkreis practioner, taking thirty-two weeks of training over a four-year period. "The Feldenkreis Method involves movement reeducation through verbally guided floorwork—awareness through movement—and gentle hands-on tablework." Adelman often works with musicians, offering whole-day music workshops once a week in Berkeley. He has also conducted workshops for the music departments of Temple University in Philadelphia and Holy Names College in Oakland, California.

Adelman analyzes a dilemma facing musicians. "Many musicians practice so compulsively that they lose sight of the love of music which first inspired them. Every musician is under an imperative to make music. Sometimes players abuse their bodies in this process by overlooking subtle cues of discomfort until they end up with overuse syndrome." According to Adelman, work with the Feldenkreis Method helps people to question the amount of effort they think is necessary for their music-making, and at the same time teaches them to play more gracefully.

Adelman explains, "I work with people to evoke the experience of music coming from their insides." This experience of making music emerges as one "gently reorganizes the emotional attitudes which are structured in the body," leading to a "deepening of self-expression."

The Feldenkreis Guild in Overland Park, Kansas, is a clearinghouse of information about the method in the United States. The guild distributes literature and audiotapes, as well as information about certification to become a practitioner.

MUSIC PROMOTION EXECUTIVE IN PUBLISHING

SUSAN FEDER is Vice President and Director of Promotion at G. Schirmer, one of the foremost publishers of classical music in the United States. Her background is that of a musicologist and violinist. After graduation from Princeton University, she taught elementary school music in Italy, studied musicology at the University of California at Berkeley, and was hired as program book editor of the San Francisco Symphony. Next she took on the project of coordinating the editing of the *New Grove Dictionary of American Music*. What was billed as a short-term job turned into a five-year project. She describes it as "trial by fire into American music." She currently writes the program notes for the New York-based American Composer's Orchestra.

Many changes had taken place at G. Schirmer around the time Feder joined the company in 1986. Most importantly, it was bought by Robert Wise, the London-based owner of Music Sales, Ltd., a publisher of popular music. He was clever enough to realize that pop music marketing skills can help promote classical music as well. The printing of serious music was in crisis at G. Schirmer, as it tends to be everywhere, largely because of the infringement of copyrights. With new management, priorities at G. Schirmer were reevaluated.

Although music continues to be printed, the trend for the future is to "take on fewer composers and help them more, in terms of commissions, performances, recordings, and career development." Feder reflects that "John Harbison's Pulitzer Prize was a turning point. We had gotten the piece out of the catalogue and into circulation. It made a difference in his career and in people's perceptions of our ability to help our composers."

Feder is responsible for keeping the G. Schirmer catalogue current, comprehensive, and appealing. She must learn all compositions thoroughly in order to promote them. She oversees the production of catalogues, brochures, newsletters, and press releases as part of the company's function as an information service on behalf of composers. In her position, Feder takes an involved, committed approach, getting to rehearsals and performances around the world of works by G. Schirmer composers. She meets conductors, music administrators, and performers, making personal contact with the decision makers of music organizations. "It is sometimes necessary to play psychologist for some composers, reassure them, a bit of hand-holding at premieres." She is also connected to the organization's role as American distributor for prestigious European publishers such as Hansen; Chester; Salabert; Sikorski; and VAAP, the copyright agency of the Soviet Union.

Feder's advice for young composers looking for a publisher? "Network, make friends, do people favors, create your own performances. Be nice—don't nudge. All manuscripts sent to G. Schirmer are looked at, even if we can only accept very few new pieces."

LAWYER

DON AIBEL is a popular New York-based tax lawyer for musicians. He is also a violinist. Aibel graduated from the Juilliard School and started out on a course familiar to many New York musicians: freelancing, subbing at the Metropolitan Opera. "But I wasn't working with great conductors. I couldn't really see myself doing this for the next fifty years." At the same time, "I never made a decision to give up music, which I'd always loved. I just wanted to add something on." The "something" he added on was law. Attending Baruch College in an M.B.A. program, he met a law professor and decided to concentrate on the law. During the 2½ years of St. John's University law school, he kept playing concerts. Better and better jobs kept coming his way. Meanwhile, he kept law school a secret from his colleagues in the music world. After law school, he continued playing and, after passing the bar, he decided to join a law firm. He was still living a double life. "I was a master of disguise. When I went to the law office, I would leave my violin with the elevator man, and at the end of the day I'd get it en route to a New Jersey Symphony concert." Later, while working as assistant counsel for the water commission, he began a small private practice with musicians and other artists on the side. Today he has a full-time practice concentrating on work with income tax returns, contracts, and real estate. There is no longer time for a professional music career. Seventy-five percent of his clients are in the arts. Does his life as a violinist help in his law practice? "I speak the same language as the musicians I represent. I can translate legal terminology." Not many lawyers have played with a world-class orchestra. Don Aibel's experience gives him an unusual perspective. "When I was fifteen I won a competition and played a concerto with the New York Philharmonic. Today I negotiate contracts and prepare tax returns for its soloists."

DIANA NICHOLSON is a New York–based lawyer specializing in trademark and copyright matters. She also has a background not often found in her profession. She was trained as an opera singer and has a Ph.D. in music education. "I was always interested in the law—especially trademarks and copyright." While working on her doctorate in music at New York University, Nicholson met Gustave Reese, the eminent Renaissance music scholar, who was also trained as a lawyer. He encouraged Nicholson to pursue her law interest. She attended St. John's University Law School, but at the same time had permission to attend graduate courses with Walter Derenberg at New York University Law School, where he had created the division of trademark and copyright law. Derenberg became a mentor for Nicholson.

After law school, Nicholson went to a small firm and offered to develop a division for them in artistic and literary property. More than ten years later she is still there, specializing in this field, and doing trademark and copyright counseling on new creations and inventions. Nicholson finds that "having a music background is an invaluable tool for work with copyright and music plagiarism. In these cases, I don't need to engage an expert to interpret the technical matters of music." She notes that "judges I come before respect this expertise."

MEDICINE: MEDICAL PROBLEMS FOR MUSICIANS

The strong connection between music and medicine has quite a history. Albert Schweitzer was an avid musician and wrote two volumes on J.S. Bach. The Russian composer Alexander Borodin was a noted chemist and M.D. But in recent decades a new relationship between music and medicine has been forged. DR. ALICE BRANDFONBRENER, head of Chicago's Medical Program for Artists at Northwestern Memorial Hospital, modestly owns up to the fact that she is one of the pioneers in the field of performing arts medicine in America. She was among the first to identify it as a specialty.

Brandfonbrener's background is in internal medicine and in student health. She is also a dedicated avocational musician, specializing in flute, piano, and Gilbert and Sullivan. Her children are professional musicians. She directed the medical program at Interlochen's National Music Camp in Michigan for the good part of a decade, but it wasn't until she worked at the Aspen Music Festival that this emerging field of medicine was first defined. The first performing arts medicine meeting, a gathering of sixty-five doctors and musicians, took place at Aspen during the summer of 1983. "In retrospect, it was amazing."

How does Brandfonbrener feel about musicians wanting to switch careers and enter this branch of medicine? "I respond with suspicion. The motivation may be neurotic rather than a healthy one—the fact that you have had problems yourself is not a good motivational factor." Does she perceive any connections between the field and music therapy? "The overlap is somewhat limited. More is different than is alike between us. It is helpful to share knowledge with others, but we need to become better at what we do before we add more to it." She keeps an open mind about other assistance to artists. "By ignoring the constructive aspects of alternative therapies as well as the alternative therapist as potential ally, we may be denying our patients an increased opportunity for successful treatment of injuries that may be resistant to traditional care alone."

In addition to Brandfonbrener's program in Chicago, the other major centers of performing arts medicine are the Miller Program for Performing Artists at New York's Roosevelt Hospital, Program for Performing Artists of University of California at San Francisco, Medical Center for Performing Artists in Cleveland, and Performing Arts Clinic of University of Texas Medical School in Houston.

The Performing Arts Medicine Association, comprised of M.D.s, helps to monitor what is going on in the field. The quarterly journal *Medical Problems of Performing Artists* is edited by Brandfonbrener.

MUSIC THERAPIST

Two associations serving this career path, the National Association for Music Therapy Inc., and the American Association for Music Therapy Inc. have placement services for their members.

CHARLES EAGLE currently teaches music therapy and music medicine at Southern Methodist University in Dallas. He founded the music therapy program there, as he had done at University of Miami. After teaching music for five years, his interest in medicine took him to a pharmaceutical company, A.H. Robins Co., where he worked for more than six years as a medical service representative. During that time, he continued to play in orchestras and dance bands, appear as guest conductor, and judge music contests.

"I wanted to know the scientific basis of the influence of music on behavior," he recalls. He enrolled in a Ph.D. program at the University of Kansas in music education. Dr. E. Thayer Gaston was a professor in music educational research and became an important influence for Eagle. How did Eagle end up in music therapy? "I fell into it." He completed a Ph.D. in music education and his certification as a music therapist. He then undertook research at the Veteran's Administration Hospital in To-peka, Kansas, on "The Effects of Music in LSD Therapy for Alcoholic Patients" while also working as a research associate of graduate training for music therapists.

Eagle explains that his mentor, Dr. Gaston, a member of the "first generation of music therapists" had been a pre-med student as well as a trumpet virtuoso. In the 1940s and 1950s music therapy was based on medical principles and Gaston served as a liaison between the National Association for Music Therapy and the American Medical Association. Later, in the 1960s and 1970s, there was a greater emphasis on behavioral psychology in the profession. In the 1980s, there has been a gradual shift back to the medical profession. Eagle says, "The path has broadened." The three sectors of the field now called Music Medicine are Conventional and Traditional Music Therapy for handicapped children and adults, meeting their psychological and physical needs through music; Performing Arts

Medicine (described previously in this chapter); and Functional Music Medicine, in which medical specialties using music in treatment are identified. In this last category Eagle has identified fifty-five medical specialties in five thousand articles printed in eight hundred medical journals in thirty-nine countries. As a theorist, he also·does research into the arcane subject of quantum musichanics, which he founded on the quantum physics relativity principle.

The International Society of Music Medicine, whose members are two-thirds M.D.'s and one-third other types of music medicine specialists, is based in Luedenscheid, West Germany. The International Arts Medicine Association, based in Philadelphia, publishes a newsletter.

MUSIC COPYIST

What a dull sounding profession! Hasn't it been made obsolete with the use of computers? Very often, those gifted in creating beautiful scores and parts for composers aren't *only* music copyists, though copying work provides a good living. Read on!

JEAN HASSE leads a varied life. Her primary occupation is copying, proofreading, and editing music, but she is also a composer and publishes her own pieces through her company, Visible Music. For four years she was manager of Margun and GunMar Music, Inc., a Newton, Massachusetts, publishing company founded by Gunther Schuller. She oversaw all aspects of the business, including editing and coordinating the production of publications. Her motto: "There is no reason why anyone with a music education should consider a job outside of music. People should not doubt what they are capable of and how a music-related job can enhance their ultimate goals."

Besides music copying, managing, and composing, her other occupations have ranged from pianist and flutist to music teacher in the public schools and ear-training instructor in colleges to producer of contemporary concerts to box office manager at the Hartt School of Music.

Hasse began copying music while a student at Oberlin College. "There was a need for someone to copy Russian political songs for a professor. I had been composing music for years, using a pencil and a Flair-tip pen. I talked to the professor and decided it was a vocation I wanted to pursue since my notation was fairly good. I had a quick lesson with a copyist and composer at Oberlin College, who told me which pens to use, and I took it from there." Working with the composer directly helps ensure accurate results. "This work is a collaboration between composer or publisher and copyist. Part of the editing process is to call the composer for clarification. Usually I copy as much as I can, and wait until I get a list, which is often a full page of questions, and review it with the composer, then fill in the blanks. The copyist has to be alert at all times to instrument ranges, meter changes, dynamics, and accidentals, and has to think as a performer would: 'Is everything clear? Do I know how loud to play it, how fast to play it? Do I know how to articulate this passage?'" When the composer is not available for consultation, Hasse tries to be as accurate as possible, working with the composer's heirs, students, or publisher.

What are the prerequisites for a copyist? "A potential copyist is a musician who can read at least two clefs. The person should have played at least one instrument so that reading music is as easy as reading your own language. Copying is a 'quiet' profession—we work alone—but we can also create our own working hours and environment, and we can take work with us when we travel or relocate."

Sure, there are tedious moments, like the time Hasse copied more than eight hundred whole notes for one composition. "After that job, I was hoping I wouldn't have to see another whole note for at least a month." But the rewards keep her upbeat. "It's important to me that contemporary music is heard. Composers with complex and graphically notated scores need good copyists. In addition, composers, publishers, and performing ensembles often need music copied on short notice. Computer engravers cannot work as quickly as hand copyists, especially for parts, which is often all that is needed for a piece. Copying and editing music is gratifying to me in many ways. As a composer, I can prepare my own pieces and I also feel good about providing the service to others."

OCCUPATIONAL THERAPIST

During my interview with Caryl Johnson, she explained some of the differences between the physical and occupational therapists. "In some facilities physical therapists rehabilitate the lower half of the body and occupational therapists rehabilitate the upper half of the body. At other treatment facilities, the current distinction is that physical therapists perform modalities on their patients, for example, using heat, whirlpool, passive stretching, electrical modalities or massage; whereas occupational therapists plan their treatment to emphasize patient function. But there is a lot of overlap between the two categories."

CARYL JOHNSON started out as a pianist at Juilliard, later teaching courses in her alma mater's literature and materials department. What was to prove a link to her later career and "added a dimension to my life" was her experience teaching music to Juilliard dancers. "I was always a dance enthusiast." Johnson figured out ways the body could be used to illustrate musical materials. "The students would express musical structures and materials through movement."

After heading the Preparatory Division of Baltimore's Peabody Conservatory, where she created a method for teaching gifted children, her husband's medical practice dictated a move to Indianapolis. "I decided to do something completely different." She worked in a hospital as a music therapist but was disappointed with the experience. Volunteering as an occupational therapist was more satisfying. One of the health professionals urged her to go back to school and become a registered therapist. After three years of science courses that were completely new to her, Johnson earned a bachelor of science in occupational therapy from the University of Indiana Medical School.

With her background of teaching musicians and dancers, "I realized I had already done body thinking." When it came time for studying hand treatment, "I found it familiar. It was like reading a book about somewhere you'd already been." There was no question in her mind that, when the family moved to New Orleans, she would specialize in hand therapy. She started a Department of Occupational Therapy for physical disabilities at New Orleans' Touro Hospital and worked as a hand therapist there for five years. In the meantime, she had become a member of the American Society of Hand Therapists.

At the time of her move back to New York, Johnson decided she wanted to work with a hand surgeon. Dr. Richard Eaton, a renowned physician and hand surgeon, needed a hand therapist. She currently works with him as well as in her own practice. Sixty percent of her clientele are musicians. She has learned that "pitchers and cellists are all performers." Research projects have brought her to baseball training camps, measuring the strength of pitchers' hands to get "a picture of normal," and likewise, to New York's opera and ballet theater pits to chart norms of "pinch and grip" for players of all orchestral instruments. The reason? So when a player in either profession is injured there will be a measured norm to use when setting goals for therapy.

SACRED MUSIC PROFESSIONAL

CANTOR

Many concert singers find satisfying positions as cantors. Sopranos Isabelle Ganz and Pamela Jordan combine concert careers with jobs as cantors. Ganz describes the cantorial field as "a seller's market." With synagogues in proliferation throughout the United States, more cantors are obviously needed. In Reform and Conservative congregations, opportunities for women are on the rise.

Professional associations available to American cantors are the American Conference of Cantors (Reform); Cantors Assembly of America (Conservative); and Cantorial Council of America (Orthodox). For a list of schools which train cantors, see page 213.

JEFFREY KLEPPER is a full-time cantor of Beth Emet The Free Synagogue in Evanston, Illinois, who "simply can't imagine doing anything else." This wasn't always the case. Originally he wanted to be a folk singer. "Folk singers like Pete Seeger and Peter, Paul, and Mary were my heroes. In the 1960s, folk songs were the liturgy of the civil rights movement. Songs like *We Shall Overcome* spoke of a world of freedom and righteousness, values which are as Jewish as they are universal." As a child he enjoyed singing but "becoming a cantor never occurred to me as I was growing up, for our synagogue, like most Reform synagogues at the time, had no cantor. At the services the professional choir, hidden behind the *bimah*, sang everything except the opening and closing hymns. While I enjoyed attending services, the old-fashioned music did not capture my imagination."

Looking back, Klepper reminisces: "I was about ten years old when Professor Abraham Wolf Binder, my synagogue's music director, walked into my Sunday school class and asked, 'Do any of you like to sing?' My hand shot up. He took me up to the organ loft and proceeded to teach me Shabbat *Kiddush*. The music was new to me and strange. I thought I would never learn it. But the months went by and I made my debut, scared and nervous, but I did it. Years later I realized how significant that experience had been." Another pivotal experience for Klepper was spending summers at the UAHC Eisner Camp-Institute in Great Barrington, Massachusetts. "We sang Hebrew songs daily at meals, services, and campfires. Guitar-playing college students called 'songleaders' strummed dozens of songs, jumping up and down as we sang and clapped. The experience changed my life." Klepper, who had played guitar since the age of eight, was soon songleading in his temple youth group. "Songleading on Shabbat evening in a packed, sweaty dining hall was the most thrilling experience I could imagine. We prayed and we experimented, creating new melodies for our prayers."

In spite of these positive experiences, Klepper still did not have an easy time making a definite career choice. "Even as I went off to college, becoming a cantor was only a remote idea. I knew I had a desire to serve the Jewish people in some way, perhaps as a rabbi. I felt my voice was too 'folksy' and untrained to be a cantor. In fact I had strained my voice by singing incorrectly. But I continued to songlead at every opportunity." Meeting fellow religious school music teacher Dan Freelander provided the impetus to write original Jewish songs. This collaboration swung Klepper in the direction of a music career. "So why did I not become a folk or pop musician? Why not be a music teacher or write advertising jingles? Those endeavors are fine things to do, but Jewish music is different. Music expresses the soul more deeply than any other art form. I came to realize that singing and writing Hebrew songs connected me more deeply with who I was as a human being and who I was as a Jew. If music had brought me closer to Judaism, perhaps it could do the same for others.

"I left college after two years and applied to the School of Sacred Music of Hebrew Union College-Jewish Institute of Religion (HUC-JIR). Now you need a bachelor's degree to apply. I did HUC the hard way. In addition to classes, I had a busy student pulpit and a Jewish music group that I had started called *Kol B'seder* [everything's OK]. Dan Freelander and I continued to write songs together."

Klepper warns young cantors-to-be that "merely graduating from a cantorial school does not guarantee immediate success as a cantor. Finding the right position and surviving in the 'real world' can be a great challenge. The life of a cantor leaves little time for quieter activities like reading, composing, and learning new music. For several years I have been working on a master's degree in voice teaching. The voice is a cantor's most precious asset. Protecting the voice from abuse, especially during the 'busy seasons' of fall and spring is important. Most cantors continue vocal studies throughout their careers." Some free-lance singers serve as cantors in synagogues for the major Jewish holidays, combining that work with other aspects of a concert career.

Klepper heartily recommends his career to those who feel suited for it. "My view of the cantorate is a very contemporary one. Even though I have a deep respect for the Jewish musical tradition, I have chosen a path which many would consider avant-garde, writing my own music and utilizing contemporary instrumentation for the services. I play guitar regularly in my services and have experimented with jazz instruments." Klepper concludes: "Being a cantor has given my life a unity. Everything I do is part of living a Jewish life through music, from teaching toddlers their first Hebrew songs to performing my compositions at Jewish events to singing at baby namings and funerals. The life cycle events, from birth to marriage to death, are perhaps the most touching aspects of my work."

MINISTER OF MUSIC AND CHURCH ORGANIST

Organizations of interest to those in the music ministry are the American Guild of Organists (AGO), the Choristers Guild, the American Choral Directors Association (ACDA), and denominational groups such as the Presbyterian Association of Musicians and the Association of Anglican Musicians.

There is good news here. "Church music is on the rise," says BILL GREEN, minister of music at First Baptist Church in Richardson, Texas. "There will be more and more jobs available in this field in the years to come. Many churches now have full time music ministers, where the job used to be combined with education or another slot. . . . The instrumental program is a rising star for music in the church." Pretty optimistic for a field where there is normally a completely lopsided ratio of supply and demand.

As a high school senior, Green was on his way to becoming an electronic engineer when he "felt a calling to the music ministry." He was already an accomplished pianist at the time and his mother was church organist. During his undergraduate studies at Oklahoma Baptist University in church music, he was music director of a small church. After already serving full-time for a number of years in music ministry, Green taught music education and served in the choral program of Odessa College.

"I feel the music ministry is a calling—not just a career, just like going into the pastorate. It is a wonderful avenue for a life's work—you work with all age groups, and have a variety of activities." Green has a music staff of nine in his church, and many are full-time. There are no less than seventeen hundred congregants enrolled in the church's choirs, orchestras, church music institute, and six hand-bell choirs.

Aside from his minister of music responsibilities, Green presents workshops and clinics in church music at music conferences; he also writes books. He wrote *Fun Book for Singing*, and co-authored *Bold Mission Music Handbook* and *Music Ministry Handbook*.

"There are far fewer limitations on what you can do in church music than in other careers. Both secular and sacred music can be performed. One is only limited by one's own interests in learning. The job can never be boring. You are not locked into one area of work—there is tremendous growth in keeping up with vocal and choral techniques. Electronic music, computerized music—all have a place in church music."

COLLEGE PRESIDENT

While studying organ, composition, choral directing, and sacred music, it never occurred to RALPH C. SCHULTZ that one day he would be a college president. What has been just as unexpected is "how valuable I have found a music background to be for the position."

Schultz, who is from the suburbs of Chicago, taught elementary school and music in Cleveland after receiving a bachelor's degree in theory and composition from Chicago's Cosmopolitan School of Music and a bachelor's degree in education from Concordia College, Rover Forest, Illinois. While in Cleveland, he earned a master's degree from the Cleveland Institute of Music and spent a summer at the University of Michigan studying organ with Robert Noehren and composition with Ross Lee Finney. In 1957, a new tracker Beckerath organ was installed at Cleveland's Trinity Lutheran Church, where he was organist. This was a turning point for Schultz, who started concertizing more seriously on this instrument. At the same time, he served as conductor of the city-wide chorus and orchestra in Cleveland.

In 1961 he came to New York to be music department chairman at Bronxville's Concordia College. While chairing the department, Schultz started his doctorate in music education at Columbia Teacher's College. However, before long, he switched to the doctoral program in sacred music at Union Theological Seminary, from which he graduated in 1967.

During 1976–77, after fifteen years as head of Concordia's music department, Schultz was asked to be acting president of the college during a search. Schultz recalls, "That was okay, but I wanted to return to my love of music. Much to my surprise, I was elected president."

How exactly has a music background provided good training for his executive position? "It turned out to be an excellent preparation because musicians always work with long range planning—the music for a concert must be ordered and rehearsed far in advance of a concert; you must know about budget, expenditures versus income; fundraising is necessary; you must know how to deal with sensitive egos—good preparation in dealing with faculty; and as a conductor, I learned how to put things together, much as a college president is required to do."

As president of Concordia College, Schultz has been a strong proponent for the arts. He initiated the creation of a fine concert hall and recording facility, the Sommer Center for Worship and the Performing Arts, which is used frequently by major record companies. "The arts are expensive to teach and don't bring in financial support, so you've got to justify that they are a wise use of resources. There is a strong emphasis of the arts on campus."

Even with all his other demands, Schultz has managed to keep up his work as a composer. "I have about 130 compositions in a file drawer I've never sent to a publisher." Besides these, though, he has had various organ pieces, hymns, and choral anthems published by Morning Star and Concordia Publishing House Presses. He has also produced a video guide called *Leading the Choir: A Guide for the Inexperienced Choir Director.* Somehow, on top of it all, with his wife he wrote the hymn for his daughter's wedding, which has since been included in *Lutheran Worship.*

U*NION OFFICIAL*

LEW WALDECK is a tuba player turned trouble shooter. He is the guy who is called in desperation in the middle of the night by musicians on tour who suddenly feel that they have been turned into hostages by exploitative management. He is head as well as creator of the symphony, opera, and ballet department, as we know it today, of the American Federation of Musicians, the national umbrella organization for all of the country's local musicians' unions. Before getting into this work, he spent twenty-five years as tuba player of the New York City Opera Orchestra. What brought him to his current position? Not surprisingly, for many years he was on the New York City Opera Orchestra committee for negotiating contracts. He learned a lot about the labor movement.

He is interested in raising the consciousness of his fellow musicians. His job is to work for the betterment of the musician's professional situation. "It is a question of self-image, of course. We have to believe we are worth more, and have the right to live respectably. We have to say 'Yes, we deserve this.' But in order to do that, we first have to give up the 'garret image' of Mimi [in the opera *La Bohème*] and it is tough to leave her. After all, we were all brought up with the image of the struggling artist."

Waldeck believes that part of the image problem stems from the fact that young musicians "exert the maximum life effort into studying and practicing their instruments in school. When they get out it's hard to find a job. They say, 'I'm afraid to give it up. And I've spent all this effort, all for naught. How can I ever be successful?' They believe they, rather than the conditions of society, are at fault. They say, 'We did everything right—where did we fail?' But it is the system that has failed them. It is an example of blaming the victim." Waldeck analyzes the root of the problem. "Classical musicians have grown up in circumstances where they feel lucky to play. This 'feeling lucky' makes them vulnerable." For most performing musicians, there has been a "fusion of identity with the fact they play an instrument. Their identity exists only when they are playing."

Waldeck strives to protect musicians and feels strongly about the dangers of exploitation. "A musician with a job is as subject to rape as the jogging victim in the park. The purpose of a union is to help people take control of their own lives. To show musicians when they need to say 'no, if we can't make this better we don't want it to exist.' The big fear of striking isn't really the loss of money. It is the stress from the identity crisis. People are afraid they won't be able to play. During a recent successful strike of the Honolulu Symphony, musicians solved that problem by giving chamber music concerts."

Where is the hope in all this? Waldeck concludes, "The business community of a city profits from the existence of a good orchestra. Real estate, tourism, retirement communities all benefit. The orchestra must sell the community a new image. Musicians who know how much they are worth can teach a lot to the board and management of their orchestra."

CHAPTER

15

Music in Media

THE career possibilities for music professionals in the world of media are wide-ranging. Of all the careers discussed in this chapter, the public is perhaps most familiar with music critics, because of their high profile and often controversial presence in print journalism. For this reason I have devoted less attention to music criticism and more to the lesser-known occupations, such as those in the film industry—composers, music editors, and recording engineers—and various sorts of music producers, for example, in the airline industry and in the realm of advertising. As we near the end of the century, the job market for musicians in media professions is bound to change quickly with technological advances. Those interested should keep current with new trends in the industry.

FILM COMPOSER

Composer ERNEST TROOST labels film composing more a craft than an art, likening it to being a "master carpenter building kitchen cabinets. Ultimately you must build them to please your employer, which in this case is the film director or producer. You've got to put yourself totally into it but also be willing to let go." We are talking about an extremely competitive profession. There probably aren't more than two hundred and fifty feature film composers in the United States who make a living at it. Ernest Troost is a relative newcomer to the field.

He started out as a songwriter. In fact, the first time Ernest Troost ever wrote music down on paper was as an undergraduate at Berklee College of Music while working on jazz arrangements. He had entered Berklee as a jazz guitar performance major, later switching to composition. His first arrangement for big band was an original song. "The teacher got upset with me; the assignment had been to *arrange* a standard." But the piece was played by the senior ensemble and was a huge success.

Troost made a discovery in his senior year of college. "I took a course in film scoring for the first time and it all came together in my head. I was so excited about that course and realized it was what I wanted to do. It was a good marriage of writing for orchestra and doing something practical—people needed you to do it. I realized writing film scores could be an art, and, if possible, I wanted to write music that would last over time. I prefer to avoid trendy, gimmicky music."

Research visits to the Boston Public Library gave Troost ideas about music for animated films. He was inspired by the European animation films using abstract music which played in Boston theaters that senior year. "It was art, not commerce, a million miles away from Hollywood." Before he graduated from Berklee, Troost had already gotten his first paycheck for writing a score for a film based on a children's picture book.

After college, he took a job in a small film production company. "I figured that if I learned more about films, I would understand more about how music is used in films, what it can do." Although he was asked to compose dramatic music behind narration for filmstrips, he had a hard time convincing the company to give him a shot at writing a score. "They wanted you to have done it before. I convinced the president of the company to make an animated film in the United States. Most of their animation had been done in other countries. So I became the film producer and they used music I had written before. The film was called *The Clown of God*. After that, they considered my music suitable for films."

After several years in the film production job, Troost decided to work free-lance, and he continued to gain experience scoring animated films. One of his most lasting memories from that period was as film editor for a Public Broadcasting System presentation of Igor Stravinsky's A *Soldier's Tale*. "It took ten months to prepare an hour show. I had to put many different skills to work and I learned a lot about film and working with people."

These experiences led to further contacts with animators, even though some knew him only as a film editor. He therefore decided to concentrate solely on composition. He worked on scores for a number of children's projects for "Sesame Street" and several other producers. "I was left to do whatever I wanted. I tried many styles and worked almost exclusively with acoustic instruments in studios. I used string quartet, a five-clarinet big band sound, Renaissance music, whatever style fit the story and pictures. There were about seventy 10–15 minute projects. But I realized I must eventually go beyond the animation world when, one year, one of the projects I worked on was nominated for an Academy Award as a composite work; the score got no particular recognition."

Breaking into feature films was very difficult. "I made fifteen phone calls a day for about a year and a half and got nowhere. I hated doing that, but I made myself. I offered to do music for demo action films for free." But during this painful time Troost also got an education about the business. "I got familiar with the companies, building files for production companies and production executives in New York and Hollywood. Even today, when things get slow, I go back to review the files. I learned that until companies want you, agents don't want you either. Also, someone told me that you can pretty much talk to anyone on the phone. They think you might be the next Steven Spielberg." But that did not guarantee any work. Finally, Troost bought a plane ticket and went out to Hollywood. "I called several producers and said 'I'm coming, I'll send a tape now, and I'll call when I arrive. If you like the tape, we'll talk then.' " Troost made many such calls, but held out hope for one studio in particular. Roger Corman's studio has a reputation of giving people first breaks. "I had called his studio for a year and finally got to talk to someone about music. She said 'Sure, send me your tape.' " This lone call eventually produced results: a chance to be the composer on a Hollywood film, *Sweet Revenge*. Several others followed, such as *Tiger Warsaw, Dead Heat, and Tremors*.

The Troost family moved to Hollywood in the late 1980s. As an up-and-coming Hollywood composer, there are constant struggles for Troost. "You must keep calling people, making cold calls. You must put energy out, let energy flow, for work to come." Many would-be film composers do not realize that there is little or no money to be made by a film composer in the starting years. For his first Hollywood project, Troost invested his own money to hire a bigger orchestra than the budget allowed. "I felt I had to build a solid reputation, even if it meant losing money. Especially in the early years I felt that I must look for a challenge rather than money." He advises young composers "to look at everything that comes your way."

Troost keeps his mind fresh by keeping up endeavors which utilize his original music impulse—song writing. Recently he wrote twenty-six children's songs for Judy Collins. Feeling down about the Hollywood life, he was thrilled to find that "she loved them. She stood for eight hours, with hardly a break, recording them." This project, a Stories to Remember production, is marketed as a book with cassette, compact disc, and home video.

Troost never stops doing research to keep aware of current film projects and come up with new ideas. Years ago, he wrote to the Library of Congress for information on careers in film music. This led him to Elmer Bernstein's newsletter, in which composers interview other composers. The honest ones are very candid about the brutality of Hollywood. Troost comments, "They realized it can be a totally abusive working atmosphere but they made the best of it. I admired this attitude and have tried to adopt it." Troost recommends reading periodicals such as *Variety*, *The Cue Sheet*, soundtrack fan magazines, and *Hollywood Reporter*, which lists all films currently in production. Helpful books on the profession are Roy M. Prendergast's *Film Music: A Neglected Art* and *Music for the Movies* by Tony Thomas. The University of Southern California library has an especially good collection of books on film music. An interesting organization to be aware of is the Society for the Preservation of Film Music in Los Angeles, whose mission is going into studios and pulling out scores and historical documents for safe keeping in museums and colleges. For example, the collection of composer Max Steiner has been given to Brigham Young University.

As he continually learns more about the profession, Troost has also learned to practice patience. "I feel I haven't done many good movies yet. But it can take a long time to gain the experience necessary to work on quality pictures, and to be given the chance."

Ten years ago DAVE NEWMAN spent a lot of time sitting in as a session violinist, recording the music for major Hollywood films. He's still involved with movie music, only now he's the composer. In the last few years he has written the music for such acclaimed films as *Throw Momma From the Train* and *War of the Roses*. He likes this work much better.

Son of legendary Hollywood composer Alfred Newman, who won fifty-four Academy Award nominations and nine Oscars, Dave Newman studied violin at the University of Southern California (USC) with Eudice Shapiro and conducting in New York with Leon Barzin. Never expecting to follow in the career track of his father, he didn't study composition. Here's his surprising point of view. "Anyone who is classically trained takes music dictation, theory, and counterpoint. Most musicians can write music. I wrote a piece for myself for my graduate recital at USC, but I was really more interested in conducting at the time."

Newman, who graduated from USC in the early 1970s, waited more than a decade to take up composing in earnest. As a session violinist he was a musician for hire. Writing his own music made him a real contributor to the creative process of filmmaking. Once he decided to make this career change, it took him about three years to build the foundation for a new life. As a first step, Newman made a demo tape—an unusual fifteen-minute orchestra piece. His music sounded original. His advice for new film composers is to "make a demo tape completely unique and different from anyone else's, so it stands out. Be sure it is an *orchestra* demo tape." He handed his tape around, got an agent, and was asked to write the music for the low budget films *Critters* and *Heathers*. *Heathers* especially was a "big industry hit, which may not be the same as a big box office hit." It was a good career vehicle, putting Dave Newman on the Hollywood map. But success did not happen overnight. In fact, Newman admits that before this break, "I learned a lot of things from being burned."

The hard thing for Newman wasn't the composing itself, but learning about the ways of Hollywood. Even growing up in the family of a prominent Hollywood composer hadn't given him inside savvy, because the elder Newman, a cultured, classically trained composer and conductor, was more apt to discuss opera and other classical music genres at home. In the beginning, Newman laments, "you don't know what you're up against. Having information about the business is crucial. Knowing how a film is made, who the important people are, where you fit in, how to appear a certain way, all of these things are important. You have to appear to know something even if you don't! You have to be hyper-vigilant about what the director's and other people's needs are. Don't be a doormat either, be a service-oriented person. Being part of a film is like being thrown into a whirlpool."

An important rule to keep in mind is "if it is anyone's thing, it is the director's thing." A director's major concern? "How the music is going to fit into *my* movie. Directors today are often yuppies in their twenties and thirties. You can't expect any real sophisticated intelligence on a musical level. There is not much more than a kindergarten mentality about music. The director just wants the music to work. Make the director feel the film can't be done without *you*." Also important is knowing "everyone's role in the process, like the role of the music editor. Relationships with people—this is how you build a career. Be part of the team—very important."

What is the best way to prepare for the career of film composer? "Go to lots and lots of movies. Go to the same movie more than once so you can really listen to the music. See what is happening, going on in film music." For education, he recommends the University of Southern California's graduate film curriculum, the University of California at Los Angeles's extension division, and BMI's film composers workshop. A very elite seminar for film composers is offered by The Sundance Institute in Utah, on whose board Newman served for several years. The institute was founded by actor Robert Redford. At Sundance, about eight composers are chosen from three hundred applicants to attend a three-week summer course filled with master classes, demonstrations, and the opportunity to work with state-of-the-art equipment and live orchestra. Working composers come from Los Angeles and tell the way it really is. Students get their work critiqued by professionals.

Newman says someone serious about composing for films must live in Los Angeles. He also recommends having an agent. "You can't do anything in L.A. without an agent. You have to have one, or a lawyer. An agent sets up your fee. A contact with one director is not enough; one director does not a career make." One entrée into the profession is putting together temporary music for a film, the background music used for production purposes before the film's original music is composed. It is one way to make contacts and get noticed.

For Newman, a film composer's career is not necessarily an end in itself. "Writing good film music can lead to other opportunities for personal projects. I have written an orchestra work and a score for the silent film *Sunrise*, and am working on an opera."

Dave Newman has proven that a mid-career change to film composer, however difficult and challenging, is certainly possible for someone with a solid musical background *and* money to live on for about two years while getting established. He stresses, "Ninety percent of what is important has to do with knowing information about the industry, understanding how things work."

FILM MUSIC EDITOR

Film composers have relatively high-profile careers. But there are some music professionals in the film industry who do not, such as music editors. Although they have an extremely important role in film production, their names won't leap out at you unless you are in the habit of watching the film credits at the end of a movie. As a lower-profile profession, it is also less competitive than film composing. There are a maximum of one hundred music editors in the United States. Salary is determined by the Film Editors' Union.

JIM HENRIKSON and NANCY FOGARTY are two music editors in Hollywood who, between them, have been responsible for putting together the music on many films turned out since the late 1950s.

Henrikson played piano and synthesizers in a band during his years at Los Angeles City College. If he stayed with the band, he was destined for a life on the road. He sensed early that it wasn't the lifestyle he wanted. But what other choices were available to him? His father, a prop man at MGM studios in Hollywood, knew an animator at Walt Disney studios. Henrikson called the animator and asked, "How can I apply my musical background to a career in film?" "Why don't you become a music editor?" the animator suggested. Animators work to a prerecorded sound track and music editing is very important in synchronizing the animated characters to the beats. And so it began.

Fogarty started out as a flutist but she felt that "playing in public was beyond my ability emotionally. I feel that as a music editor I can use my background in a productive way."

Henrikson outlines two basic skills needed by music editors: first, film editing techniques, knowing about the mechanics of film equipment and the dramatics of film; and second, a musical background, knowing how to read a score and being able to speak the same musical language as the film composer. Active music editors take on four to six film projects a year and can be booked from six months to as much as two years in advance. There used to be music editors on staff at studios but no longer. Henrikson was on staff at Universal Studios from 1959 to 1964.

There is often temporary music used to accompany a film's action in the early stages of production before the film composer has been selected. It is with this music that the director shows the rough edit of the film to the studio heads, distributor, and marketing personnel. Although most of the music editor's work takes place after the final shooting, at this early stage the editor may be consulted on the temporary music, as well as singing and dancing parts of the film. Henrikson remembers working on the film *Spartacus* in the late 1950s, where much of the action footage was filmed silently and, because of that, it seemed too long. The film editor said, "I have to show a rough cut to the director. In the projection room it won't work. I need you to put music with it." This was the beginning of a trend that has become standard practice in today's film making.

The largest role of the music editor begins with the music spotting session after the composer is hired. A blueprint is drawn up outlining where music will be required in the underscore of the film. There is a general exchange of ideas in which compositional approaches, character of the music, and instrumentation are discussed and the composer talks about his initial ideas. It is the music editor's responsibility to write an outline of the notes from the meeting and give it to the composer, director, and producer. Next, the editor supplies the composer with a "continuity breakdown" where each sequence of the underscore is broken down into tenths of a second, the unit used in film composition. In writing this "continuity," a particular skill is needed from the editor to free the composer from useless details. Henrikson and Fogarty both warn editors, "Don't bury someone in minutia. Always see the big picture even though you're dealing with small units. This is where understanding dramatics, knowing how to tell a story, comes in. It all amounts to good, long phrases, just like in music."

The composer uses this continuity, usually in conjunction with a videotape of the film, to write the film score. The completed score is sent to the music editor with indications of tempos and visual cues needed for conducting. At this stage of production, the music editor's job gets very busy: working with the orchestrator and the music copyist; preparing the print or video of the film with the composer's cues for the recording session; and establishing variable tempo tracks where needed, with the use of computer, that will determine the sliding of beats necessary for synchronization of music and visuals. The musicians performing the film score will have these beats, called a click track, in their earphones during the recording session. The music is then recorded in sessions while a print of the film is being shown. There is interaction between the music editor and the recording engineer. The multi-track tape is mixed down and transferred to a magnetic film stock. The editor synchronizes the new mixdown to the visuals of the film. Then the music, dialogue, and sound effects are mixed onto the master sound track, balancing levels to keep the music under the dialogue. Henrikson states, "At the very end of this entire process the director or producer may say 'I wish the music did this over here.'" Enter the role of music editor as reconstructive surgeon. "Something like this almost always happens."

Both Henrikson and Fogarty caution that a music editor, who serves as a liaison among many aspects of post-production, should be prepared for the "haphazard aspect of dealing with creative people. It happens somewhere but you never know where. Sometimes you need to be the buffer between director and composer. You are dealing with people who are sensitive, volatile, and often have a lot of ego. There are sometimes crises but, if the music editor remains calm, other people are also helped by it. The composer benefits if you can be a problem-solver rather than a problem maker. Sometimes they want you to shut up, sometimes they want your ideas. You must be flexible."

This profession clearly requires more than just a musical background. "You need to be part psychiatrist, part negotiator, and part linguist-translator." How is it learned? "There aren't formal courses in the United States. You really have to beat the drum and assist all over the place to learn the skills. But people aren't often drawn to music editing as a career. It is not a mogul road. Maybe that's why those of us doing it are almost always consistently employed."

*F*ILM RECORDING ENGINEER

SHAWN MURPHY is one of the busiest film musicians in Los Angeles. His colleagues say Murphy is the best film recording engineer in Hollywood. He records the music for films and integrates it with the dialogue and sound effects.

Starting out as a trombone player, Murphy switched to tuba during college. While a student at San Francisco State and Stanford, he worked with sound systems of theatrical productions, but was still active as a player in local orchestras. He earned a Master of Fine Arts in lighting and sound design from Stanford University. What does a sound designer do? "Selects, adapts, and edits music and sound effects, live and taped, making it work dramatically." Murphy had a background as a performer that he augmented with technical training and work in the theater. He then worked as a recording engineer in recording studios and gradually started doing the same for films. The performance background helps him "know what musicians expect." Murphy describes his place in the film world. "What I do is a tiny corner of the industry. There are fewer than ten engineers in the world recording music for films." He works on many films in L.A. and as the industry shifts, he goes to other parts of the world, such as England, Munich, and Budapest, to record music for films.

What do you need to be a good recording engineer? "The first thing is to think of the music, then the technical end, and then finally to integrate knowledge of the two. It is an interdisciplinary art." Suggestions of where to get trained? He mentions three schools where engineering programs are connected to the music programs: Berklee College of Music, University of Miami, and University of Southern California. Any periodicals of interest? *Film Score* gives reviews of film scores and includes related feature articles.

FILM MAKER

ALLAN MILLER, the Academy Award-winning film maker, has this fantasy: One day the first oboist of a major American orchestra walks down a city street and a little boy yells out "Hey, great Mahler Fifth last night!" much like the greeting accorded today's baseball heroes. Will the arts ever become that popular to mainstream America? Miller is certainly trying to come up with innovative ways to reach that goal. He has consistently worked to humanize the arts, build audiences, and help make the arts as accessible as possible to large groups. In films such as *The Bolero* and *High Fidelity* he has shown musicians to be real people with everyday problems and concerns. He took an old movie theater on New York's Upper West Side and helped create a new kind of concert hall, Symphony Space, which presents an array of different types of concerts. There have even been marathon celebrations where anyone off the street could come and join in. In 1990 Miller was moderator for the series *Face the Music* at Symphony Space, comprising three evenings of "performance and probing conversation," a meeting of the minds between musicians and literary figures.

Miller graduated from Harvard and then stayed on to get his M.A. in music. He was active during that period as a conductor of orchestras and choruses. After graduate school, he was a conducting apprentice to Herman Scherchen in Switzerland. Two years later he was back in New York, uncertain where his future was taking him. In the early 1960s, while doing some free-lance conducting, he got a job working on music programs for New York's Channel 13 Public Broadcasting Station, which specialized in cultural programming. He eventually became music director. Miller realized that "nothing could reproduce the feeling of a concert," but that a filmed concert could create its own interesting process, helping to "lead the eye to the ear."

In 1972 the National Endowment for the Arts considered creating a public media division. Several film makers submitted ten-minute projects on music topics. Miller was chosen to make a pilot film in music. Out of that emerged the Academy Award-winning film *The Bolero*, a documentary introducing Zubin Mehta conducting the Los Angeles Philharmonic. In humanizing the players, he hoped to take musicians "out of the remote community of strangers" for audiences. During the next few years, Miller created several half-hour public television programs. "The Secret Life of an Orchestra," "Romeo and Juliet in Kansas City," "Ancient

Voices of Children," and "Music for Prague" each featured a different American ensemble. In 1976 he directed and produced *Amazing Grace: America in Song*, a documentary of American songs. Two Carnegie Hall specials and the televising of Beethoven's nine symphonies with the Detroit Symphony followed the next year. In 1979 Isaac Stern and entourage returned from a three-week trip to China with two hundred thousand feet of film. Ten months later the film *From Mao to Mozart* was completed. The eighty-four minute feature film had been created in the cutting room by Miller and his editor-colleague Tom Haneke.

In addition to his film endeavors, Miller has continued conducting activities and since 1979 has been Artistic Director of Symphony Space. He directed an "American Masters" special for PBS, documenting the lives of selected American composers, and created *High Fidelity: The Adventures of the Guarneri String Quartet*. Making music more accessible to the listener, a constant theme throughout Miller's career, was a motivating factor in producing this film. "Each performance is put in the film following a new revelation of their [the Guarneri Quartet's] relationship that you will be unconsciously mulling over as the film goes on. You're not just listening to the music. You're listening to it in the context of what you've just discovered about music and music making. My belief is that the more you know about these people, the more you're interested in what they're doing."

THE JINGLE WORLD

According to Fred Miller in his book *Music in Advertising*, a jingle is "a melody with lyrics, designed to be a memorable and recognizable part of a television or radio commercial." His book and *Through the Jingle Jungle* by Steve Karmen provide a good introduction to this world. There are about six hundred jingle or music houses in the United States. Jingle houses are hired by advertising agencies to take on the product of a client. Some composers work for only one jingle house, while others free-lance their work to different houses. When an ad campaign is being mounted, the finished product must be delivered quickly. Composers work fast and often conduct the sessions themselves, while making changes in the score. It is not uncommon for session musicians to be hired just twenty-four hours in advance of the job.

Contrary to what many musicians assume, the head of one New York music house contends that "using synthesizers instead of acoustic instruments for a project is not a cost-cutting measure. The decision of instrumentation is based on the type of sound a client has described." Whatever the reasons, there is much less session work for musicians these days and employment prospects for instrumentalists in this market are limited. There are, however, opportunities for good composers and music producers at advertising agencies.

MUSIC PRODUCER AT AN ADVERTISING AGENCY

CRAIG HAZEN is one of five music producers at the New York advertising agency of Young & Rubicam. About twenty-five music producers are employed in agencies in the United States. Hazen, a graduate of Brown University and Mills College, where he worked with many West Coast artists, races in and out of a room strewn with scribbled-on papers and pictures. Records and tapes are everywhere you look. This is definitely the room of someone who has lots going on. It's not hard to feel a buzz. Hazen is always testing out ideas for ad campaigns for agency clients. The creative team which develops concepts for commercials includes an art director and copywriter. As part of the team, the producer organizes the creation of the music that will be identified with a particular product. At any time, Hazen may be working on fifteen to thirty ad campaigns. He acts as the liaison between the music house which produces the jingle and the client. "Finding the right composer is the most important thing." The music producer describes what the client is looking for. The composer translates these thoughts into music using instrumentation or synthesizer sounds needed for the message. Then the pressure is really on. Within just a few days the music must be written and recorded. Hazen, a former composer, recording engineer, and performance artist, explains that "commercials are a reactive art. To get attention they must be creative in some way." He happily recalls a successful Goodyear ad campaign that he had helped put together not long ago. It used a fresh musical form. His secret for satisfaction? "Go out on a limb. Be proud of what you do."

MUSIC CRITIC

MICHAEL WALSH, the music critic of *Time* Magazine, describes himself as a "self-educated zealot." The first music he remembers hearing is Burl

Ives, bagpipes, and country and western. His introduction to classical music was "hearing second-hand classical records brought home by my father by accident." What made the biggest impression on him in his formative years? The celeste and the dance of the sugar plum fairies in a live performance of Tschaikovsky's *Nutcracker Suite.*

His mother insisted on piano lessons and he had developed into a pianist and composer by the end of high school. But when he entered the Eastman School of Music as a freshman, he felt "left behind. I didn't have the cultural background of other students. But Eastman was challenging. I had a lot of catching up to do." Walsh says he has always had the ability to take on a lot. "I feel I can do anything I put my mind to." Eastman was a testing ground for him.

He knew he could write words as well as music, since he had been writing stories since he was a child. Why not write about music? By his second year at Eastman he knew he would be a music critic; he had an understanding of musical structure and knew how to listen. He feels that being a good listener has been one of his strongest attributes as a critic.

He never took a music criticism course but learned about his future profession by reading reviews in record magazines. He has mixed feelings about formal courses in criticism, and a bit of cynicism creeps in. "What's the point? There are no jobs." But he admits such courses can teach a student specific skills and some professional short cuts.

"Music criticism is really bad in America. It has to be connected to live art, but it isn't. There is no excitement in criticism any more." He deplores the fact that not enough critics love music. "Often they are not reviewing something that means anything to them. What results are dead reviews. There are no strong opinions."

Walsh feels that musicians should be proud to serve their local communities. He remembers listening to an enjoyable performance of the Oregon Symphony in Portland. Later, while chatting with the conductor, James DePreist, Walsh sensed the maestro was getting ready to think about the next career step. "Why? What is the big deal about coming to New York?" Another pet peeve is the elitism of classical music. "Music is about communicating directly with people. You look for the art. All you see is the commerce. Why do we just want to reach the same people all the time? We should look to play for people who really appreciate it. Isn't that what music is all about?"

Walsh is proud to say that he first came to music as an amateur. He has a distinguished list of credits as former critic of Rochester's *Democrat and Chronicle* and the *San Francisco Examiner,* and now critic of one of the most influential magazines in the world. Through it all, his perspective about music has managed to stay fresh and even rather innocent, if slightly eccentric. One of his books is called *Who's Afraid of Classical Music?* Its message is simple but surprisingly unusual. "It is important to tell people that music is for everybody. We have to stop frightening them away."

MUSIC PRODUCER

CATHY WALDMAN is a Juilliard-trained pianist, so why put her in a section called Music in Media? This could be a comment from one of her past colleagues. For indeed Waldman is known as a pianist and a very accomplished one. But in mid-career she has discovered new gifts and is utilizing them fully. Together with partners Paul Levi, a composer, and Mark Lipson, a cantor and music electronics expert, she has formed a music production company in Connecticut.

But this is not the first time she has ventured into other musical worlds. In the past, while teaching piano and performing, she wrote and narrated children's theater pieces and composed incidental music for the theater. Now this spirit of adventure has been transformed into a more committed endeavor. The woman who remembers "I was never interested in electronics. I didn't know or care what synthesizers could do" has, with her partners, written the title music and lyrics for the PBS production "First Things First." Not only that, Waldman also sang the show's theme song. Other projects range from composing the title theme for the "Cooking Show" on PBS and an ABC after school movie called "Divorce Kids Blues," to providing music for slide shows at industrial sales meetings, to writing the script and the music for a video on relaxation targeted to a mass market, to producing recording sessions for classical musicians. In the meantime she has lost her fear of computers, and even enjoys composing on them.

"It is exciting to take new steps in mid-life. Just because you get trained as a pianist, why should it limit you? Now when I feel I'm burning out on something I go in new directions. I don't resent anything I do." Waldman also plays piano in production projects. "I'm growing and learning and my listening skills are sharper. My piano playing is better. I now realize a lot of it is in your head, not your fingers. I'm not where I thought I'd be, but I'm a hell of a lot happier."

MUSIC PRODUCER FOR AIRLINE INFLIGHT ENTERTAINMENT PROGRAMS

JEFF BORGESON is manager of inflight programming services for AEI Music Network Inc. of Seattle. He creates inflight audio entertainment programs for many of the leading airlines. His goal is "to enhance a passenger's time onboard the plane." Another part of AEI Music Network is the "foreground music" division. Music is put together to "enhance an atmosphere" in restaurants, fashion outlets, and a variety of locations. AEI, with thousands of clients nationwide, has the biggest operation in the field.

In his airline work, Borgeson works with a contact person from each airline to create programs that fit the needs of the airline. Program concepts devised for flights in the United States and abroad are the result of market research on passenger demographics, different cultures and nationalities represented, and seasonal considerations. For example, since more children fly in the summer, special interest programs are provided for them during this time. Sibelius is often programmed for Finnair flights and, not surprisingly, the British West Indian carrier features Caribbean music. Interviews with performing artists, part of inflight programming, are also in Borgeson's domain.

Borgeson began his career as a recording engineer in Los Angeles, working with a variety of artists, including Michael Jackson, Elton John, and Chicago. He also produced a syndicated radio production which led him to his position with AEI. "Radio production skills are very connected to inflight production skills. Most of our producers have radio backgrounds." How do you find out about jobs in this field? "Read inflight magazines of the different airlines. Note the names of the firms who provide this specialized music service. Contact them."

RADIO PRODUCER

Martin Goldsmith, the host of "Performance Today" on National Public Radio, says, "Classical music never was and never will be mass entertainment. Neither should it be considered the province of an imagined elite." While some radio executives worry about classical listenership waning, there are plenty of success stories in the medium: Bill McGlaughlin with his "St. Paul Sunday Morning," distributed by American Public Radio;

John Schaefer's program called "New Sounds," distributed by National Public Radio; Robert Sherman, with an array of different programs on New York's WQXR; and Goldsmith's program, the only daily national music program featuring concert performances recorded around the country.

This is a time of flux in the world of radio. It is no longer a secure medium. Perhaps we can make something positive out of that. After all, sometimes it is uncertainty that can open the door for something new. Adventurous performers can experiment with program proposals and, with hard work, get funding to do a pilot. Potential radio professionals, in production and as broadcasters, may find it is the right moment to start something really innovative.

RICH KLEINFELDT is a producer of classical music and fine arts programs at Voice of America, a branch of the United States Information Agency. While in high school, Kleinfeldt started private lessons on the tenor saxophone, participated in the state choir, and attended summer music camp. By the time he went to college, he knew he would have a career in music.

At Millikin University in Illinois Kleinfeldt was a music education major. In the late 1960s the university sponsored tours of its jazz band to the Middle East and South America, where Kleinfeldt met U.S. cultural affairs officers. This experience made a lasting impression.

Kleinfeldt taught junior high school music and eventually joined the Army band, while at the same time earning a master's degree in music at Catholic University in 1973. It was in Washington, D.C., that he got his first radio experience, as a narrator for the band. As a part-time employee at Voice of America, he learned how to direct a broadcast. His previous work as a conductor helped, but his ear had to be trained in a new way. He learned that the shape of the broadcast was very important—timing, balance, creating a beginning, middle, and end. "Leave them wanting more" was the slogan.

Kleinfeldt worked at Voice of America part-time until 1983, when he started a full-time job in the news department. Two years later he became host of the morning show, which included discussion of cultural activities. Given his background, he made sure music topics were included in the programming. Since 1987 Kleinfeldt has been in charge of the Voice of America programs "Concert Hall" and "Critic's Choice," whose emphasis used to be about films, but under Kleinfeldt's tenure has become an arts magazine of cultural news from around the country.

As a radio producer, Kleinfeldt carries over the musician's discipline to the medium of radio. He lends his musical skills to the dissemination of American culture all over the globe.

*R*ECORD *PRODUCER*

Sitting in STEVE EPSTEIN's office is a pure delight. He is a record producer at Sony Classical, formerly CBS Masterworks. Peering out from the walls of his office are the smiling faces of everyone from Isaac Stern to Mandy Patinkin. I was there to get ideas about making records. But more than that happened. A respected record producer in the classical music industry showed me how much he loves his work.

Sony Classical, where Epstein is one of three producers, is an international label. Therefore artists with an international career and an active touring schedule record on this label. Epstein produces about fifteen records a year.

Epstein studied violin as a child and "loved technical things." He wanted to be a record producer from an early age. During high school he phoned Tom Frost, then a producer at CBS, and asked for advice on an education for the profession. Frost made some suggestions on courses which would be useful. Epstein eventually went to Long Island's Hofstra University, majored in music, and augmented that study with courses in acoustics and physics. "The musical education is the most important. You can learn specifics about technical matters later."

What are the requirements for a good record producer? "A good ear is essential, and you must understand music and how to read a score." Epstein explains his role in the recording process. "The producer works with the engineer and together they decide on microphones to be used, recording venue, how many tracks, and the general approach to recording." His ultimate goal is "to realize on record what the conductor or artist is trying to get across in the most natural acoustic setting." Sometimes getting there requires delicate and diplomatic tactics with artists who have sensitive egos.

Resources he recommends for the aspiring record producer are *Billboard*'s annual resource issue which lists studios and their engineers and producers throughout the world. Epstein reads the trade publications *Audio Magazine*, *Billboard*, and *The Gramophone*, among others. He recommends that aspiring recording engineers and record producers join the Audio Engineering Society. He finds the society's *AES Journal* a good technical reference for the field.

CONCLUDING THOUGHTS

We are musicians. But *why?* Some of us chose this enigmatic profession before the age of ten. We could say the profession chose us because of special gifts we had from birth. This may be partly true, but it isn't the whole story. A passive explanation is of no benefit to those who have yet to find their place. We don't *have* to be musicians. But many of us would feel lost without a sturdy connection to music, our professional identity.

It is helpful to figure out why we have chosen this calling. In the process, an important fact is likely to emerge. That the definition of who we are and what it means to be a musician changes over a lifetime. We grow.

I admire musicians who grow. Their playing improves, they contribute more, and they have happier, more fulfilling professional lives. A large number of the people I interviewed for this book were not satisfied with the status quo. Many went back to school in a music-related field or learned new skills on the job. They discovered ways to have stimulating lives and be needed in a profession. Sometimes it took a bit of trial and error and the growth process was often a little scary. After all, you don't always end up exactly where you had envisioned. Cynthia Hoover never expected to be a curator at the Smithsonian Institution. As she said, "Life is what happens when you have planned something else." While studying singing, Hillary Mayers did not know she would one day become an Alexander teacher for fellow musicians. During his undergraduate study at Brown University, Richard Cohn would not have predicted that he would become a music theorist. Organist-choral conductor-composer Ralph C. Schultz never dreamed he would one day be a college president, but has found that a background in music provided excellent preparation for running an institution. As a Juilliard instructor for musicians and dancers, Caryl Johnson never imagined she would become a hand specialist, treating many illustrious baseball pitchers and musicians. But it felt right, "like a place you have been before."

How do you get in touch with what you want to do and be? This may be the hardest task of all. Laura Jeppesen, while a graduate student at Yale University, was encouraged to figure out what was really important to her. This exercise in the late 1960s academic environment at Yale was given great importance, and appropriately so. With an open-minded attitude, she realized she loved history and utilized an accessible resource, Yale's collection of instruments, to begin playing the viola da gamba. Things clicked for her and a life's course was initiated. She had found a niche in music where she could make her own distinctive contribution. Likewise, all the above-mentioned musicians found their professional identities by being open to new ideas and discovering what suited them and what didn't.

After some years as principal violist of an orchestra, I realized a full-time orchestral career was not for me. Soul-searching uncovered my real wish: to have opportunities as a solo recitalist and to write about music. This discovery surprised me as much as anyone. Part of me never imagined I could actually write a book or be a soloist with an orchestra or make a solo record. It was all a kind of fantasy. But I wanted to do these things so very much. Over a period of years I worked hard, learned an enormous amount, and thrived on the struggle to achieve these goals. All these things eventually came to pass. The universe of music is so expansive. I feel lucky to be involved in more than one aspect of it. The important part of my story? I did not ignore the nagging impulse to go beyond where I thought I would end up.

We can do so very much for ourselves. An abundance of resources is available to help us achieve our most valued goals. There are wonderful libraries and collections of instruments to inspire our imaginations. There are expert people in service organizations to answer questions and even do some occasional hand-holding. Professional associations offer all types of benefits, from networking opportunities to a helpful assortment of newsletters and journals. The government can help, too. Each time I return from a United States Information Agency assignment abroad, I feel as if I've been revitalized, given a shot in the arm of pure enthusiasm for life. For that matter, any travel to different parts of the world, whether for the purpose of study or work, is almost guaranteed to provide a fresh and healthy perspective on life and career. Sometimes these are the pivotal experiences of a lifetime for musicians.

Performers don't have to have management or wait by the telephone to be asked to perform in Carnegie Hall. Without fame or fanfare, they can offer clever programs to foreign embassies or the American Musicological Society or countless other presenters "in the cracks." Why not pick alternative career boosters where the main objective is to be the best *you* can be? A young American quartet approached the president of a small New England college with a proposal to become the quartet in residence. There was no such position advertised. The idea is being seriously considered. Remember Steven Stucky and Bert Lucarelli? They went out and were determined to use their gifts, unsolicited, to help their careers. In the meantime they also brought joy to countless others.

If we lack faith in the way things are, we can change them. Arts International heard a number of complaints from American composers who couldn't afford the travel expenses to attend performances of their works abroad. As a result, the organization's Musica program is awarding travel fellowships to composers to enable them to hear their foreign premieres. I am troubled with the dearth of fresh ideas in the foundation world. Maybe this book will reach someone in a position to do something about it. If not, knocking on a few executive doors may be in order. Career issues need more attention in university curricula, and I am not shy about stating my views when invited to lecture at higher education institutions. Getting back to the constant refrain of the book: We have a lot to say about our own destinies.

How precious it is to feel vital! To wake up in the morning full of excitement about a project, a job, or an endeavor which poses both challenge and reward. We all have the right as well as an obligation to ourselves to be ambitious, to discover and develop gifts throughout life, and to be single-minded—even downright stubborn—about realizing our most important aspirations, even if it means forging a path as yet undiscovered.

RESOURCE GUIDE

The Resource Guide contains material germane to the text of this book. In no way is it a definitive list of organizations or bibliographic references. All entries and commentary reflected the taste of the author.

APPENDIX A:
EDUCATIONAL INSTITUTIONS

RESOURCES ABOUT INSTITUTIONS

BOOKS

Brookhart, Edward. *Music in American Higher Education: An Annotated Bibliography.* Warren, Michigan: Harmonie Park Press, 1988.
   This comprehensive bibliography is distributed by the College Music Society.

Clark, J. Bunker. *Music at KU: A History of the University of Kansas Music Department.* Lawrence, Kansas: The University of Kansas, 1986.
   Everything you ever wanted to know about music at the University of Kansas, which is known for its research in music education and music therapy programs.

Directory of Music Faculties in Colleges and Universities, U.S. and Canada. 1988–90 ed. Boulder: The College Music Society, 1989.
   Valuable reference for all American and Canadian higher education institutions teaching music.

Guide to Ethnomusicology Programs in the United States and Canada, compiled by Anthony Seeger for the Executive Board of the Society for Ethnomusicology, Inc.
   Comprehensive resource for students and scholars.

Suber, Charles. *1986 Guide to Business-of-Music Schools and Careers.* Chicago: Charles Suber & Associates, Inc., 1986.
   Useful guide to schools with a music business orientation.

Thompson, Annie F., comp. *Directory of Library School Offerings in Music Librarianship.* 2d ed. Canton, Massachusetts: Music Library Association, August, 1986. [Corrected Sept. 1987]
   Excellent reference for those pursuing a music librarian career.

Uscher, Nancy. *The Schirmer Guide to Schools of Music and Conservatories Throughout the World.* New York: Schirmer Books, 1988.

PERIODICAL
The Chronicle of Higher Education
Subscription Service
PO Box 1955
Marion, Ohio 43306
   A unique publication; thorough coverage of goings-on at higher education institutions. Listings for music faculty positions are included.

ARTICLE
Roberts, Don L. "Education for Music Librarians in the United States and Canada." *Fontis Artis Musicae* 32 (1985): 59–62.

SPECIAL PROGRAMS OUT OF THE MAINSTREAM

There are a number of universities in the United States with distinguished musicology, ethnomusicology, and music theory departments. Likewise, a significant number of colleges, universities, and conservatories offer strong performance and composition programs. The student looking for an institution in which to study one of these disciplines should undertake research and find out where an admired scholar, composer, or performer teaches. The programs listed below are specialized and offered only at selected institutions.

ACOUSTICS
Penn State University
University Park, PA 16802
(814) 865-0431

ARTS ADMINISTRATION
University of California at Los Angeles
Management in the Arts Program
John E. Anderson Graduate School of Management
405 Hilgard Avenue
Los Angeles, CA 90024
(213) 825-1946

State University of New York at Binghamton
MBA in Arts Administration Program
MBA/Arts School of Management
SUNY at Binghamton
Binghamton, NY 13901
(607) 777-2630

Indiana University Arts
Administration Program
Indiana University School of
Business
Room 660 F
Bloomington, IN 47405
(812) 855-0282

University of Wisconsin at
Madison
Center for Arts Administration
1155 Observatory Drive
Madison, WI 53706
(608) 263-4161

New York University
Performing Arts Administration
239 Greene Street, Room 300
New York, NY 10003
(212) 998-5500

CANTORIAL STUDY

Reform:
Hebrew Union College
School of Sacred Music
1 West 4th Street
New York, NY 10012
(212) 674-5300

Conservative:
Jewish Theological Seminary
Cantors Institute
3080 Broadway
New York, NY 10027
(212) 678-8036

Orthodox:
Philip and Sarah Belz
School of Jewish Music
at Yeshiva University
Schottenstein Center
560 West 185th Street
New York, NY 10033
(212) 960-5353

CAREER CURRICULUM (Includes Music Career or Career Development Courses)

Hartt School of Music
University of Hartford
West Hartford, CT 06117
(203) 243-4467

Oberlin College
Conservatory of Music
Oberlin, OH 44074
(216) 775-8200

Manhattan School of Music
120 Claremont Avenue
New York, NY 10027
(212) 749-2802

University of Miami
School of Music
PO Box 248165
Coral Gables, FL 33124
(305) 284-2161

New England Conservatory
290 Huntington Avenue
Boston, MA 02115
(617) 262-1120

FILM MUSIC

Berklee College of Music
1140 Boylston Street
Boston, MA 02215
(617) 266-1400

University of Southern California
University Park School of Music
Los Angeles, CA 90089-0851
(213) 743-6935

University of California at Los
Angeles
Department of Music
405 Hilgard Avenue
Los Angeles, CA 90024
(213) 825-4761

Sundance Institute
19 Exchange Place
Salt Lake City, UT 84111
(801) 521-9330

GRADUATE STRING QUARTET PROGRAMS

Eastman School of Music
26 Gibbs Street
Rochester, NY 14604
(716) 274-1000

University of Arizona
School of Music
Tucson, AZ 85721
(602) 621-1655

Hartt College of Music
University of Hartford
West Hartford, CT 06117
(203) 243-4467

Yale School of Music
96 Wall Street
New Haven, CT 06520
(203) 432-4162

MILITARY MUSIC

School of Music
Naval Amphibious Base
Little Creek
Norfolk, VA 23521
(804) 464-7501

This school is used by the Army, Navy, and Marines branches of the armed forces. After acceptance in a music program of one of these branches, a musician goes through a program of up to twenty-three weeks to gain skills necessary for being a musician in the military. There are also advanced military courses offered.

MUSIC CRITICISM

McMaster University
Department of Music
Hamilton, Ontario L8S 4M2
Canada
(416) 525-9140

Peabody Institute of Music
1 East Mt. Vernon Place
Baltimore, MD 21202-2397
(301) 659-8100

MUSIC THERAPY

The University of Kansas
Department of Music
Murphy Hall
Lawrence, KS 66045-2279
(913) 864-3436

Southern Methodist University
Division of Music
School of the Arts
Dallas, TX 75275
(214) 692-2587

RECORDING ENGINEERING

Berklee College of Music
1140 Boylston Street
Boston, MA 02215
(617) 266-1400

Peabody Institute of Music
1 East Mt. Vernon Place
Baltimore, MD 21202-2397
(301) 659-8100

Cleveland Institute of Music
11021 East Boulevard
Cleveland, OH 44106
(216) 791-5165

University of Southern California
School of Music
Los Angeles, CA 90007
(213) 743-6935

University of Miami
School of Music
Coral Gables, FL 33124
(305) 284-2161

VIOLIN MAKING

These schools offer full three-year violin-making curricula:

Chicago School of Violin Making
3446 North Albany Street
Chicago, IL 60618
(312) 478-0505

The Violin Making School of
    America
308 East 200 South
Salt Lake City, UT 84111
(801) 364-3651

North Bennet Street School
39 North Bennet Street
Boston, MA 02113
(617) 227-0155

The schools below offer one-year programs in instrument repair of violins and guitars:

Red Wing Technical College
Highway 58 and Pioneer Road
Red Wing, MN 55066
(612) 388-8271

Chimneys Violin Making School
614 Lerew Road
Boiling Springs, PA 17007
(717) 258-3203

Summer Sessions

Summer Violin Craftmanship
   Institute
University of New Hampshire
Brook House
24 Rosemary Lane
Durham, NH 03824
(603) 862-1088

Oberlin College
Conservatory of Music
Oberlin, OH 44074
(216) 775-8206

OTHER PROGRAMS

The Banff Centre for the Arts offers a Winter Music Program for individual musicians and ensembles. This is a program for professionals who have completed training and wish to work on personal artistic projects, such as preparing for auditions, recitals, solo orchestral engagements, and competitions. Summer offerings include the Academy of Chamber Music, Master Classes, and programs in singing, opera, and musical theater. In addition to the arts programs, there is also The Banff Centre for Management, which offers courses in arts administration, fund-raising, and other aspects of arts management.

For information, contact:
Office of the Registrar
The Banff Centre for the Arts
St. Julien Road
Box 1020
Banff, Alberta Canada T0L 0C0
(403) 762-6180

APPENDIX B:
LOOKING FOR MONEY

Much of the information here is discussed in chapter 2: Knowing About Career Resources and chapter 5: Indian Chief Syndrome: The Role of Foundations And Corporations In Getting The Arts Paid For In America.

*R*EFERENCE COLLECTIONS: THE FIRST STEP FOR GRANT-SEEKERS

The Foundation Center
79 Fifth Avenue
New York, NY 10003.
(212) 620-4230

The Foundation Center
1001 Connecticut Avenue NW
Washington, D.C. 20036
(202) 331-1400

The Foundation Center
Kent H. Smith Library
1442 Hanna Building
1422 Euclid
Cleveland, OH 44115
(216) 861-1933

The Foundation Center
312 Sutter Street
San Francisco, CA 94108
(415) 397-0902

For cooperating collections, see: *Foundation Fundamentals*, 3rd ed. Patricia E. Read, ed. The Foundation Center: New York, 1986, Appendix G. To check on new locations and current information, call (800) 424-9836

ORGANIZATIONS

Arts and Business Council, Inc.
130 East 40th Street
New York, NY 10016
(212) 683-5555

The Grantsmanship Center
1031 South Grand Avenue
Los Angeles, CA 90015
(213) 749-4721

Business Committee for the Arts,
   Inc.
1775 Broadway
Suite 510
New York, NY 10023
(212) 664-0600

Council on Foundations
1828 L Street NW
Washington, D.C. 20036
(202) 466-6512

FINANCING OF MUSICAL INSTRUMENTS

Mr. Nigel Brown
N.W. Brown & Co.
25 City Road
Cambridge CB1 1DP
ENGLAND
(0223) 65732

As explained in chapter 2, investment manager Nigel Brown has created
an innovative method for financing expensive instruments.

RESOURCES ABOUT GRANTS AND
PHILANTHROPY

BOOKS

Corporate Philanthropy. Washington, D.C.: Council on Foundations,
1982.
    Overview of corporate funding.

Cummings, Milton C., Jr., and J. Mark Davidson. *Who's to Pay for the
Arts? The International Search for Models of Support*. New York: ACA
Books, American Council for the Arts, 1989.
    Not very easy to read but worth trying.

DiMaggio, Paul J. *Nonprofit Enterprise in the Arts: Studies in Mission &
Constraint.* New York: Oxford University Press, 1986.
   Quite a scholarly approach to the subject.

Directory of Research Grants 1990. Phoenix: Oryx Press, 1990.
   Comprehensive volume.

Ford Foundation Support for the Arts in the United States. New York:
Ford Foundation Office of Reports, 1986.
   Explanation of the Ford Foundation funding interests.

The Foundation Center. *The Foundation Directory.* 12th ed. New York:
The Foundation Center, 1990.
   The bible for grantseekers.

Foundation Grants to Individuals. 6th ed. New York: The Foundation
Center, 1988.
   There aren't many grants that fall in this category. Read this so as not
to waste time applying for those that don't.

National Guide to Funding in Arts and Culture. New York: The Foundation Center, 1990.
   A good volume to use in conjunction with other Foundation Center
publications.

The Grants Register. New York: St. Martin's Press, 1988.
   A useful reference.

Green, Laura R., ed. *Money for Artists.* New York: ACA Books, 1987.
   Excellent. There is nothing quite like this.

Guzzardi, Walter, Jr. *The Henry Luce Foundation: A History: 1936–1986.*
Chapel Hill: The University of North Carolina Press, 1988.
   An interesting history of a foundation.

Hillman, Howard, and Karen Abravanel. *The Art of Winning Foundation
Grants.* New York: The Vanguard Press, Inc., 1975.
   Dated but worth reading.

Jeffri, Joan. *ArtsMoney.* Minneapolis: University of Minnesota Press, 1983.
   A good resource for adminstrators of not-for-profit organizations.

Millsaps, Daniel. *Grants and Aid to Individuals in the Arts.* Washington, D.C.: Washington International Arts Letter, 1983.
A bit dated, but a valuable resource.

Neilsen, Waldemar A. *The Golden Donors: A New Anatomy of the Great Foundations.* New York: E.P. Dutton, 1989.
Excellent and comprehensive.

Oclendahl, Teresa J. *Charity Begins at Home: Generosity and Self-Interest Among the Philanthropic Elite.* New York: Basic Books, 1990.
The author introduces a provocative argument about the philanthropic upper classes.

Partners: A Practical Guide to Corporate Support of Artists. New York: Cultural Assistance Center, Inc., 1982.
Good for understanding the corporate mentality.

Read, Patricia E., ed. *Foundation Fundamentals.* 3d ed. New York: The Foundation Center, 1986.
A useful introduction to the world of foundations.

Skloot, Edward, ed. *The Nonprofit Entrepreneur.* New York: The Foundation Center, 1988.
Mildly amusing.

White, Virginia L. *Grants for the Arts.* New York: Plenum Press, 1980.
Good but dated.

Wyszomirski, Margaret Jane, and Pat Clubb. *The Cost of Culture: Patterns and Prospects of Private Arts Patronage.* New York: ACA Books, American Council for the Arts, 1989.
An insightful look at arts support.

PAMPHLET
Basic Guide to Grants for Minnesota Artists. Minnesota State Arts Board, United Arts/Resources and Counseling, St. Paul, MN, 1987.
Extremely useful resource. Has good ideas for those outside Minnesota as well.

DISSERTATION

Parker, Ellen. "An Investigation of the Practices of Selected Manhattan-Based Corporations and Private Foundations in Assessing the Eligibility of Performing Arts Groups for Funding." Ph.D. diss., New York University, 1988.

Extremely informative. The appendices are full of rich material including the names of influential contributions officers of major corporations.

NEWSLETTERS

Grantsmanship Center News
and
The Grantsmanship Center Whole Nonprofit Catalog
The Grantsmanship Center
1031 South Grand Avenue
Los Angeles, CA 90015
(213) 749-4721

ANNUAL REPORTS

The foundations listed below have a past or current record of arts support.

Bush Foundation
E-900 First National Bank
   Building
332 Minnesota Street
Saint Paul, MN 55101
(612) 227-0891

The Mary Flagler Cary Trust
Room 6622
350 Fifth Avenue
New York, NY 10118
(212) 563-6860

The Ford Foundation
320 East 43rd Street
New York, NY 10017
(212) 573-5000

The John D. and Catherine T.
   MacArthur Foundation
140 South Dearborn Street
Chicago, IL 60603
(312) 726-8000

The Andrew W. Mellon
   Foundation
140 East 62nd Street
New York, NY 10021
(212) 838-8400

The Pew Charitable Trusts
Suite 501
Three Parkway
Philadelphia, PA 19102-1305
(215) 568-3330

The John Simon Guggenheim
   Memorial Foundation
90 Park Avenue
New York, NY 10016
(212) 687-4470
   This foundation gives assistance
to individuals through fellowships.
Fellowships in music are awarded
to composers and scholars in the
history and theory of music.

Jerome Foundation
West 1050 First National Bank
   Building
332 Minnesota Street
St. Paul, MN 55101
(612) 224-9431

Readers Digest Foundation
Pleasantville, NY 10570
(914) 241-5370

The Rockefeller Foundation
1133 Avenue of the Americas
New York, NY 10036
(212) 869-8500

APPENDIX C:
PERFORMANCE AIDS

Material relating to this section of the Resource Guide can be found in chapter 2: Knowing About Career Resources; chapter 3: Orchestral Auditions; chapter 4: Ready To Perform; chapter 6: Where to Go for Help: Organizations That Serve Artists; and chapter 9: A Record Can Be Your Calling Card.

*R*ECITAL SPONSORS

COMPETITIONS LEADING TO DEBUTS

Concert Artists Guild
  International New York
  Competition
850 Seventh Avenue, Suite 1003
New York, NY 10019
(212) 333-5200
  Concert Artists Guild sponsors a workshop called Career Moves in association with a number of colleges, universities, and conservatories throughout the United States.

East & West Artist Prize for New
  York Debut
310 Riverside Drive
No. 313
New York, NY 10025
(212) 222-2433

Pro Musicus Sponsorship Award
140 West 79th Street
No. 9F
New York, NY 10024
(212) 787-0993

Young Concert Artists
  International Auditions
250 West 57th Street
New York, NY 10019
(212) 307-6655

Mae M. Whitaker International
  Competition
c/o Saint Louis Conservatory of
  Music
560 Trinity
St. Louis, MO 63130

NEW YORK RECITAL LOCATIONS

These locations are ideal for trying out a recital program. An artist can arrange an appearance at one of these halls without services of management. Usually a letter and audition tape, or live audition, are required.

American Landmark Festivals
26 Wall Street
New York, NY 10005
(212) 866-2086

BACA Sunday Afternoon Concert
   Series
The Brooklyn Museum
200 Eastern Parkway
Brooklyn, NY 11238
(718) 783-4469, 783-3077

The Donnell Library
20 West 53rd Street
New York, NY 10019
(212) 621-0613

Hospital Audiences Incorporated
   (HAI)
220 West 42nd Street
New York, NY 10036
(212) 575-7681

Library & Museum of the
   Performing Arts
111 Amsterdam Avenue
New York, NY 10023
(212) 870-1613

New York Public Library
Office of Adult Services
455 Fifth Avenue
New York, NY 10016
(212) 340-0913

Saint Bartholomew's Church
109 East 50th Street
New York, NY 10022
(212) 751-1616

Saint John's in the Village
224 Waverly Place
New York, NY 10014
(212) 243-6192

Saint Peter's Church
619 Lexington Avenue
New York, NY 10022
(212) 935-2200

Service to the Aging
Brooklyn Public Library
2115 Ocean Avenue
Brooklyn, NY 11229
(718) 376-3577

Trinity Church Music Office
74 Trinity Place
New York, NY 10006
(212) 602-0760

SERVICES FOR PUBLICITY AND CONCERT PRODUCTION

Comprehensive lists of publicity services can be found in:
Musical America: International Directory for the Performing Arts. New York: Musical America Publications, 1990.
and
Stern's Performing Arts Directory. New York: DM Inc., 1990.

Agnes Bruneau Associates
155 West 68th Street
Suite 1010
New York, NY 10023
(212) 724-7550

John Dudich, Public Relations
PO Box 2017, Cathedral Station
New York, NY 10025
(212) 222-1363

Mary Lou Falcone, Public
  Relations
155 West 68th Street
Suite 1114
New York, NY 10023
(212) 580-4302

Suzanne L. Ford Public Relations
220 West 98th Street
Suite 5H
New York, NY 10025
(212) 864-8271

Jay K. Hoffman & Associates
136 West 57th Street
Suite 801
New York, NY 10022
(212) 371-6690

Shirley Kirshbaum & Associates
711 West End Avenue
Suite 5LN
New York, NY 10025
(212) 222-4843

New York Recital Associates
155 West 68th Street
Suite 2101
New York, NY 10023
(212) 769-0133

Shear Performing Arts Services
180 West End Avenue
No. 28-P
New York, NY 10023
(212) 496-9418

Steorra
243 West End Avenue
Suite 907
New York, NY 10023
(212) 799-5783

Beverly Wright & Associates, Inc.
157 West 57th Street
Suite 1100
New York, NY 10019
(212) 333-7735

PERFORMING ORGANIZATIONS FOR YOUNG PROFESSIONALS

National Orchestral Association
475 Riverside Drive
Suite 249
New York, NY 10115
(212) 870-2009

New Music for Young Ensembles,
   Inc.
Suite 9E
12 West 72nd Street
New York, NY 10023
(212) 601-0085

New York Youth Orchestra
881 Seventh Avenue
New York, NY 10019
(212) 581-5933

The New World Symphony
541 Lincoln Road
Miami Beach, FL 33139
(305) 673-6749

New York Philharmonic Music
   Assistance Fund
Orchestra Fellowship Program
Avery Fisher Hall
Broadway at 65th Street
New York, NY 10023
(212) 580-8700

SERVICE ORGANIZATIONS

Affiliate Artists
37 West 65th Street
New York, NY 10023
(212) 580-2000

American Choral Director's
   Association
PO Box 6310
Lawton, OK 73506
(405) 355-8161

American Federation of Musicians
1501 Broadway
New York, NY 10036
(212) 869-1330

American Guild of Musical Artists
1727 Broadway
New York, NY 10019-5214
(212) 265-3687

American Symphony Orchestra
   League
777 14th Street NW
Suite 500
Washington, D.C. 20005
(202) 628-0099

Chamber Music America
545 Eighth Avenue
New York, NY 10018
(212) 244-2772

Concert Artists Guild
Career Moves Workshops
850 Seventh Avenue
Suite 1003
New York, NY 10019
(212) 333-5200

National Advancement in the Arts
3915 Biscayne Boulevard
Miami, FL 33137
(305) 573-0490

Opera America
1010 Vermont Avenue NW
#702
Washington, D.C. 20005
(202) 347-9262

Volunteer Lawyers for the Arts
1285 Avenue of the Americas
3rd Floor
New York, NY 10019
(212) 977-9273

*I*NSTRUMENT SOCIETIES

American Harp Society
6331 Quebec Drive
Los Angeles, CA 90068-2831

American String Teachers
  Association
Georgia University Station Box
  1066
Athens, GA 30612-0066
(404) 542-2741

American Viola Society
Brigham Young University Music
  Department
Provo, UT 84601
(801) 378-3083

International Double Reed Society
10 Broadview Place
Fort Thomas, KY 41075
(606) 781-3797

International Horn Society
2220 North 1400 East
Provo, UT 84604
(801) 377-3026

International Society of Bassists
Northwestern University School of
  Music
Evanston, IL 60208
(312) 491-4764

International Trombone
  Association
University of North Texas
School of Music
Denton, TX 76203
(817) 565-3720

Keyboard Teachers Association
   International
361 Pin Oak Lane
Westbury, NY 11590
(516) 333-3236

Lute Society of America
PO Box 1328
Lexington, VA 24450

National Flute Association
Northwestern University
School of Music
Evanston, IL 60201
(312) 491-4775/7228

Percussive Arts Society
Box 697
214 West Main
Urbana, IL 61801
(217) 367-4098

Viola da Gamba Society of
   America
31 Kilburn Road
Belmont, MA 02178
(617) 484-5676

Violin Society of America
85-07 Abington Road
Kew Gardens, NY 11415
(718) 849-1373

Violoncello Society Inc.
340 West 55th Street
Suite 5D
New York, NY 10019
(212) 246-3267

CAREER RESOURCES FOR VOCAL ARTISTS

Central Opera Service
Metropolitan Opera
Lincoln Center
New York, NY 10023
(212) 799-3467

The Central Opera Service publishes the *Career Guide for Young American Singers*, as well as *Opera/Music Theater Companies and Workshops in the United States and Canada, 1989–90*. The COS List of Publications contains many useful resources.

Other helpful publications are *The Professional Singer's Guide to New York* and *Towards a Career in Europe*, both by Richard Owens. Periodicals about opera and vocal arts include *Opera News*, *The Opera Quarterly*, and *The New York Opera Newsletter* (see p. 233).

Camerata Opera Theater offers young singers opportunities to learn opera roles and present staged performances at schools and community centers. Contact:

Rita Dreyfus, Director
Camerata Opera Theater
1006 Kingston Drive
Cherry Hill, NJ 08034
(609) 428-7999, (215) 233-1911

*M*AKING A RECORD

Material on this topic is discussed in chapter 9: A Record Can Be Your Calling Card. A comprehensive list of record companies can be found in the annual resource issue *Billboard's International Buyer's Guide.*

Arabesque Recordings
60 East 42nd Street
New York, NY 10165
(212) 983-1414

Cappella Records
7001 Discovery Boulevard
Dublin, OH 43017
(614) 761-2000

Dorian Recordings
17 State Street
Suite 2E
Troy, NY 12180
(518) 274-5475

Musical Heritage Society
1710 Highway 35
Asbury Park, NJ 07712
(201) 531-7000

Newport Classics Ltd.
106 Putnam Street
Providence, RI 02909
(401) 421-8143

New World Records
701 Seventh Avenue
New York, NY 10036
(212) 302-0460

Nonesuch Records
75 Rockefeller Plaza
21st Floor
New York, NY 10019
(212) 484-7275

Northeastern Records
271 Huntington Avenue
Boston, MA 01701
(617) 536-9096

Smithsonian Folkways Records
Smithsonian Institution
Washington, D.C. 20560

Telarc Records
23307 Commerce Park Road
Beachwood, OH 44122-5810
(216) 464-2313

Virgin Classics (USA)
30 West 21st Street
New York, NY 10010
(212) 463-0980

PERFORMANCE CAREER LITERATURE

RESOURCES ON AUDITIONS

BOOKS

Akos, Katherine, Marshall Burlingame, and Jack Wellbaum. *Facing the Maestro: A Musician's Guide to Orchestral Audition Repertoire*. Washington, D.C.: American Symphony Orchestra League, 1983.
Invaluable resource for all instrumentalists.

Dunkel, Stuart Edward. *The Audition Process: Anxiety Management and Coping Strategies*. Stuyvesant, New York: Juilliard Performance Guides, No. 3, Pendragon Press, 1990.
New resource full of good advice.

Sharp, Erica. *How to Get an Orchestra Job . . . And Keep It*. Encinitas, California: Encinitas Press, 1985.
Short but snappy, with introduction by Glen Dicterow.

PERFORMANCE CAREER RESOURCES

BOOKS

Career Guide for Young American Singers. 5th ed. New York: Central Opera Service, 1985.

Gibson, James. *Getting Noticed, A Musician's Guide to Publicity & Self-Promotion*. Cincinnati: Writer's Digest Books, 1987.
Geared to commercial musicians but contains good ideas for all musicians.

————. *How to Make Money in Music: A Free Lance Guide.* Atlanta: Workbooks Press, 1985.
> Common sense advice.

Highstein, Ellen, ed. *Guide to Competitions.* New York: Concert Artists Guild, Inc., 1987.
> A comprehensive and useful booklet.

Hoover, Deborah A. *Supporting Yourself as an Artist.* 2d ed. New York: Oxford University Press, 1989.
> An outstanding resource, beautifully and carefully written.

Insights on Jazz: A Musician's Guide to Increasing Performance Opportunities. Minneapolis: Arts Midwest, 1989.
> An excellent compilation of resources for jazz artists and those teaching jazz.

Musical America: International Directory of the Performing Arts. New York: Musical America Publications, 1990.
> Excellent directory lists both American and international resources for musicians.

Opera/Music Theater Companies and Workshops in the United States and Canada, 1989–90. New York: Central Opera Service, 1989.

Owens, Richard. *Towards a Career in Europe.* Dallas, Texas: American Institute for Musical Studies, 1983.
> Lists agents and auditioning procedures for opera houses in Austria, Germany, and Switzerland.

Owens, Richard. *The Professional Singer's Guide to New York.* Dallas, Texas: American Institute of Musical Studies, 1984.
> A useful guide for singers living in New York.

Papolos, Janice. *The Performing Artists Handbook.* Cincinnati: Writer's Digest Books, 1984.
> Has provided much-needed information to musicians. A valuable book for performing artists.

Stern's Performing Arts Directory 1990. New York: DM Inc., 1990.
Once primarily a directory for the dance industry, it is now a directory for music and dance. A valuable resource.

Summers-Dossena, Ann. *Getting It All Together: A Handbook for Performing Artists in Classical Music and Ballet.* Metuchen, NJ: The Scarecrow Press, Inc., 1985.
Sketchy and superficial. Advice from a manager's point of view. Has some good anecdotes.

SELF-HELP APPROACHES FOR PERFORMERS

BOOKS
Gallwey, W. Timothy. *The Inner Game of Tennis.* New York: Random House, 1974.
The original "Inner Game" book about how to do your best is so universal in concept, its ideas can be applied to almost anything in life.

Green, Barry, with W. Timothy Gallwey. *The Inner Game of Music.* Garden City, New York: Anchor Press/Doubleday, 1986.
A musical adaptation of *The Inner Game of Tennis* offering helpful advice to performers.

Ristad, Eloise. *A Soprano on Her Head.* Moab, Utah: Real People Press, 1982.
An original and refreshing volume offering methods for overcoming psychological blocks.

EARLY MUSIC

BOOKS
Boyden, David D. *The History of Violin Playing from its Origins to 1761.* 2 vols. London: Oxford University Press, 1965.
The definitive history of the violin.

Crum, Alison, with Sonia Jackson. *Play the Viol.* London: Oxford University Press, 1989.
Fun reading for avid viol players.

Donington, Robert. *Baroque Music: Style and Performance.* New York: W.W. Norton, 1982.

Dreyfus, Laurence. *Bach's Continuo Group.* Cambridge: Harvard University Press, 1987.
Scholarly work on the subject of J.S. Bach's continuo practices.

Geminiani, Francesco. *The Art of Playing the Violin, 1751.* Facsimile Edition, London: Oxford University Press, 1751.
Sheds light on baroque performance practice.

Mozart, Leopold. *A Treatise on the Fundamental Principles of Violin Playing.* Translated by Editha Knocker. London: Oxford University Press, 1756.
W.A. Mozart's father wrote an important treatise that gives insight into eighteenth-century performance practice.

Quantz, Johann Joachim. *On Playing the Flute.* New York: Schirmer Books, 1966.
An important treatise on eighteenth-century performance practice.

JOURNALS
Early Music. Edited by Nicholas Kenyon. London: Oxford University Press, 37 Dover Street, London W1X 4AH, England.

Historical Performance. Publication of Early Music America, 250 West 54th Street, Suite 300, New York, New York 10019.

SHOP
Early Music Shop of New
   England
65 Boylston Street
Brookline, MA 02146
(617) 277-8690
   This establishment carries materials for the early music performer, including instruments, strings, and sheet music.

MUSIC MAGAZINES

American Music Teacher	*Opera News*
617 Vine Street, Suite 1432	Metropolitan Opera Guild
Cincinnati, OH 45202	1865 Broadway
	New York, NY 10023

American String Teacher
PO Box 49-0039
Key Biscayne, FL 33149

Billboard
1515 Broadway
New York, NY 10036

*Double Reed: The Journal of the
  International Double Reed
  Society*
University of Idaho School of
  Music
Moscow, ID 83843

The Instrumentalist
200 Northfield Road
Northfield, IL 60093

The Opera Quarterly
14832 Hart Street
Van Nuys, CA 91405

Strings
PO Box 767
San Anselmo, CA 94960

Symphony Magazine
American Symphony Orchestra
  League
777 14 Street NW, Suite 500
Washington, D.C. 20005

The New York Opera Newsletter
PO Box 278
Maplewood, NJ 07040

APPENDIX D:
ASSORTED CAREERS

The material in this section is related to chapter 2: Knowing about Career Resources, chapter 6: Where to Go for Help: Organizations That Serve Artists, and to the section entitled Musical Portraits.

SPECIFIC CAREERS: SOCIETIES, SERVICE ORGANIZATIONS, PROFESSIONAL JOURNALS, AND LITERATURE

ALEXANDER METHOD

ORGANIZATIONS
Affiliates for the Performing Arts
220 West 98th Street #12A
New York, NY 10025
(212) 865-0556
(212) 866-8233

North American Society of
  Teachers of the Alexander
  Technique (NASTAT)
PO Box 806
New York, NY 10023-0806
(212) 866-5640

Information about international societies of the Alexander Technique can be obtained from NASTAT.

ARTICLES
Babits, Linda, and Hillary Mayers. "A Balanced Approach: The Alexander Method." *Music Educators Journal*, November 1987: 51–54.

———. "The Path to Productive Practicing: An Introduction to the Alexander Technique." *American Music Teacher*, November/December 1988: 24–26, 60.

ARTS ADMINISTRATION

ORGANIZATIONS

The National Arts Job Bank
207 Shelby Street
Suite 200
Santa Fe, NM 87501
(505) 988-1166

Korn/Ferry International
237 Park Avenue
New York, NY 10017
(212) 687-1834

ArtSEARCH
Theatre Communications Group
   Inc.
355 Lexington Avenue
New York, NY 10017
(212) 697-5230

BOOKS

Christensen, Warren, ed. *National Directory of Arts Internships.* Los Angeles: National Network for Artist Placement, 1988/89.

Cohen, Lilly, and Dennis Young. *Careers for Dreamers and Doers: A Guide to Management Careers in the Nonprofit Sector.* New York: The Foundation Center, 1989.

Langley, Stephen, and James Abruzzo. *Jobs in Arts and Media Management.* New York: Drama Book Publishers, 1986.

MAGAZINE

International Arts Manager
Martin Huber, Publisher
20 Horsford Road
London SW2 5BN
England

COMPOSITION

ORGANIZATIONS

American Composers Alliance
(ACA)
170 West 74th Street
New York, NY 10023
(212) 362-8900

American Music Center (AMC)
30 West 26th Street
Suite 1001
New York, NY 10010
(212) 366-5260
   The American Music Center
publishes the *AMC Newsletter*
and *Opportunity Update.*

American Society of Composers,
   Authors and Publishers
   (ASCAP)
1 Lincoln Plaza
New York, NY 10023
(212) 595-3050

Broadcast Music, Inc. (BMI)
320 West 57th Street
New York, NY 10019
(212) 586-2000

Meet the Composer
2112 Broadway
Suite 505
New York, NY 10023
(212) 787-3601

Minnesota Composers Forum
MarketHouse 206
289 East 5th Street
St. Paul, MN 55101
(612) 228-1407

Playwrights Horizons
Director of Development
416 West 42nd Street
New York, NY 10036
(212) 564-1235

Playwrights Horizons, based in New York, created a Musical Theater Program in 1979. It was needed to fill the void for a professional workshop where composers and lyricists could test and refine their work. At a time when producing musicals in the nonprofit theater has been considered too costly and too difficult, Playwrights Horizons has provided new institutional interest in musical theater. *Sunday in the Park with George* by Stephen Sondheim and James Lapine is an example of a work generated by the program. Each year, at least one major musical is produced in the Mainstage season, and two to five other new works are done in staged readings/workshops.

Society of European Stage
  Authors and Composers Inc.
  (SESAC)
156 West 56th Street
New York, NY 10019
(212) 586-3450

BOOKLETS
Iossa, Lauren, and Ruth Dreier. *Composers in the Marketplace: How to Earn a Living Writing Music.* Edited by Mindy Levine. New York: Meet the Composer, Inc., 1989.

Ward, Norman. *How to Submit Music Manuscripts to Publishers.* Dix Hills, NY: Hollow Hills Press, 1984.

PERIODICAL
Living Music. Desert Hot Springs, California: Minuscule University Press, Inc.

CONDUCTING

ORGANIZATION
Conductors' Guild Inc.
P.O. Box 3361
West Chester, PA 19381

BOOKS
Del Mar, Norman. *Anatomy of the Orchestra.* Berkeley: University of California Press, 1983.

Osborne, Richard. *Conversations with Karajan.* New York: Harper & Row, 1990.

Rudolf, Max. *The Grammar of Conducting: A Practical Guide to Baton Technique and Orchestral Interpretation.* 2d ed. New York: Schirmer Books, 1980.

CURATOR

ORGANIZATION
American Musical Instrument
   Society
c/o The Shrine to Music Museum
414 East Clark
Vermillion, SD 57069-2390
(605) 677-5306

INSTRUMENT COLLECTIONS
Crosby Collection
c/o Metropolitan Museum of Art
New York, NY 10028
(212) 570-3919

Musical Instruments Collection
The Museum of Fine Arts, Boston
465 Huntington Avenue
Boston, MA 02115
(617) 267-9300

Division of Musical History
National Museum of American
   History, Room 4123
Smithsonian Institution
Washington, D.C. 20560
(202) 375-1707

Shrine to Music Museum
414 East Clark
Vermillion, SD 57069-2390
(605) 677-5306
   *The Shrine to Music Museum
Newsletter* is published quarterly
for members of the Museum

Stearns Collection of Musical
   Instruments
School of Music
University of Michigan
Ann Arbor, MI 48109-2085
(313) 764-6527
(313) 763-4389

Yale University Collection of
   Musical Instruments
15 Hillhouse Avenue
New Haven, CT 06520
(203) 432-0822

PUBLICATIONS
Bessaraboff, Nicholas. *European Musical Instruments.* Cambridge, Massachusetts: Harvard University Press, 1941.

Good, Edwin. *Giraffes, Black Dragons and Other Pianos.* Palo Alto, California: Stanford University Press, 1982.

"Instruments, Collections of." In *Grove's Dictionary of Music and Musicians*, 6th ed. London: Macmillan Publishers Ltd, 1980, p. 245–254.

Jenkins, Jean. *International Directory of Musical Instrument Collections.* The Netherlands: Buren (Gld.), Frits Knuf, 1977.

Lichtenwanger, William, Dale Higbee, Cynthia Adams Hoover, and Phillip T. Young, Eds. *Survey of Musical Instruments Collections in the United States and Canada.* Canton, Massachusetts: Music Library Association, 1974.

ETHNOMUSICOLOGY

ORGANIZATIONS
Society for Ethnomusicology, Inc.
Business Office
Morrison Hall 005
Indiana University
Bloomington, IN 47405
(812) 855-6672

East-West Center
1777 East-West Road
Honolulu, HI 96848
(808) 944-7111 (General)
(808) 944-7735 (Awards Office)

For information of all the music disciplines taught at the university level, contact:

The College Music Society
202 West Spruce Street
Missoula, MT 59802
(406) 721-9616

CMS PUBLICATIONS
The *CMS Newsletter* is the College Music Society's monthly publication.

   College Music Symposium is the annual journal of the College Music Society.

SOCIETY PUBLICATIONS
Ethnomusicology, the SEM journal, is published three times a year.

Society for Ethnomusicology Newsletter is published quarterly.

Guide to Ethnomusicology Programs in the United States and Canada, compiled by Anthony Seeger for the Executive Board of the Society for Ethnomusicology, Inc.

BOOKS
Hood, Mantle. *The Ethnomusicologist.* New York: McGraw Hill.

Nettl, Bruno. *The Study of Ethnomusicology.* University of Illinois Press, 1983.

———. *The Western Impact on World Music.* New York: Schirmer Books, 1985.

Titan, Jeff. *Worlds of Music.* New York: Schirmer Books, 1984.

FELDENKREIS METHOD

ORGANIZATION
The Feldenkreis Guild
PO Box 13285
Overland Park, KS 66212-3285
(913) 492-1444

The Feldenkreis Guild provides information about Feldenkreis practitioners, training programs, and literature and audio-tapes.

PUBLICATIONS
Brickey, Michael. *Self-Tuning for the Whole Musician.* Overland Park, Kansas: The Feldenkreis Guild, 1983.

"The Feldenkreis Method: An Interview with Anat Beniel," *Medical Problems of Performing Artists* (December 1989): 159–162.

Feldenkreis, Moshe. *Awareness Through Movement: Health Exercises for Personal Growth.* New York: Harper & Row, 1977.

———. *The Potent Self.* New York: Harper & Row, 1985.

ORGANIZATION
Society for the Preservation of
   Film Music
10850 Wilshire Boulevard
Suite 770
Los Angeles, CA 90024
(213) 474-5225
   The Cue Sheet is a publication of the Society for the Preservation of
Film Music.

PUBLICATIONS
Film Quarterly
University of California Press
Berkeley, CA 94720
(415) 642-6333
   Journal about film topics.

Hollywood Reporter
6715 Sunset Boulevard
Hollywood, CA 90028
(213) 464-7411
   Lists all films currently in production.

Variety
154 West 46th Street
New York, NY 10036
(212) 869-5700
   Weekly newspaper about the entertainment industry.

Prendergast, Roy M. *Film Music: A Neglected Art*. New York: W.W.
Norton & Co., 1977.

Thomas, Tony. *Music for the Movies*. Cranbury, New Jersey: A.S. Barnes
& Co., Inc., 1973.

LIBRARY
Margaret Herrick Library of the
   Academy of Motion Picture
   Arts and Sciences
8949 Wilshire Boulevard
Beverly Hills, CA 90211
(213) 278-4313

The library of the Academy of Motion Picture Arts & Sciences has a telephone reference service. Librarians will answer questions about film resources as well as supply research materials for film projects.

JINGLES

PUBLICATIONS
Frerickson, Scott, and Darwin Fredrickson. "The Jingle Business: An Interview with John Bahler." *Jazz Educators Journal*, Oct/Nov 1984.

Karmen, Steve. *Through the Jingle Jungle*. New York: Billboard Books, 1989.

Miller, Fred. *Music in Advertising*. New York: Amsco Publications, 1985.

MUSICOLOGY

ORGANIZATION
American Musicological Society
201 South 34th Street
Philadelphia, PA 19104-6313
(215) 898-8698

SOCIETY PUBLICATIONS
Journal of the American Musicological Society is published quarterly.

The *AMS Newsletter* is published twice annually.

PUBLICATIONS
Journal of Musicology Business Office: University of California Press, 2120 Berkeley Way, Berkeley, CA 94720.

Donaldson, Christine F., and Elizabeth A. Flynn. *Alternative Careers for Ph.D.'s in the Humanities: A Selected Bibliography*. New York: Modern Language Association, 1982.

Humanities Ph.D's and Nonacademic Careers: A Guide for Faculty Advisors. Evanston, Illinois: The Committee on Institutional Cooperation, 1983.

Kerman, Joseph. *Contemplating Music*. Cambridge, Massachusetts: Harvard University Press, 1985.

Lindenberger, Herbert. *Opera: The Extravagant Art*. Ithaca, New York: Cornell University Press, 1984.

Lockwood, Lewis. "Communicating Musicology: A Personal View." *College Music Symposium* 28 (1988).

Robinson, Paul. *Opera and Ideas*. New York: Harper & Row, 1985.

Taruskin, Richard. "On Letting the Music Speak for Itself: Some Reflections on Musicology and Performance." *The Journal of Musicology*, Vol 1, No 3. Pages 338–49.

Verba, Cynthia. *The Ph.D. and Your Career: A Guide for Musicologists*. Prepared for The Office of Career Studies, Harvard University, and adapted for the American Musicological Society, 1980. (Available from the American Musicological Society; see JAMS.)

MUSIC CRITICISM

ORGANIZATION
Music Critics Association, Inc.
National Office
6201 Tuckerman Lane
Rockville, MD 20852
(301) 530-9527

MUSIC EDUCATION

ORGANIZATIONS

Music Educators National
    Conference (MENC)
1902 Association Drive
Reston, VA 22091
(703) 860-4000

National Association of Jazz
    Educators
P.O. Box 724
Manhattan, KS 66502
(913) 776-8744

Music Teachers National
    Association (MTNA)
617 Vine Street, Suite 1432
Cincinnati, OH 45202-1420
(513) 421-1420

National Association of Teachers
    of Singing Inc.
2800 University Boulevard North
Jacksonville, FL 32211
(904) 744-9022

PUBLICATIONS

Lee, Patricia Taylor. A *Business Manual for the Independent Music Teacher*. Dallas: National Piano Foundation, 1980.

*Journal of Research in Music
    Education*
University of Kansas
Department of Art & Music
    Education & Music Therapy
311 Bailey Hall
Lawrence, KS 66045-2344

MUSIC LIBRARIANSHIP

ORGANIZATION

Music Library Association Inc.
Business Office
P.O. Box 487
Canton, MA 02021
(617) 828-8450

PUBLICATIONS

Journal of Research in Singing & Applied Vocal Pedagogy. International Association for Research in Singing. Texas Christian University, Music Department, Fort Worth, TX 76129.

Notes is the quarterly journal of the Music Library Association.

Directory of Library Offerings in Music Librarianship. Education Committee, Music Library Association.

Burkat, Leonard. "The Challenge of Music Librarianship in a Public Library." *Notes* 38 (1981): 7–13.

Mann, Alfred, ed. *Modern Music Librarianship: Essays in Honor of Ruth Watanabe.* Festschrift Series No. 8. New York: Pendragon Press, 1989.

Watanabe, Ruth. "American Music Libraries and Music Librarianship: An Overview in the Eighties." *Notes* 38 (1981) 239–56.

MUSIC THEORY

ORGANIZATION
The Society for Music Theory
Mary H. Wennerstrom, Treasurer
School of Music
Indiana University
Bloomington, IN 47405

SOCIETY PUBLICATIONS
Music Theory Spectrum is the journal of the Society for Music Theory.

SMT Newsletter is a biannual publication of the Society for Music Theory.

PUBLICATIONS
Journal for Music Theory, published by Yale School of Music, 96 Wall Street, New Haven CT 06520.

Music Analysis. Basil Blackwell Ltd., 108 Cowley Road, Oxford OX4 1JF England.

19th Century Music, University of California Press, Berkeley, CA 94720.

Browne, Richard. "The Inception of the Society for Music Theory." *Music Theory Spectrum* 1 (1979): 2–5.

Cone, Edward. *Musical Form and Musical Performance*. New York: W.W. Norton, 1968.

Meyer, Leonard. *Emotion and Meaning in Music*. Chicago: University of Chicago Press, 1956.

MUSIC THERAPY

ORGANIZATIONS
American Association for Music
  Therapy
66 Morris Avenue
Springfield, NJ 07081
(201) 379-1100

National Association for Music
  Therapy, Inc. (NAMT)
505 11th Street SE
Washington, D.C. 20003
(202) 543-6864
  Journal of Music Therapy is a quarterly publication of the National Association for Music Therapy.

PERFORMING ARTS MEDICINE

JOURNAL
Medical Problems of Performing Artists
Alice G. Brandfonbrener, M.D., Editor
Hanley & Belfus, Inc.
210 South 13th Street
Philadephia, PA 19107

RECORDING AND ELECTRONIC MUSIC

ORGANIZATION
Audio Engineering Society Inc.
60 East 42nd Street, Room 2520
New York, NY 10165-0075
(212) 661-8528

PUBLICATIONS
Audio Magazine. 1515 Broadway, New York, NY 10036.

Horn, Delton T. *Creative Sound Recording on a Budget.* Blue Ridge Summit, Pennsylvania: Tab Books Inc., 1987.

Newquist, H.P. *Music and Technology.* New York: Billboard Books, 1989.

Wadhams, Wayne. *A Dictionary of Music Production and Engineering Terminology.* New York: Macmillan, 1988.

White, Adam, ed. *Inside the Recording Industry: An Introduction to America's Music Business.* Washington, D.C.: Recording Industry Association of America, Inc., 1988.

ELECTRONIC MUSIC

Back Stage
330 West 42nd Street
New York, NY 10046
(212) 947-0020

Electronic Musician
6400 Hollis Street
Emeryville, CA 94608
(415) 653-3307

Electronic Music Educator
200 Northfield Road
Northfield, IL 60093

Fiddle & Dance Newsletter
RD 1 Box 489
West Hurley, NY 12491
(914) 338-2996

Keyboard
500 Howard Street
San Francisco, CA 94105
(415) 397-1881

Music Technology
22024 Lassen Street
Chatsworth, CA 91311
(818) 407-0744

SACRED MUSIC

ORGANIZATION
American Conference of Cantors
One Kalisa Way, Suite 104
Paramus, NJ 07652
(201) 599-0910

PUBLICATIONS

Green, William. *Bold Mission Music Handbook*. Nashville, Tennessee: Convention Press, 1982.

————. *Music Ministry Plan Book*. Nashville, Tennessee: Convention Press, 1990.

Mitchell, Robert. *Ministry and Music*. Philadelphia, Pennsylvania: Westminster Press, 1978.

Routley, Eric. *Church Music and the Christian Faith*. Carol Stream, Illinois: Agape, 1978.

Slobin, Mark. *Chosen Voices: The Story of the American Cantorate*. Champagne-Urbana: University of Illinois Press, 1989.

Thayer, Lynn W. *The Church Music Handbook*. Grand Rapids: Zondervan Publishing House, 1971.

Walton, Janet. *Worship and Art: A Vital Connection*. New York: Union Theological Seminary, 1990.

VIOLIN AND BOW MAKING

ORGANIZATION
American Federation of Violin and Bow Makers
288 Richmond Terrace
Staten Island, N.Y. 10301
(718) 816-7711

BOOKS

Baines, A. *European & American Musical Instruments*. London: Batsford Ltd., 1966.

Bessaraboff, Nicholas. *Ancient European Musical Instruments*. New York: Museum of Fine Arts, Boston, October House Inc., 1964.

Bolander, John A. *Violin Bow Making*. San Mateo, California: Coyd Poulsen, 1969, 1981.

Boyden, David. *Catalog of the Hill Collection of Musical Instruments at the Ashmolean Museum*. London: Oxford University Press, 1969.

Hamma, W. *Meister Italienischer Geigenbaukunst*. Stuttgart: Shuler Verlagsgesellschaft MBH, 1964.

Hill, W.H., A.F., & A.E. *The Violin Makers of the Guarneri Family (1626–1762)*. London: Holland Press, 1965.

Hill, W.H., A.F., F.S.A., & A.E. *Antonio Stradivari, His Life and Work*. New York: Dover Publications, 1963.

Jalovic, Karel. *Encyclopedia of Violin-Makers*. 2 Vols. Translated by J.B. Kozak. Edited by Patrick Hanks. London: Paul Hamlyn, 1968.

Lebet, Claude. *Dictionnaire Universel des Luthiers*. Brussels: Les Amis de la Musique, 1985.

Millant, R. *J.B. Vuillaume, His Life and Work*. London: W.E. Hill & Sons, 1972.

Moller, M. *Violin Makers of the Low Countries*. Amsterdam: N V J K Smit & Zonen, 1955.

Rehairing of Bows. Lincolnwood, Illinois: William Lewis and Son, 1959.

Retford, William C. *Bows and Bow Makers*. London: The Strad, 1964.

Roda, Joseph. *Bows for Musical Instruments of the Violin Family*. Chicago: William E. Lewis & Son, 1959.

Sacconi, S.F. *The "Secrets" of Stradivari*. Cremona: Libreria del Convegno, 1979.

Wenberg, Thomas James. *The Violin Makers of the United States*. Mount Hood, Oregon: Mount Hood Publishing Company, 1986.

Woodcock, Cyril. *Dictionary of Contemporary Violin and Bowmakers*. Brighton, England: The Southern Publishing Co. Ltd., 1965.

Vatelot, E. *Les Archets Francais*. 2 Vols. Paris: Sernor, 1985.

MAGAZINES

The Strad
Novello & Co. Ltd.
8 Lower James Street
London W1R 4DN
England

Strings
PO Box 767
San Anselmo, CA 94960

ASSOCIATIONS FOR ARTISTS

Artist Trust
517 Jones Building
1331 3rd Ave.
Seattle, WA 98101
(206) 467-8734
   This is a regional organization, primarily concerned with helping artists residing in Washington state. However, its quarterly publication, *Artist Trust*, is a helpful resource for all artists.

American Council for the Arts (ACA)
1285 Avenue of the Americas
3rd Floor
New York, NY 10019
(212) 245-4510
   ACA publishes books useful to artists, a number of which are listed in this Resource Guide. In addition, it publishes *Vantage Point*.

National Association of Artists
Organizations (NAAO)
918 F Street NW
Washington, D.C. 20004
(202) 347-6350
   The NAAO publishes the *National Directory of Artists' Organizations*.

United Arts Resources and Counseling
411 Landmark Center
75 West 5th Street
Saint Paul, MN 55102
(612) 292-4381

This association is oriented toward Minnesota artists, but it can provide useful information for all artists. In addition to publishing helpful books and pamphlets, it offers seminars and counseling to individual artists on such topics as grant writing, career planning, and financial management.

LITERATURE ABOUT MUSIC CAREER EXPLORATION

BOOKS

The Art of Deduction. 7th ed. San Francisco: California Lawyers for the Arts, 1989.
   A good tax guide for artists.

Baskerville, David. *Music Business Handbook and Career Guide.* 4th ed. Los Angeles: The Sherwood Company, 1985.
   Emphasizes copyright and performing rights issues in the publishing and recording industries.

Beatty, Richard H. *The Complete Job Search Book.* New York: John Wiley & Sons, 1988.
   Contains resume and letter formats, and general information.

Bolles, Richard Nelson. *The 1990 What Color Is Your Parachute?* San Francisco: Ten Speed Press, 1990.
   Outstanding and universal. Updated annually.

Dearing, James W. *Making Money Making Music (No Matter Where You Live).* Cincinnati: Writer's Digest Books, 1982.
   Strong on the commercial side of the music industry.

Falkner, Robert R. *Hollywood Studio Musicians: Their Work and Careers in the Recording Industry.* Lanham, Maryland: University Press of America, 1985.
   Very interesting historical and sociological account of Hollywood musicians.

Feder, Judith. *Exploring Careers in Music.* New York: Rosen Publishing Group, Inc., 1982.

Dated and limited in scope, but with a comprehensive list of institutions offering degrees in music therapy.

Field, Shelly. *Career Opportunities in the Music Industry*. New York: Facts on File, 1986.
Quite superficial, but outlines various music professions, including the more commercial fields.

Fink, Michael. *Inside the Music Business: Music in Contemporary Life*. New York: Schirmer Books, 1989.
An excellent addition to the literature, with historical background about the music profession, as well as practical information.

Gerardi, Robert. *Opportunities in Music Careers*. Lincolnwood, Illinois: VGM Career Horizons, 1984.
Part of career series, contains very general descriptions of occupations in the music profession. Good for high school students and college freshmen looking for an overview of the field.

Hanson, Jo. *Artists' Taxes: The Hands-on Guide, An Alternative to Hobby Taxes*. San Francisco: Vortex Press, 1987.
Very useful guide for all artists.

Klayman, Toby Judith, with Cobbett Steinberg. *The Artist's Survival Manual*. New York: Charles Scribner's Sons, 1984.
Interesting information, especially for composers.

Luther, Judith. *For the Working Artist: A Survival Guide for Artists*. Developed for the Office of Placement and Career Development, California Institute of the Arts, 1986.
Good ideas included.

Messman, Carla. *The Art of Filing*. Saint Paul, Minnesota: United Arts, 1987.
Excellent resource for all artists.

National Directory of Artists' Organizations. Washington, D.C.: National Association of Artists' Organizations.
A useful reference on the subject.

Navaretta, Cynthia. *Whole Arts Directory*. New York: Midmarch Arts Books, 1987.
Very useful compilation of resources.

Rachlin, Harvey. *The Encyclopedia of the Music Business*. New York: Harper & Row Publishers, 1981.
Commercially oriented.

Schuller, Gunther. *Musings: The Musical Worlds of Gunther Schuller*. New York: Oxford University Press, 1986.
Brilliant volume of essays. Should be required reading for all musicians.

Shemel, Sidney, and M. William Krasilovsky. *This Business of Music*. 4th ed. New York: Billboard Publishers, Inc., 1979.
Law and business oriented. Useful for composers.

Shipley, Lloyd. *Information Resources in the Arts, A Directory*. Washington, D.C.: Library of Congress, National Referral Service, 1986.

Weissman, Dick. *The Music Business: Career Opportunities and Self-Defense*. New York: Crown Publishers, Inc., 1979.
Not very relevant for classical musicians.

Zalkind, Ronald. *Getting Ahead in the Music Business*. New York: Schirmer Books, 1979.
Dated, with a commercial orientation.

DISSERTATION

Marty, Quentin Gerard. *Influences of Selected Family Background, Training, and Career Preparation Factors on the Career Development of Symphony Orchestra Musicians: A Pilot Study*. Eastman School of Music, 1982.

PAMPHLETS

Career Skills Publication Series from New England Conservatory of Music, Boston, Massachusetts, 1988:

Achieving a Professional Image. Compiled by Sylvia S. Han and Rob Lee.

Bibliography of Music Career Resources. Compiled by Sylvia S. Han.

The Composer's Resource Guide. Compiled by Robin A. Wheeler with Sylvia S. Han and Paul Hoffman.

Financial Management for Musicians. Compiled by Robin A. Wheeler with Edward Donahue, CPA.

A Practical Guide for Music Teachers. Compiled by Sylvia S. Han.

Survival Packet for Musicians: A Practical Job Search Guide. Compiled by Robin A. Wheeler.

A wonderful series, available for just a few dollars per volume, from New England Conservatory of Music, 290 Huntington Avenue, Boston, MA 02115, Phone: (617) 262-1120.

MUSIC RESEARCH

BOOKS

Berger, Melvin. *Guide to Chamber Music.* New York: Dodd, Mead & Company, 1985.

Esoteric chamber works, as well as the more popular ones, are discussed.

Byrne, Frank P., Jr. *A Practical Guide to the Music Library.* Cleveland: Ludwig Music Publishing Co., 1987.

Good for the music library novice.

Cobbett's Cyclopedic Survey of Chamber Music. 3 vols. 2nd ed. London: Oxford University Press, 1929.

Decades after publication, nothing has yet replaced this quintessential chamber music reference.

Drusedow, John E., Jr. *Library Research Guide to Music.* Ann Arbor: Pieram Press, 1982.

Another help for new music library users.

Duckles, Vincent H., and Michael A. Keller. *Music Reference and Research Materials.* 4th ed. New York: Schirmer Books, 1988.

An essential volume for every musician, recently updated.

Grove's Dictionary of Music and Musicians. 6th ed. London: Macmillan Publishers, Ltd., 1980.
> The most comprehensive music reference now available.

Slonimsky, Nicholas. *Baker's Biographical Dictionary.* New York: Schirmer Books, 1988.
> A wonderful reference and a great help when writing program notes.

Watanabe, Ruth T. *Introduction to Music Research.* Englewood Cliffs, New Jersey: Prentice-Hall, Inc., 1967.
> A must for every music researcher.

DISSERTATION SERVICES

University Microfilms
  International
300 North Zeeb Road, Box 61
Ann Arbor, Michigan 48106-1346
(800) 521-0600

Library of Congress Telephone
Reference for Division of
Music: (202) 707-5507

*W*RITING AND PUBLISHING TOOLS

BOOKS

Bunin, Brad, and Peter Beren. *The Writer's Legal Companion.* Reading, Massachusetts: Addison-Wesley Publishing Company, Inc., 1988.
> Comprehensive in outlining a free-lance writer's legal protections. Nothing here specifically deals with music.

The Chicago Manual of Style. 13th ed. Chicago: The University of Chicago Press, 1982.
> This style guide is the one usually used by American university presses and commercial publishers.

Curtis, Richard. *How to Be Your Own Literary Agent.* Boston: Houghton Mifflin Company, 1984.
> Interesting for those who wish to get a book published.

Gorn, Janice L. *The Writer's Handbook.* New York: Simon & Schuster, Inc., 1984.
> A fine, sensible, easy-to-use style guide.

Helm, E. Eugene, and Luper, Albert T. *Words and Music*. Valley Forge, Pennsylvania: European American Music Corporation, 1982.
Valuable guide to writers on musical subjects.

Holoman, D. Kern. *Writing About Music*. A Style Sheet from the editors of *19th Century Music*. Berkeley: University of California Press, 1988.
May not be germane to all journals' styles, but offers useful suggestions about foreign language writing, musical examples, and tables and illustrations.

Jacobs, Hays B. *Writing and Selling Nonfiction*. Cincinnati, Ohio: Writer's Digest Books, 1985.
A helpful book for writers.

Literary Market Place. New York: R.R. Bowker, 1990.
The definitive resource about the publishing world.

Resume Basics. 3rd ed. New York: Office of Career Planning & Placement Services, Manhattan School of Music, 1989.
A most useful publication from the Manhattan School of Music.

Writer's Market. Cincinnati, Ohio: Writer's Digest Books, 1990.
Particularly useful for writers looking for magazine outlets.

Much of the information in this section is discussed in chapter 7: Government and the Arts.

DEPARTMENT OF EDUCATION

Alliance for Arts Education (AAE)
The John F. Kennedy Center for
the Performing Arts
Washington, D.C. 20566
(202) 416-8800

Fulbright-Hays Seminars Abroad
Program
Center for International Education
U.S. Department of Education,
Mail Stop 3308
400 Maryland Avenue, SW
Washington, D.C. 20202
(202) 732-3292/3293
This is the contact address for
those applying to participate in the
Seminars.

Office of Educational Research
and Improvement (OERI)
U.S. Department of Education
Washington, D.C. 20202
Public Affairs Office:
(202) 732-4576
This is the address for the
Educational Research Grant
Program.

Very Special Arts
The John F. Kennedy Center for
the Performing Arts
Washington, D.C. 20566
(202) 662-8899

NATIONAL ENDOWMENT FOR THE ARTS

Music Program, Room 702
National Endowment for the Arts
Nancy Hanks Center
1100 Pennsylvania Avenue NW
Washington, D.C. 20506
(202) 682-5445

OTHER NATIONAL ENDOWMENT FOR THE ARTS PROGRAMS:
Inter-Arts (202) 682-5444
Media Arts (202) 682-5452
Opera-Musical Theater (202) 682-
5447

NATIONAL ENDOWMENT FOR THE HUMANITIES

National Endowment for the
   Humanities
1100 Pennsylvania Avenue NW
Washington, D.C. 20506

Division of Research Programs:
Texts (202) 786-0207
Reference Materials (202) 786-0358
Interpretive Research (202) 786-0210
Regrants (202) 786-0204

UNITED STATES INFORMATION SERVICE

The Office of Public Liaison
United States Information Agency
301 4th Street SW
Washington, D.C. 20547
(202) 485-2355

Fulbright Teacher Exchange
   Program
U.S. Information Agency
301 4th Street SW
Washington, D.C. 20547
(202) 485-2555

MILITARY BANDS

ARMY

Office of the Chief, Army Bands
Department of the Army
Building 600
Fort Benjamin Harrison, Indiana
  46216-5070
(317) 542-4724

Commander
The United States Army Band
PO Box 24074
Washington, D.C. 20024-1374

Army Bands Sergeant Major (202)
  325-5092

Public Affairs Office for United
  States Army Band
PO Box 70565
Washington, D.C. 20024-1374
(202) 696-3718

NAVY

Raymond A. Ascione
Commander, U.S. Navy
Assistant Director
Community Programs and Public
  Liaison Division
Department of the Navy
Office of Information
Washington, D.C. 20350-1200
(202) 697-9344

Head, Music Branch (NMPC-654)
Navy Military Personnel
  Command
Washington, D.C. 20370-5110
(202) 746-7000

U.S. Navy Band
Washington Navy Yard
Washington, D.C. 20374-1052
(202) 433-2865/3366

AIR FORCE

Chief, Bands and Music Branch
  (SAF/PAGB)
Department of the Air Force
Washington, D.C. 20330-1000
(202) 695-0019

MARINE CORPS
United States Marine Corps
Commandant of the Marine
Corps
O-I-C Field Military Music
Section
Code MPC-60
Washington, D.C. 20380
(202) 433-4044

COAST GUARD
Operations Officer
The United States Coast Guard
Band
U.S. Coast Guard Academy
New London, Connecticut 06320-
4195
(203) 444-8466

*R*ESOURCES ON GOVERNMENT AND THE ARTS

BOOKS
Biddle, Livingston. *Our Government and the Arts.* New York: ACA Books, 1988.
   A comprehensive account by a former head of the National Endowment for the Arts about how the Endowments were created.

Catalog of Federal Domestic Assistance. Washington, D.C.: U.S. General Services Administration, 1988.
   There may be some interesting funding ideas for artists here.

Netzer, Dick. *The Subsidized Muse: Public Support for the Arts in the United States.* Cambridge: Cambridge University Press, 1980.
   An informative volume on the subject of arts support.

Straight, Michael. *Nancy Hanks: An Intimate Portrait.* Durham and London: Duke University Press, 1988.
   A tribute to Nancy Hanks by a former deputy.

Wyszomirski, Margaret Jane, ed. *Congress and the Arts: A Precarious Alliance?* New York: ACA Books, 1988.

Worth reading if you want to know more about government arts support.

PERIODICALS

Federal Register is a daily newsletter published by the United States Government. This is where all public forums of the Endowments are announced.

UNPUBLISHED ARTICLES

Brenner, Janet. "An Historical Perspective of Music Theater Support by the National Endowment for the Arts." Paper presented to the Opera-Musical Theater Program, April 1983.

An informative history of the OMT program. This publication can be obtained directly from the National Endowment for the Arts.

The Nation and the Arts: Presidential Briefing Paper. Prepared by the Independent Committee on Arts Policy. New York, August 1988.

Produced by the Twentieth Century Fund during the campaign for the 1988 Presidential election.

STATE ARTS COUNCILS

Information about Artist-in-Education and Artist-in-Residence programs can be obtained by writing to state arts councils. Newsletters published by the arts councils are extremely informative, often offering a national perspective on career opportunities. One example is the publication *FYI: For Your Information*, published by the New York Foundation for the Arts.

ALABAMA
Alabama State Council on the
   Arts
1 Dexter Avenue
Montgomery, AL 36130-5801
(205) 261-4076

ALASKA
Alaska State Council on the Arts
619 Warehouse Avenue
Suite 220
Anchorage, AK 99501-1682

ARIZONA
Arizona Commission of the Arts
417 North Roosevelt Street
Phoenix, AZ 85003
(602) 255-5882

ARKANSAS
Arkansas Arts Council
Heritage Center
225 East Markham
Suite 200
Little Rock, AR 72201
(501) 371-2539

CALIFORNIA
California Arts Council
1901 Broadway
Suite A
Sacramento, CA 95818-2492
(916) 445-1530

COLORADO
Colorado Council on the Arts
770 Pennsylvania Street
Denver, CO 80203
(303) 894-2617

CONNECTICUT
Connecticut Commission on the
  Arts
227 Lawrence Street
Hartford, CT 06101
(203) 566-4770

DELAWARE
Delaware State Arts Council
820 North French Street
Wilmington, DE 19801
(302) 571-3540

DISTRICT OF COLUMBIA
District of Columbia Commission
  on the Arts & Humanities
410 8th Street NW
Fifth Floor
Washington, D.C. 20004
(202) 724-5613

FLORIDA
Arts Council of Florida
The Capitol
Tallahassee, FL 32399-0250
(904) 487-2980

GEORGIA
Georgia Council for the Arts
2082 East Exchange Place #100
Tucker, GA 30084
(404) 493-5780

HAWAII
State Foundation on Arts
335 Merchant Street
Room 202
Honolulu, HI 96813
(808) 548-4145

IDAHO
Idaho Commission on the Arts
304 West State Street
c/o Statehouse Mall
Boise, ID 83720
(208) 334-2119

ILLINOIS
Illinois Art Council
State of Illinois Center
100 West Randolph
Suite 10-500
Chicago, IL 60601
(312) 814-6750

INDIANA
Indiana Arts Commission
47 South Pennsylvania
6th Floor
Indianapolis, IN 46204
(317) 232-1268

IOWA
Iowa Arts Council
State Capitol Complex
Executive Suites
Des Moines, IA 50319
(515) 281-4451

KANSAS
Kansas Arts Commission
700 Jackson
Suite 1004
Topeka, KS 66603
(913) 296-3335

KENTUCKY
Kentucky Arts Council
Berry Hill
Frankfort, KY 40601
(502) 564-3757

LOUISIANA
Louisiana State Arts Council
PO Box 44247
Baton Rouge, LA 70804
(504) 342-8180

MAINE
Maine State Commission on Arts
55 Capitol St.
State House Station 25
Augusta, ME 04333
(207) 289-2724

MARYLAND
Maryland State Arts Council
15 West Mulberry Street
Baltimore, MD 21201
(301) 685-6740

MASSACHUSETTS
Massachusetts Cultural Council
80 Boylston Street
Room 1000
Boston, MA 02116
(617) 727-3668

MICHIGAN
Council for the Arts
1200 6th Avenue
11th Floor
Detroit, MI 48226-2461
(313) 256-3717

MINNESOTA
Minnesota State Arts Board
432 Summit Avenue
St. Paul, MN 55102
(612) 297-2603

MISSISSIPPI
Mississippi Arts Commission
239 North Lamar Street
Suite 207
Jackson, MS 39201
(601) 359-6030

MISSOURI
Missouri Council on the Arts
Wainwright Office Complex
111 North Seventh Street
Suite 105
St. Louis, MO 63101
(314) 444-6845

MONTANA
Montana State Arts Council
48 North Last Chance Gulch
Helena, MT 59624
(406) 443-4338

NEBRASKA
Nebraska State Arts Council
1313 Farnam-on-the-Mall
Omaha, NE 68102-1873
(402) 554-2122

NEVADA
Nevada State Arts Council
329 Flint Street
Reno, NV 89501
(702) 789-0225

NEW HAMPSHIRE
New Hampshire Commission on
    the Arts
40 North Main Street
Concord, NH 03301-4974

NEW JERSEY
New Jersey State Council on the
    Arts
4 North Broad Street
CN 306
Trenton, NJ 08625
(609) 292-9213

NEW MEXICO
New Mexico Arts Division
224 East Palace Avenue
Santa Fe, NM 87501
(505) 827-6490

NEW YORK
New York State Council on the
    Arts
915 Broadway
New York, NY 10010
(212) 614-2900

New York Foundation for the Arts
5 Beekman Street
New York, NY 10038
(212) 233-3900

NORTH CAROLINA
North Carolina Arts Council
Dept. of Cultural Resources
Raleigh, NC 27601-2807
(919) 733-2821

NORTH DAKOTA
North Dakota Council on the Arts
Black Building
Suite 606
114 Broadway
Fargo, ND 58102
(701) 237-8962

OHIO
Ohio Arts Council
727 East Main Street
Columbus, OH 43205
(614) 466-2613

OKLAHOMA
State Arts Council of Oklahoma
640 Jim Thorpe Building
2110 North Lincoln Boulevard
Oklahoma City, OK 73105
(405) 521-2931

OREGON
Oregon Arts Commission
835 Summer Street NE
Salem, OR 97301
(503) 378-3625

PENNSYLVANIA
Pennsylvania Council on the Arts
216 Finance Building
Harrisburg, PA 17120-1323
(717) 787-6883

RHODE ISLAND
Rhode Island Council on the Arts
95 Cedar Street
Suite 103
Providence, RI 02903-1034
(401) 277-3880

SOUTH CAROLINA
South Carolina Arts Commission
1800 Gervais
Columbia, SC 29201
(803) 734-8696

SOUTH DAKOTA
South Dakota Arts Council
108 West 11 Street
Sioux Falls, SD 57102
(605) 339-6646

TENNESSEE
Tennessee Arts Commission
320 6th Avenue North
Suite 100
Nashville, TN 37243-0780
(615) 741-1701

TEXAS
Texas Commission on the Arts
PO Box 13406
Capitol Station
Austin, TX 78711
(512) 463-5535

UTAH
Utah Arts Council
617 East South Temple Street
Salt Lake City, UT 84102
(801) 533-5895

VERMONT
Vermont Council on the Arts
136 State Street
Montpelier, VT 05602
(802) 828-3291

VIRGINIA
Virginia Commission on the Arts
James Monroe Building
101 North 14th Street
17th Floor
Richmond, VA 23219
(804) 225-3132

WASHINGTON
Washington State Arts
   Commission
9th & Columbia Building
Mail Stop GH-11
Olympia, WA 98504-4111
(206) 753-3860

WEST VIRGINIA
West Virginia Department of
Culture and History
Arts and Humanities Division
The Cultural Center
Capitol Complex
Charleston, WV 25305
(304) 348-0240

WYOMING
Wyoming Council on the Arts
2320 Capital Avenue
Cheyenne, WY 82002
(307) 777-7742

WISCONSIN
Wisconsin Arts Board
131 West Wilson Street
Suite 301
Madison, WI 53702
(608) 266-0190

The National Assembly of State Arts Agencies serves as a communications network, information clearinghouse, and advocacy organization for the individual state arts councils. The Assembly publishes a variety of materials, including a *Directory of State Arts Agencies*.

National Assembly of State Arts
Agencies
1010 Vermont Avenue NW
Suite 920
Washington, D.C. 20005
(202) 347-6352

The following are regional arts organizations which are partially funded by government funds. Each has an annual conference where concert presenters look for talent to fill programs.

Arts Midwest
Hennepin Center for the Arts
528 Hennepin Avenue
Suite 310
Minneapolis, MN 55403
(612) 341-0755
   Serves Iowa, North Dakota, Minnesota, South Dakota, and Wisconsin.

Consortium for Pacific Arts & Cultures
2141C Atherton Road
Honolulu, HI 96822
(808) 946-7381
   Serves Alaska, Hawaii, California, Guam, American Samoa, and the Northern Marianas.

Mid-America Arts Alliance
912 Baltimore Avenue
Suite 700
Kansas City, MO 64105
(816) 421-1388
   Serves Arkansas, Kansas, Missouri, Nebraska, Oklahoma, and Texas.

Mid Atlantic States Arts Foundation
11 East Chase Street
Suite 2-A
Baltimore, MD 21202
(301) 539-6656
   Serves New York, Pennsylvania, New Jersey, Maryland, Delaware, West Virginia, District of Columbia, and Virginia.

Southern Arts Federation
1293 Peachtree Street NE
Suite 500
Atlanta, GA 30309
(404) 874-7244
   Serves Alabama, Florida, Georgia, Kentucky, Mississippi, Louisiana, North Carolina, Tennessee, and South Carolina.

Western States Arts Foundation
207 Shelby Street
Suite 200
Santa Fe, NM 87501
(505) 988-1166
   Serves Arizona, Colorado, Idaho, Montana, Nevada, New Mexico, Oregon, Utah, Washington, and Wyoming.

The following are regional arts institutes which focus on art in education.

Nashville Institute for the Arts
123 30th Avenue South
Nashville, Tennessee 37212
(615) 329-6740

Capital Region Center Institute for
Arts in Education
State University, PAC 146
Albany, NY 12222
(518) 442-4240

Western New York Institute for
Arts in Education
Cassety Hall Room #208
1300 Elmwood Avenue
Buffalo, NY 14222
(716) 881-6057

Western Oregon Institute for Arts
in Education
Suite 402
44 West Broadway
Eugene, OR 97401
(503) 683-4324

Texas Institute for Arts in
Education
3220 Audley Street
Houston, TX 77098
(713) 528-7424

The Delaware Institute for the
Arts and Education
Glasgow High School
1901 South College Avenue
Newark, DE 19711
(302) 454-2217

Lincoln Center Institute
Lincoln Center for the Performing
Arts
140 West 65th Street
New York, NY 10023
(212) 877-1800

Arts in the Schools Institute
6th Floor
2714 Union Avenue extended
Memphis, TN 38112-4402
(901) 452-2787

Aesthetic Education Institute
500 University Avenue
Rochester, NY 14607
(716) 271-5070

Harwelden Institute
2210 South Main Street
Tulsa, OK 74114
(918) 584-3333

Arts in Education Institute
259-261 Genesee Street
Utica, NY 13501
(315) 724-1113

Arts Unlimited
300 McFall Center
Bowling Green State University
Bowling Green, OH 43403
(419) 372-8181

San Diego Institute for Arts
   Education
PO Box 1910
San Diego, CA 92112-1910
(619) 232-2552

Southern Tier Institute
PO Box 13902
Binghamton, NY 13902
(607) 723-5030

Central New York Institute for the
   Arts in Education
411 Montgomery Street
Syracuse, NY 13202
(315) 425-2115

The National Assembly of Local Arts Agencies is an association which helps local arts agencies. Like the National Assembly of State Arts Agencies, it provides communications, information, and advocacy services. Its publications include *The Arts in Rural Areas Information Exchange* and *Arts & Education Handbook: A Guide to Productive Collaborations*.

National Assembly of Local Arts
   Agencies
1420 K Street NW
Suite 204
Washington, D.C. 20005
(202) 371-2830

APPENDIX F:
INTERNATIONAL OPPORTUNITIES

This section contains the particulars about material discussed in chapter 10: The International Musician.

LITERATURE ABOUT STUDY ABROAD

BOOKS

Barton, Marianne, ed. *British Music Education Yearbook*. London: Rhinegold Publishing Ltd.
   An excellent resource about studying music in the United Kingdom. Published annually.

Commonwealth Universities Yearbook. London: Association of Commonwealth Universities.
   This resource, published annually, presents a comprehensive list of universities and their departments (including music) in commonwealth countries. A good companion to the *International Handbook of Universities*. Not specifically geared toward arts institutions, but does list programs and names of faculty.

Hill, Deborah J., ed. *Study Abroad in the Eighties*. Columbus, Ohio: Renaissance Publications, 1986.
   A group of essays on study abroad. Dated, and quite far removed from concerns of musicians, but some may find the material interesting.

Howard, Marguerite, ed. *Academic Year Abroad*. New York: Institute of International Education, 1989-90.
   Not specifically geared to music but an adequate overview on American institutions' foreign programs.

————. *Studying in the United Kingdom and Ireland*. New York: Institute of International Education, 1987-88.

Not geared to music, but gives ideas about study in this part of the world.

————. *Vacation Study Abroad*. New York: Institute of International Education, 1987.

Like the rest of the Institute of International Education volumes, not particularly geared to music, but informative.

International Handbook of Universities. 10th ed. Paris: Stockton Press for The International Association of Universities, 1986.

One of the main reference works on international higher education institutions. Includes information about a number of music institutions.

Scholarships, Fellowships, & Grants for Programs Abroad. Houston: American Collegiate Service, 1989.

Nothing else covers this material as concisely.

Studying Music in the Federal Republic of Germany. Mainz, West Germany: B. Schott's Söhne, 1990-91.

The Federal Republic of Germany (West Germany) is the only country I know of that publishes such a volume—found at all German embassies, consulates, and cultural centers. Very informative.

Uscher, Nancy. *The Schirmer Guide to Schools of Music and Conservatories Throughout the World*. New York: Schirmer Books/ Macmillan, 1988.

Includes information about 750 institutions worldwide.

*S*PECIALIZED CAREERS: SCHOOLS AND ASSOCIATIONS

ALEXANDER TECHNIQUE

Society for Teachers of the
   Alexander Technique (STAT)
10 London House
266 Fulham Road
London SW10 9EL
England
(01) 351-0828

VIOLIN MAKING

Staatliche Berufsfach und
Fachschule für Geigenbau und
Zupfinstrumentenmacher
Mittenwald
Partenkirchener Strasse 24
D-8102 Mittenwald
Germany
0 88 23/13 53

The Entente Internationale
Des Maitres Luthiers Et Archetiers
D'Art
c/o Mads Hjorth, President
Ny Vestergade 1
1471 Copenhagen K
Denmark
(45) 1123989

Instituto Professionale Artigianato
Liutario e del Legno (Scuola
Internazionale de Liuteria)
Palazzo dell'Arte
Via Bell' Aspa 3
Cremona
Italy
2 71 76

Newark School of Violin Making
Newark Technical College
Chauntry Park
Newark, Notts
England
(063) 6705921

Tokyo Violin Making School
141 Shinagawa-ku
Higashi-Gotanda
4-6-13 Tokyo
Japan
344 14017

ORCHESTRAL STUDIES

The Secretary
National Centre for Orchestral
Studies
Univeristy of London
Goldsmiths' College
21 St. James'
London SE14 6AD
England

ORGANIZATIONS SPONSORING CULTURAL EXCHANGE

Center for International Exchange
U.S. Department of Education
Washington, D.C. 20202
(202) 732-3283

Council for International
Exchange of Scholars (CIES)
11 Dupont Circle
Suite 300
Washington, D.C. 20036-1257
(202) 939-5400

Fulbright Teacher Exchange
Programs
U.S. Information Agency
301 4th Street SW
Washington, D.C. 20547
(202) 485-2555

Institute of International
Education (IIE)
U.S. Student Programs Division
809 United Nations Plaza
New York, NY 10017-3580
(212) 984-5330

Institute of International
Education
1400 K Street NW
Suite 650
Washington, D.C. 20005
(202) 898-0600

Arts International
Institute of International
Education
809 United Nations Plaza
New York, NY 10017-3580
(12) 984-5564

The International Research and
Exchanges Board (IREX)
126 Alexander Street
Princeton, NJ 08504-7102
(609) 683-9500

The Japan Foundation
342 Madison Avenue
New York, NY 10173
(212) 949-6360

Rothmans Foundation
7th Floor
139 Masquerie Street
Sydney, New South Wales
2000 Australia

RECRUITMENT FOR TEACHING POSTS ABROAD

American Field Service
Intercultural Programs USA
313 East 43rd Street
New York, NY 10017
(212) 949-4242

International Schools Services
PO Box 5910
Princeton, NJ 08543
(609) 452-0990
452-2690

The ISS Directory of Overseas Schools. 1988/89 Edition. Princeton: International School Services, 1988/89.

Office of Overseas Schools (A/OS)
Room 234, SA-6
U.S. Department of State
Washington, D.C. 20520
(703) 875-6220

Peace Corps Recruiting Office
633 Indiana Avenue NW
Room 600
Washington, D.C. 20004
(202) 376-2550

Department of Defense
  Dependents School
Recruitment and Assignments
  Section
Hoffman Building I
2461 Eisenhower Avenue
Alexandria, VA 22331-1100
(202) 325-0885

Semester at Sea/Institute for
  Shipboard Education
University of Pittsburgh
2E Forbes Quadrangle
Pittsburgh, PA 15260
(800) 854-0195
(412) 648-7490

RADIO STATIONS ABROAD

Address letters to the particular department of radio stations relevant to your query; for example, the chamber music or contemporary music department.

ORF
Landesstudio
Ernste Musik
Sponheimerstrasse 13
9010 Klangenfurt
Austria

ORF
Studio Wien
Musikabteilung
Argentinierstrasse 30 A
1041 Wien
Austria

British Broadcasting Corporation
Broadcasting House
London W1A 1AA
England

Oy Yleisradio Ab.
Unionkatu
Helsinki
Finland

Radio France
Société Nationale de
    Radiodiffusion
116 Avenue du Président Kennedy
75786 Paris
France

Radio Bremen
Postfach
D-2800 Bremen 33
Germany

Radio SFB
Haus des Rundfunk
Masurenallee 8-14
D-1000 Berlin 19
Germany

RIAS
Kufsteinerstrasse 69
D-1000 Berlin 62
Germany

Saarlaendischer Rundfunk
D-6660 Saarbrucken
Germany

Suddeutscher Rundfunk Stuttgart
Neckarstrasse 230
D-7000 Stuttgart 1
Germany

Radio Telefís Eireann
Donnybrook
Dublin 4
Ireland

NCRV Radio/Television
Schuttersweg 8-10
P.O. Box 121
1200 JE Hilversum
The Netherlands

Sveriges Radio
The Swedish Broadcasting
   Corporation Music Department
Oxenstierngatan 20
S-105 10 Stockholm 1
Sweden

Radio della Svizzera Italiana
Societa Svizzera di
   Radiotelevisione
6903 Lugano
Switzerland

Radio DRS
Studio Basel
Postfach
4024 Basel
Switzerland

*I*NTERNATIONAL CAREER RESOURCES

BOOKS

Barton, Marianne, ed. *British Music Yearbook*. London: Rhinegold Publishing Ltd.

A wonderful resource about music in the United Kingdom. Outstanding for its breadth and detail. Published annually.

Billboard's 1990 International Buyer's Guide. New York: BPI Communications, Inc., 1990.

A useful directory including record companies and music associations and professional organizations throughout the world.

Diplomatic List. Washington, D.C.: United States Department of State, 1984.

This directory gives office and home telephone numbers of all foreign diplomats based in Washington, D.C.—including cultural attachés and information officers, who will (hopefully) be helpful in providing information about cultural institutions abroad.

Ford, Trevor, ed. *The Musician's Handbook*. London: Rhinegold Publishing, 1986.

An interesting book of articles pertaining to professional musical life in the United Kingdom. An interesting and multifaceted little handbook.

Kurabayashi, Yoshimasa, and Yoshiro Matsuda. *Economic and Social Aspects of the Performing Arts in Japan: Symphony Orchestras and Opera*. Tokyo: Kinokuniya Company Ltd./Oxford University Press, 1988.

A scholarly tome about Japan's cultural institutions. Not an easy read but a valuable research document.

McGee, Timothy J. *The Music of Canada*. New York: W.W. Norton & Co., 1985.

A valuable introduction to music in Canada, including good career resources.

Musical America: International Directory of the Performing Arts. 1990 Edition. New York: Musical America Publications, 1990.

Expensive (in 1990 the price was $60, but it tends to rise annually) but actually worth the money for all the information found in the directory —both national and international in scope.

Owens, Richard. *Towards a Career in Europe*. Dallas: American Institute of Musical Studies, 1983.

A good resource for singers who are interested in doing the European opera and management audition circuit.

Permanent Missions to the United Nations No. 253. New York: United Nations Protocol and Liaison Service, 1983.

Like the *Diplomatic List*, this book gives information about missions to the United Nations. Especially valuable when looking for information about countries that do not have diplomatic relations with the U.S.

Who's Who in Arts Management. London: Rhinegold Publishing Ltd.

Directory of arts managers in the United Kingdom and British managers working abroad. Very useful. Published annually.

MAGAZINES

Classical Music Magazine
Rhinegold Publishing Ltd.
241 Shaftsbury Avenue
London WC2H 8EH
England

Das Orchester
B. Schott's Söhne Verlag
Postfach 3640 Weihergarten 1-11
D-6500 Mainz
Germany
   An invaluable source for
audition information about
orchestras worldwide, though
focusing on Europe and most
particularly, Germany.

The Gramophone
General Gramophone
   Publications Ltd.
177-9 Kenton Road
Harrow
Middlesex HA3 OH A
England

International Arts Manager
Martin Huber, Publisher
20 Horsford Road
London SW2 5BN
England

International Musician
American Federation of Musicians
1501 Broadway
Suite 600
New York, NY 10036
   This is where you find out
about auditions for American,
Canadian, and, on occasion,
foreign orchestra positions.

Musical Opinion
Denby Richards, Editor
8/9 Red Barn Mews, High Street
Hastings
East Sussex TN33 0AG
England

Music Teacher
c/o Rhinegold Publishing Ltd.
241 Shaftsbury Avenue
London WC2H 8EH
England

The Musical Times
Novello & Company Ltd.
8 Lower James Street
London WIR 4DN
England

The Strad
Novello & Company Ltd.
8 Lower James Street
London WIR 4DN
England

Tempo
Boosey & Hawkes Ltd.
295 Regent Street
London WIR 8JH
England

INTERNATIONAL MUSIC SERVICE ORGANIZATIONS

This list is composed of music information centers and arts councils, where information about a country's musicians, concert venues, and concert presenters can be found. Musicological resources are included in specific countries. For further information, there is a comprehensive directory of international organizations in *Musical America*. Cultural attachés and information officers at embassies and consulates are another source, as are American diplomats (mentioned in the USIA section of chapter 7: Government and the Arts) posted abroad. Names and addresses of organizations in Eastern European countries may have changed.

AUSTRALIA

The Australian Music Centre
Room 405, 4th Floor
3 Smail Street
Broadway
Sydney
(02) 212-1611

Australia Council
168 Walker Street
North Sydney NSW 2060
(02) 923-3333

AUSTRIA

Internationale Gesellschaft für
  Neue Musik
(Austrian Society for New Music)
Ungargasse 9/3
A-1030 Vienna
(0222) 73 70 40

International Music Centre
  Vienna (IMZ)
Lothringerstr 20
A-1030 Vienna
(0222) 72 57 95

BELGIUM

Seminar for Musicology, State
  Univ., & Institute for
  Psychoacoustics and Electronic
  Music (IPEM)
Blandijnberg 2
B-9000 Ghent
(091) 25 75 71

Société Belge des Auteurs,
  Compositeurs & Editeurs
  (SABAM)
75-77 Rue d'Arlon
B-1040 Brussels
(02) 230 26 60

BOLIVIA
Sociedad Boliviana de Autores &
Compositores de Musica
(Sobodaycom)
Figueroa 788
Depto. 1, 2nd fl.
La Paz
(02) 36-6514

BRAZIL
Sociedade Brasileira de Música
Contemporânea (SBMC)
SQS 105, Bloco B, Ap. 506
70344 Brasilia, D.F.
(061) 242-9036

Sociedade Independente de
Compositores & Autores
Musicals (SICAM)
Largo Paissandú 51, 10th, 11th
and 16th fl.
01034 São Paulo
(011) 222-4381, 223-8555

BULGARIA
Union of Bulgarian Composers
Ivan Vazov Street 2
1000 Sofia
88 15 60

Union of Bulgarian Musicians
Alabin Street 52
Sofia

CANADA
Canadian Music Centre/Centre de
musique
20 St. Joseph Street
Toronto, Ontario M4Y 1J9
(416) 961-6601

Canadian Music Council
189 Laurier Avenue East
Ottawa, Ontario K1N 6P1
(613) 238-5893

CHILE
Consejo Chileno de Música
Ricardo Matte 485
Santiago
223-6383

CHINA (PEOPLE'S REPUBLIC OF)
Chinese Musicians' Association
Nong zhanguan Nan Li, No. 10
Beijing 100026
5004524

COLOMBIA
Comité Nacional de Música
Calle 11, No. 5-51, 2nd fl.
Bogota, D.E.

CZECHOSLOVAKIA
Music Information Center
Besedni 3
118 00 Prague 1
539-720, 534-234

Union of Czechoslovak
   Composers
Skroupovo nám. 9
130 000 Prague 3
270-785, 270-418

Music Information Centre of the
   Slovak Music Fund
Fučikova 29
811 02 Bratislava
333-569

DENMARK
Danish Music Information Center
Vimmelskaftet 48
DK-1161 Copenhagen K
(01) 33 11 20/66

Union of Danish Musicians
Vendersgade 25
DF-1363 Copenhagen K
(01) 13 46 61

ECUADOR
Casa de la Cultura Ecuatoriana,
Sede Nacional
Apartado 67
Quito

EL SALVADOR
Centro Nacional de Artes
2a Avenida Norte Pje. Contreras,
   No. 145
San Salvador
25-9092, 25-4605

FINLAND

Finnish Music Information Centre
Runeberginkatu 15 A 6
SF-00100 Helsinki 10
409-134

Society of Finnish Composers
Runeberginkatu 15 A 11
SF-00100 Helsinki 10
(0) 445-589

Musicological Society in Finland
Töölönkatu 28
SF-00260 Helsinki 26
(0) 408-166/257

FRANCE

International Music Council
   (UNESCO)
1 Rue Miollis
F-75732 Paris Cédex 15
(1) 45 68 25 50

Société des Auteurs, Compositeurs
   & Editeurs de Musique
   (SACEM)
225 Av. Charles de Gaulle
F-92521 Neuilly-sur-Seine
(1) 47 47 56 50

GERMANY

Verband der Komponisten &
   Musikwissenschaftler der DDR
(Association of Composers and
   Musicologists of the GDR)
Leipzigerstr 26
DDR-1080 Berlin
220-2051

Gesellschaft für Musikforschung
   eV
(Society for Musical Research)
Heinrich Schütz Allee 35
D-3500 Kassel-Wilhelmshöhe
(0561) 31050

Gesellschaft für Neue Musik eV
(Society of Contemporary Music)
Bendergasse 3, Schirn am
   Römerberg
D-6000 Frankfurt 1
(069) 20038

GREECE
Association for the Dissemination
of Greek Music
Kountouriotou, Ersis &
Poulcherias Streets
Athens
(1) 881-1930

GUATEMALA
Asociación Guatemalteca de
Autores & Compositores
(AGAYC)
14 Calle 11-42, Zona 1
Guatemala City
(2) 84-921/251

HONG KONG
Hong Kong Government Music
Office
25/F Wanchai Tower One, 12
Harbour Rd.
Wanchai
Hong Kong
(5) 823-5333

HUNGARY
Editio Musica Budapest
(State Music Publisher)
Vörösmarty tér 1
H-1051 Budapest
(01) 184-228

Institute for Musicology of the
Hungarian Academy of
Sciences
Táncsics Mihály utca 7
H-1014 Budapest
(01) 566-858

ICELAND
Iceland Music Information Centre
Freyjugotu 1
P.O. Box 978
121 Reykjavik
1 23 22

Society of Icelandic Composers
Laufásvegur 40
101 Reykjavik
(1) 2 49 72

INDIA
Inter-National Cultural Centre
205 Tansen Marg
New Delhi 1
389470

INDONESIA
Cipta Indonesia
Jalan Gandaria VII/9
Jakarta 12130
(6221) 818093

IRELAND
Irish Composers Centre
Liberty Hall, Rm. 804
Dublin 1
(01) 740070

ISRAEL
Music Information Centre of
Israel (Is MIC)
PO Box 3004
61030 Tel Aviv
(03) 544-0219

ITALY
Anglicum
(Concerts, publications, records)
Piazza Sant'Angelo 2
1-20121 Milan
(02) 655 17 12, 659 27 48

Sindicato Musicisti Italiani
(National Union of Musicians)
Via di Villa Albani 8
I-00198 Rome

JAPAN
Council of Musical Education &
Research
c/o Kyoiku Shuppan 2-10, Jimbo-
cho
Kanda, Chiyoda-ku
Tokyo 101
(03) 261-0191

Japanese Composers Society
Ogawa Bldg., 3-7-15 Akasaka
Minato–ku
Tokyo 107
(03) 585-4970

KOREA

Korean Composers' Association
5 Muhak-dong, Chung-ku
Seoul
(02) 233-6333

Music Association of Korea
1-117 Dongsoong-dong, Chongro-
ku
Seoul
(02) 744-8060

MEXICO

Sociedad de Autores &
  Compositores de Música S de
  A (SACM)
San Felipe 143, Col. General
  Anaya
03330 Mexico, D.F.
(905) 660-2285, 524-1934

THE NETHERLANDS

Genootschap van Nederlandse
  Componisten
(Society of Dutch Composers)
Prof. E.M. Meijerslaan 3
1183 AV Amstelveen
(020) 540-7405

NEW ZEALAND

Composers Association of New
  Zealand
PO Box 4065
Wellington
(4) 893-415

The Information Centre
Queen Elisabeth II Arts Council
  of New Zealand
PO Box 3806
Wellington
(4) 730-880

NORWAY

Norsk Musikkinformasjon
(Norwegian Music Information
  Centre)
Toftesgaten 69
N-0552 Oslo 5
(02) 37 09 09

Norsk Komponistforening
(Society of Norwegian Composers)
Postboks 9171 Vaterland
N-0134 Oslo 1
(02) 17 01 90

PARAGUAY
Juventudes Musicales
c/o Miguel Echeverria
R.I., 3 Corrales 516
Asunción
45 169

PERU
Asociacion Peruana de Autores &
Compositores (APDAYC)
Jiron Washington 1206
Lima
23 0954

THE PHILIPPINES
National Music Council of The
Philippines
c/o UP College of Music,
Dillman
Quezon City
97 69 63

Philippine Society for Music
Education
Philippine Normal College
Taft Ave.
Manila

POLAND
Polish Music Centre/Polish Music
Council
Rynek Starego Miasta 27
00-272 Warsaw
31 06 07

Stowarzyszenie Polskich
Artystów Muzyków (SPAM)
(Association of Polish Musicians)
Krucza 24/26
00-526 Warsaw
(022) 21-86-47; 21-28-02

PORTUGAL
Sociedade Portuguesa de Autores
Avda. Duque de Louie 3
1098 Lisbon Codex
578570, 578370

Sindicato dos Músicios
Av. D. Carlos 1 72, 2nd floor
1200 Lisbon Codex
(1) 66-6551

ROMANIA
Uniunea Compozitorilor din
    Republica Socialistă Romania
(Composers Union of the Socialist
    Republic of Romania)
Str. Constanin Esarcu 2
Bucharest
(90) 16 37 47

SINGAPORE
Musicians & Singers' Association
Block 3, 03-628, Rochor Centre,
Rochor Road, c/o SMMWU
Singapore 0718
296-3417

SOUTH AFRICA, REPUBLIC OF
South African Society of Music
    Teachers
PO Box 5318
Walmer 6065
Cape Province
(041) 36-1534

SPAIN
Centro Para la Difusion de la
    Música Contemporanea
Santa Isabel 52
28012 Madrid
(01) 468 23 10

Sociedad Española de Musicologia
    (SEM)
Juan Alvarez Mendizabal 65, 3rd
    Floor
28008 Madrid
(01) 241-31-65

SWEDEN
Swedish Music Information
    Center
Box 27327
S-102 54 Stockholm
(08) 783 88 00

Svenska Samfundet for
    Musikforskning
(Swedish Society for Musicology)
Musicology Dept. Ovre
    Slottsgatan 4-6
S-752 20 Uppsala
(018) 12 45 82

SWITZERLAND
International Musicological
   Society
P.O. Box 1561
CH-4001 Basel

Swiss Music Council
Bahnhofstr 78
CH-5000 Aarau
(064) 25 11 22

TAIWAN (REPUBLIC OF CHINA)
Pacific Cultural Foundation
Palace Office Building
Suite 807
346 Nanking East Road, Sec. 3
10543 Taipei
(02) 752-7424

USSR
Union of Composers of the USSR
Ul. Nezhdanovoi 8
Moscow K-9
or
Ul. Gertsena 45
Leningrad

UNITED KINGDOM
British Music Information Centre
10 Stratford Place
London W1N 9AE
(01) 499-8567

Welsh Music Information Centre
PO Box 78
University College Cardiff
Cardiff CF1 1XL
(0222) 874000 Ext. 5126

Scottish Music Information
   Centre
1 Bowmont Gardens
Glasgow, Scotland G12 9LR
(041) 334-6393

URUGUAY
Sociedad Uruguaya e Música
   Contemporanea
Casilla de Correo 1328
Montevideo
(02) 36 15 13

VENEZUELA

Instituto Interamericano de
  Etnomusicologia & Folklore
  (INIDEF)
Urb. Colinas de Charallavito
Calle Miranda
Qta. San Jose
Caracas 1080
77 11 10

Sociedad de Autores &
  Compositores de Venezuela
  (SACVEN)
Edif. Vam, entrada Oeste, 9th
  floor
Avenida, Andrés Bello
Caracas 1050
(02) 573-1589

YUGOSLAVIA

Music Information Center
PO Box 438
Trnjanska bb
YU-41001 Zagreb
539-955, 422-138

INDEX